# NINETEENTH-CENTURY BRITAIN

# NINETEENTH-CENTURY BRITAIN

England, Scotland, and Wales
The Making of a Nation

*The Ford Lectures*
*Delivered in the University of Oxford*
*1986–1987*

KEITH ROBBINS

Oxford   New York
OXFORD UNIVERSITY PRESS
1989

Oxford University Press, Walton Street, Oxford OX2 6DP

Oxford New York Toronto
Delhi Bombay Calcutta Madras Karachi
Petaling Jaya Singapore Hong Kong Tokyo
Nairobi Dar es Salaam Cape Town
Melbourne Auckland

and associated companies in
Berlin Ibadan

Oxford is a trade mark of Oxford University Press

First published 1988 by Oxford University Press
First issued as an Oxford University Press paperback 1989

British Library Cataloguing in Publication Data
Robbins, Keith
Nineteenth-century Britain: England,
Scotland and Wales: the making of a nation.
1. Great Britain. Social life, 1837–1901
I. Title
941.081
ISBN 0–19–285122–5

Library of Congress Cataloging in Publication Data
Data available

Printed in Great Britain by
The Guernsey Press Co. Ltd.
Guernsey, Channel Islands

# Preface

As a sixth-former, I listened to a broadcast of Mr A. J. P. Taylor's Ford Lectures. The experience confirmed my desire to read history at Oxford. I was fortunate enough to have Mr Taylor as a tutor. It never occurred to me then that thirty years later I might myself deliver the Ford Lectures. I am most grateful to the electors for their invitation.

My theme, made even more topical by events since the lectures were written, was not difficult to choose. 'Born and bred a west-countryman, thank God,' to quote the young Tom Brown, I have been privileged to teach at universities in Yorkshire, Wales, and Scotland. A historian of modern Britain, with such a background, has accumulated debts which extend beyond the world of professional scholarship acknowledged in the textual notes, but they are no less real.

The content of some of the lectures has been rearranged. There has also been a modest inclusion of material which could not be squeezed into an hour. These small changes apart, the lectures are published in the form in which they were delivered.

Professor Sir Michael Howard courteously concerned himself with my welfare, and Dr A. D. Macintyre, acting President of Magdalen College, kindly arranged accommodation in my old college. The hospitality also extended by other friends and colleagues made my weekly experience of the integration and diversity of Britain most enjoyable.

K.G.R.
*University of Glasgow*

# Contents

# I

## The Identity of Britain

'In Britain,' declared the Prime Minister in an interview in September 1984, 'certainly since the time of Elizabeth I, our geographical boundaries have never been big enough to contain the fundamental British character and British spirit.'[1] In the time of Elizabeth I, it might be observed, a fundamental *British* character and *British* spirit could at best have been a distant gleam in the royal eye. Confusion, or carelessness, however, is not confined to Downing Street. Jan Morris has recently described Wales as a country which 'for some 700 years . . . has been absorbed into the political entity of Great Britain, with its seat of power in London.' However, as a political entity, Great Britain has not existed 'for some 700 years'.[2] Many other examples of looseness in talking about Britain could be provided. Such slips point to the palpably inadequate understanding of British identity to be found in the press, on radio and television, and even in parliament. Historians, however, have no reason to be smug in this matter. British writers, with rare exceptions, have not been seriously interested in interpreting *Britain*. It may well be that the emphasis at Oxford and Cambridge upon *English* history, narrowly conceived, has stood in the way of a comprehensive grappling with the dimensions of 'Britishness'. English history is central to the history of Britain, but is not synonymous with it.

The chapters that follow seek to explore these dimensions in a thematic fashion by examining the identity of Britain as it was manifested in language and literature, in religion, in politics and business, in education and the life of the mind, in music and sport. They culminate in a consideration of the First World War when national cohesion was put to the supreme test. 'Integration' appeared to be attained, but diversity was not eliminated. The creation of 'the British nation' seemed to be a success. It has been more often taken for granted than explained. Yet the present

[1] Margaret Thatcher, *Daily Telegraph*, 19 Sept. 1984.
[2] J. Morris, *The Matter of Wales* (Oxford, 1984), 1.

existence of the United Kingdom of Great Britain and Northern Ireland is a reminder of failure. Although there remains an Irish dimension (of a kind) within the United Kingdom and a British identity (of a kind) within Northern Ireland, the island of Ireland did not become 'West Britain'. Our concern is therefore with the blending of 'the English', 'the Scots', and 'the Welsh' to produce 'the British'. The fact that, despite 'union', 'the Irish' could not, as a whole, be coerced or induced into accepting 'Britishness' is a salutary reminder that there was nothing inevitable about the process. On the other hand, a number of Irish historians have been reluctant to accept that political separation was the only destiny of the Irish nation. Professor Lyons drew attention to the many facets of 'Irishness' in his Ford lectures. It scarcely needs to be said that the achievement of an acceptable balance between 'integration' and 'diversity' in that island remains as elusive as ever. The theme of this book, in a sense, matches (for Britain) the concerns of Professor Lyons. It suggests that there was no monolithic British entity confronting a monolithic Irish identity. The cleavages within 'the British Isles' frequently do not follow the neat patterns of political stereotype. In this context, the time is approaching when the British–Irish (not merely Anglo-Irish) relationship needs to be approached in a new historical framework. The fact that the 'Irish dimension' is formally excluded from this treatment of Britain should not therefore be taken to imply that the issues it raised were marginal. The 'integration/non-integration' of Ireland requires a book in itself.

The investigation of the curious triangular relationship *between* England, Scotland, and Wales on the one hand, and the internal dynamics *within* England, Scotland, and Wales on the other, as it evolved during the nineteenth century has a fresh interest in the late twentieth century. The end of the British Empire, a common enterprise, has led to a concern, almost an obsession, with 'roots'. Where do 'the British' belong? For much of the nineteenth century it appeared that they were to become an 'imperial race' scattered across the globe in Greater Britain. That 'destiny' has disappeared. The 'British nation' might therefore be thought a construct for a purpose which no longer exists. It is, in my view, too simple to explain the 'crisis of the British state', which some detected in the 1960s and 1970s, as a direct consequence of the post-1945 loss of empire.[3] Nevertheless, after centuries in which conquest or settlement overseas had been a common British activity, it became pertinent to ask again what 'Britishness' was supposed to mean. Whether or not 'devolution' reappears on the political agenda, how both integrity and diversity are to be maintained is a fundamental aspect of contemporary life in Britain. Awareness of its nineteenth-century background can only assist that discussion.

There is, too, a sense in which we are all Europeans now. Britain is caught up in a process of European 'integration', though it is by no means clear either what Europe is or what we mean by 'integration'.[4] This term perplexes both historians and political scientists. We have no model of perfect integration to guide us. Societies which seemed cohesive have suddenly fallen apart and we are no longer sure what we mean by 'national unity'. In the early 1960s, for example, Karl Deutsch and other political scientists were noting that Englishmen, Scotsmen, and Welshmen had preserved their distinct identity despite the fact that they had, for centuries, 'made up the British people and the British nation'.[5] Britain at that point evidently appeared from the United States to be one of the most 'integrated' of states, whether measured by political, linguistic, cultural, religious, or economic criteria. Ten years later, however, when 'Britain' appeared to some observers to be falling apart, it was far from clear what 'integration' it was that these criteria had supposedly established.[6]

The concept of 'integration' may be perilous, but we do need some terminology. Earlier generations would have contented themselves with 'unity' or 'Union' as a way of describing the coming together, primarily politically, of territories which were formerly distinct. The 'unification' of Germany or Italy was frequently thought to be an inexorable and largely beneficial process. Of course, post-1945 historiography has questioned this interpretation. As a result, formerly much-vaunted 'unity' has been seen as patchy and partial. A German consciousness or an Italian identity

[3] K. G. Robbins, '"This Grubby Wreck of Old Glories": The United Kingdom and the End of the British Empire', *Journal of Contemporary History*, 15 (1980), 81–95.

[4] G. Ionescu (ed.), *Between Sovereignty and Integration* (1974).

[5] K. W. Deutsch and W. J. Foltz (eds.), *Nation-Building* (New York, 1966), 7.

[6] S. Neumann (ed.), *Small States and Segmented Societies: National Political Integration in a Global Environment* (New York, 1976). Confidence is not increased by the editor's statement that 'Scotland, Wales and Britain [*sic*] were constitutionally joined in 1707 by the Act of Union that formed the Kingdom of Great Britain' (p. 39n.).

did not merely have to find appropriate institutional expression. It had to be deliberately forged. Peasants living in 'France' were often sublimely ignorant of the fact that they were 'Frenchmen' and had to be made aware of their inheritance. There remained a gap between the rhetoric of national unity and the reality of a diversity that remained only tenuously 'national'. We need only a nodding acquaintance with the academic literature on 'nation-building' and an awareness of the developing world to see how difficult it is, in any political system, to maintain the 'right' balance between a centralizing tendency (which emphasizes the necessity for standardization in the interests of parity and efficiency) and a decentralizing tendency (which stresses the benefits to be gained from local knowledge and individuality). In the making of contemporary Europe both a 'push' and a 'pull' operate; so it was also in nineteenth-century Britain.

Subsequent chapters will focus on the interplay of such forces in specific contexts. This chapter has a more fundamental concern with issues of identity. We know from social psychology that it is no easy matter to determine what is meant by personal or by collective identity. Professor Mackenzie notes that the concept of a man's 'crisis of identity' was familiar to the Romantic Age. Many writers have seen in the emergence of nationalism the social extension of this personal crisis, though Mackenzie notes that the term 'identity crisis' does not appear in a dictionary before 1973, and then has a personal rather than social reference.[7] Particularly during an epoch of social and economic change, it has been asserted, human beings need a specific identification with a particular community. The individual depends upon the community; the community depends upon the individual. 'I belong to Glasgow', in the words of the song, is matched by 'and Glasgow belongs to me.' There is no need to quarrel with such general assertions, but it is also apparent that human beings differ widely in their 'belongingness'. It may, in practice, be limited to family or immediate locality or it may extend to a 'region' or a 'nation'. It may be 'weak' or 'strong'. Most people belong to a plurality of communities and these allegiances can conflict.

At the beginning of the nineteenth century, therefore, it was

[7] W. J. M. Mackenzie, *Political Identity* (Harmondsworth, 1978), 25–6 and *passim*; J. Lee makes some helpful comments in his editorial introduction to *Ireland: Towards a Sense of Place* (Cork, 1985).

possible to envisage various ways in which a 'modern' British identity might emerge. One metaphor which had a certain currency was that of 'blending'. John Gibson Lockhart, writing to Sir Robert Peel, expressed the view that Samuel Johnson might be thought 'the last specimen of the pure Englishman' and Sir Walter Scott the *ultimus Scotorum* since the two nations, the English and the Scots, were blending so rapidly.[8] Blending implied a fusion of elements drawn from both peoples in creating a British identity. Britishness was an amalgam which transcended 'Englishness' and 'Scottishness'. The components of that mixture will be subsequently considered, but as the century wore on there were those who were not entirely happy with how that process was developing. Addressing the University of Edinburgh in 1882, Lord Rosebery dwelt on the difficulty of reconciling the desire simultaneously to preserve a separate nationality and maintain a unitary state. In the case of Britain, the blending could not take place between equals. He noted that Englishmen generally eschewed the terms 'British' and 'Great Britain'. They tended to think that every part of the United Kingdom was 'English'. This self-possession, characteristic, he thought, of dominant races, had indeed made England what it was, but it was a dangerous guide. 'Where nations do not readily blend,' Rosebery added. 'their characters and humours must be studied. It is open to argument whether you should blend or not.' There was, he believed, more variety, more depth, more stimulus, and more points of comparison from the fact that the island of Britain contained both Englishmen and Scotsmen (Welshmen rarely rated a specific mention!). The fascination of Scotland, in his opinion, would not be so great if it were to be colonized with the inhabitants of Surrey and Middlesex. His example, of course, was merely illustrative. No major northern migration was impending. The arrival of settlers from the North was the more usual pattern. Rosebery's case, however, was that every part of Britain should be 'self-reliant'. Scotland was an old country and had attained her majority, as he put it, when other countries were still in their political 'teens'.[9]

'Blending' might therefore be an ideal—but an impossible one. 'Self-reliance' in every part of Britain might be a goal but what if it

[8] Cited by F. R. Hart, *Lockhart as Romantic Biographer* (Edinburgh, 1971), 16.

[9] A. Stodart-Walker (ed.), *Rectorial Addresses Delivered before the University of Edinburgh, 1859–1899* (1900), 210–17.

appeared to produce, or at least perpetuate, social and economic disparities? Central to this dilemma was the relationship between England and Scotland. The demographic facts speak for themselves. In round figures, the population of England stood at 8.5 million and that of Scotland at over 1.5 million. In 1911, however, the figures had changed to 33.5 million and 4.75 million respectively. England had steadily become the more populous partner as the nineteenth century developed. Weight of numbers had wide political implications. The population of England was not, of course, entirely 'English' by origin, but that did not detract from England's commanding role within the structure of Britain. In such circumstances, the 'blending of Britain' could appear to be merely a euphemism for 'assimilation into England'.

Weight of population seemed to tell even more strongly against the survival of Wales, which had only half a million inhabitants in 1801. Habitual reference, in both London and Edinburgh, to 'the two kingdoms' had appeared to exclude Wales from any distinct consideration.[10] Yet, in just over a century after 1801, the population of the principality quintupled. In 1911 its population was half as big as that of Scotland whereas in the early nineteenth century it was only a third as big.

It is conventional, and up to a point useful, to draw attention to these shifts in the underlying constituents of nineteenth-century Britain. Difficulty arises when we move from talking about the relative populations of England, Scotland, and Wales to talking about 'Englishmen', 'Scotsmen', and 'Welshmen'. Mobility between one part of Britain and another, and intermarriage, diluted the 'purity' of the Englishman, the Scot, or the Welshman. It is an oversimplification, in other words, to take borders and frontiers too seriously. They existed to be crossed—in both directions.

There is an even deeper problem. To suppose that the identity of Britain emerged from the fusion, at various levels and to various degrees, of Scottish, Welsh, and English identities presupposes their existence. There was a general belief that they did, but it was not easy to define their essence. A fractured identity is perhaps most apparent in the cases of Wales and Scotland. There is an element of mythology in supposing that Wales and Scotland on the

---

[10] For some reflections on the Welsh–Scottish relationship see K. G. Robbins, 'Wales and the Scottish Connexion', *Transactions of the Honourable Society of Cymmrodorion* (1985), 57–69.

eve of the First World War were spiritually the 'same' as they had been at the beginning of the nineteenth century. Parts of both countries had undergone massive industrial transformation accompanied by substantial immigration (from England and Ireland respectively). The implications of these developments will be discussed subsequently. It is important to add, however, that such changes brought fresh stresses for countries whose own internal unity had been, historically, only precariously established. The historical experience of 'North' Wales had not been the same as 'South' Wales and more than geographical factors made it difficult to assert and maintain a single Welsh identity. Recent work has re-emphasized (on the basis of examining blood groups) that 'the Welsh' were not of a common stock. Two processes were therefore at work: on the one hand, the establishment of what was taken to be an authentically Welsh tradition and, on the other, the impress of that identity in the context of Britain. The two processes could work in unison or they could conflict.[11] Was the 'true' Wales the pub in Port Dinorwic (Gwynedd) where men talked avidly of sea serpents, or Merthyr Tydfil, which George Borrow also visited, where sea serpents were less in evidence?[12] In the days of its independence, too, Scotland had been riven by conflicts of interest and outlook, of which that between 'Gaelic' and 'English' Scotland, between Highland and Lowland, was only the best known. Scottish identity needed the existence of an alien England to keep its own fissiparous tendencies in check. By the beginning of the nineteenth century these historic antinomies had by no means lost all their vitality. The concentration of population and industry reinforced old polarities. Although little more than forty miles separated the cities of Glasgow and Edinburgh, they were very different in ethos. Even their Victorian architecture differed markedly and it was a fact that few of the leading architects of the period executed work in both cities.[13] Who spoke for Scotland? Was its true voice in the big cities in which its population was increasingly located or in

[11] K. O. Morgan, *Wales: Rebirth of a Nation, 1880–1980* (Oxford and Cardiff, 1981).

[12] D. Williams, *A World of his Own: The Double Life of George Barrow* (Oxford, 1982), 155–6; A. M. Fraser, 'George Barrow's *Wild Wales*: Fact and Fabrication', *Transactions of the Honourable Society of Cymmrodorion* (1980), 163–73.

[13] J. G. Dunbar, *The Architecture of Scotland* (1978), 144–5. For Patrick Geddes's attempts to renew Edinburgh and to shake off the 'deteriorative influences of London' see M. Cuthbert, 'The Concept of Province and Metropolis in British Town Planning', in G. Gordon (ed.), *Regional Cities in the UK, 1890–1980* (1986), 234.

Inverness or a small town in the Borders? Edinburgh, it was true, remained the 'capital' city of Scotland, but what did that signify in the Britain that seemed to be evolving? Wales did not possess a 'capital' city and the fact that there was no agreement on what might be the capital was a further commentary on the uncertainty surrounding Welsh nationhood.[14] This difference, however, served to symbolize a deep-seated psychological contrast between Scotland and Wales, however tempting it is to see both countries as sharing the common experience of rejecting or accepting pressures from England. Scotland had not been conquered and had possessed the institutions of statehood. Wales had been conquered and had not possessed the institutions of statehood. The nineteenth-century blending of Britain reflected both sets of facts.

English identity, by contrast, appeared self-confident. In the nineteenth century it drew upon a national continuity within the same political frontiers over a longer period than any other contemporary European state. Yet there were two fundamental problems which grew more grave as the decades passed.

London constituted the first difficulty. It was the capital of England, the capital of Britain, and the hub of the British Empire. It was almost *sui generis*. Its very size, the complexity of its internal sub-divisions and the varied origins of many of its inhabitants made it at once 'representative' and 'unrepresentative' of Britain as a whole. Many contemporaries shared Henry James's notion that there was simply too much of London. Human contacts were coming to resemble 'the momentary concussion of a million of atoms.'[15] The government of the 'Great Wen' was becoming ever more intractable. By 1911, 'Greater London' contained as large a population as that of Scotland and Wales put together.[16] What was the function of such a capital? Was it a monster out of control?[17] There were some who believed not that London 'spoke' for Britain but merely for itself. According to the 1851 census, half the 'foreign-

---

[14] M. J. Daunton, *Coal Metropolis: Cardiff 1870–1914* (Leicester, 1977); N. Evans, 'The Welsh Victorian City: The Middle Class and Civic and National Consciousness in Cardiff, 1850–1914', *Welsh History Review*, 12 (1984–5), 367; for a contrast see P. E. Jones, *Bangor 1883–1983: A Study in Municipal Government* (Cardiff, 1986).

[15] Cited by F. Sheppard, 'London and the Nation in the Nineteenth Century', *Transactions of the Royal Historical Society*, 5th ser. (1985), 58. The article does not identify the 'nation' to which London relates.

[16] P. J. Waller, *Town, City and Nation: England 1850–1914* (Oxford, 1983), 25 and chap. 2.

[17] D. Owen, *The Government of Victorian London 1855–1889* (1982).

ers' who had settled in England and Wales lived in London, consti-
tuting approximately one per cent of its population. For the
remainder of the century it was to London that those seeking
asylum came, at least in the first instance.[18] That in itself gave the
capital a distinct character, or at least parts of it. For many foreign
visitors, the life of London was the life of Britain. Ralph Waldo
Emerson was not among them. He wrote:

What we think of as English traits really reduces itself to a small district. It
excludes Ireland and Scotland and Wales and reduces itself at last to
London, that is to those who come and go thither. The portraits that hang
on the walls in the Academy Exhibition at London, the figures in *Punch*'s
drawings of the public men or of the club-houses, the prints in the shop-
windows, are distinctive English ... but it is a very restricted nationality.
As you go north ... the world's Englishman is no longer found.[19]

'The North' was the second aspect of English identity about which
there was much concern. The pattern of industrial growth was
changing the balance of power within the country. 'Manchester is
the place for money-making business,' wrote the southerner,
Richard Cobden, to his brother.[20] The gap between 'the North' and
'the South', familiar to contemporaries, has been the subject of
much speculation. An Australian has devised an elaborate set of
metaphors in an attempt to encapsulate the difference. The
'northerner' is 'pragmatic, empirical, calculating, Puritan, bourgeois,
enterprising, adventurous, scientific, serious.' He believes in
struggle. The 'southerner' is 'romantic, illogical, muddled, divinely
lucky, Anglican, aristocratic, traditional, frivolous.' He believes in
order.[21] Such images, though they must not be taken too seriously,
imply a cleavage within England as profound as any that might
exist between 'England' and 'Scotland'. John Thornton in Mrs
Gaskell's novel *North and South* certainly thought that, unlike the
men of Oxford, who reverenced the past, the men of the North
could be defined as those who wanted 'something which can apply
to the present more directly.' His 'Milton' might be situated in
deepest 'Darkshire', but he was confident that it pointed the way to
the England of the future. The men of his county hated to have

[18] B. Porter, *The Refugee Question in Mid-Victorian Politics*, (Cambridge, 1979), 3–5.
[19] R. W. Emerson, *English Traits* (1913 edn.), 55.
[20] W. Hinde, *Richard Cobden: A Victorian Outsider* (1987), 12–13.
[21] M. J. Wiener, *English Culture and the Decline of the Industrial Spirit, 1850–1980* (Harmondsworth, 1985), 41–3.

their laws made at a distance, that is to say in the South. They were thorough Teutons, amongst whom there was little mingling of alien blood—unlike elsewhere—and they stood up for self-government and opposed centralization.[22] We must be on our guard, however, against too simple a contrast. There were many 'Norths' and many 'Souths' and the boundary was not fixed. Different criteria, as will become apparent, produce different 'frontiers'.

'National character' is a term which makes a modern historian either timid or angry. The last substantial volume which essayed to write about *The Character of England* was published forty years ago by Sir Ernest Barker.[23] We are rightly chary of 'racialist' implications lurking in much Victorian discussion of this subject. Yet, even if we avoid the term 'national character', we must recognize that it stood for an attempt to grapple with the total culture of a society, such as would now be attempted by social anthropologists using more complex language. 'Character', both individual and national, was of great interest to Victorians and observations upon it could range from the crude to the sophisticated.[24] The Revd Thomas Jones, for example, was reported in the *South Wales Press* in July 1900 as believing that men of sober and upright virtue inhabited the rural areas of Wales while the southern industrial valleys had been corrupted 'through the influence of English people and their vicious habits.'[25] Such a bold ascription of character does not, perhaps, take us very far. Mrs Oliphant was more circumspect when she wrote about the national character of the Scots in *Blackwood's Edinburgh Magazine* in 1861. She noted that three images were widespread, but she felt unable to decide which was the most accurate. In one, the Scots were seen as a nation of adventurers, not over-scrupulous as to the means by which they obtained the good things that came within their reach. In a second, they were a nation of the sourest ascetics—mean, vulgar, and sullen—whose asceticism was not softened by those gleams of light which made monks and convents tolerable. In a third, they were furious patriots, defying all the world

[22] E. Gaskell, *North and South* (1973 edn.), 334.

[23] E. Barker (ed.), *The Character of England* (Oxford, 1947).

[24] The notion of 'character' and its implications is explored by S. Collini, 'The Idea of "Character" in Victorian Political Thought', *Transactions of the Royal Historical Society*, 5th ser. (1985), 29–50.

[25] Cited by D. J. V. Jones, 'The Welsh and Crime, 1801–1891' in C. Emsley and J. Walvin (eds.), *Artisans, Peasants and Proletarians* (1985), 100. Jones's paper provides an effective commentary on the quotation.

to prove them anything but perfection.[26] Attempts to define the English ran into even greater difficulty. David Hume was not the only man to find them quite remarkable. Continental states, he suggested, tended to possess a single, or at least a dominant, social, political, or religious pattern, but that was not the case in England. He was struck by 'a wonderful mixture of manners and characters in the same nation, speaking the same language and subject to the same government.' He was driven, in conclusion, to a paradox: '. . . the English, of any people in the universe, have the least of a national character, unless this very singularity may pass for such.'[27]

Hume's wise recognition of the plurality of English worlds should make us pause before too readily assuming, as many historians have done, that 'anglicization' in nineteenth-century Britain is a simple and uniform process: a matter of assimilation, under some degree of duress, into what is believed to be *the* dominant English mode. It is my contention, to be illustrated in subsequent chapters, that the blending of Britain was a far more complicated affair.[28] Scotland and Wales were not 'absorbed' by 'England' in any simple fashion. The singularity of England was indeed to be found in its cultural diffuseness. The cohesion of Britain, in so far as it was attained, was not achieved by the simple imposition of 'England' upon Scotland and Wales. English identity was itself undergoing constant change during precisely the same period. Peripheral counties were entering into new relationships with the rest of the country. New regional balances emerged as new major regional cities constantly sought to extend their influence.[29] And border counties, straddling the boundaries between England and Wales and England and Scotland, frequently had more in common with each other than they had with their respective national hinterlands.

The task before us, therefore, is to explain how contemporaries came to understand the dense complexity that lay behind 'Britain'

[26] 'Scotland and her Accusers', *Blackwood's Edinburgh Magazine* (Sept. 1861), 269.

[27] D. Hume, 'On National Characters', in *Essays, Moral, Political and Literary* (1903 edn.), 212.

[28] P. Corrigan and D. Sayer, *The Great Arch: English State Formation as Cultural Revolution* (Oxford, 1985), attempt an ambitious investigation of England, but my approach is much more that of the 'conventional history book' which they emphatically deny they have written.

[29] D. Read, *The English Provinces* c.1760–1960 (1964); C. Dellheim, 'Imagining England: Victorian Views of the North', *Northern History*, 22 (1986), 216–30.

and 'the British'. How could such a small island off the coast of mainland Europe still contain such a bewildering mixture of ingredients? Where was the 'essence' of Britain to be found? Historians need to be aware of their own 'mental maps'.[30] Our own sense of place determines our own preconceptions more often than we care to admit. The history of the whole of Britain is so difficult to write precisely because there is no ideal vantage point from which to survey it.[31] It is a paradox that the 'centre' of Britain is located in the South of England. 'British' history, which is very often little more than English history, has often been written by historians resident in the South, even if they themselves have been of northern origin. What follows in this chapter is an examination of how the Victorian 'image' of Britain was formed.

The 'look' and 'feel' of the country was captured on canvas by painters. They brought distant scenes to urban English drawing-rooms. From the end of the eighteenth century, artists were increasingly enthralled by the beauty of Britain. In August 1792, fresh from sketching in Conwy, J. M. W. Turner travelled westwards over the Sychnant Pass and found the view of shore, sea, and the distant Isle of Anglesey framed between the hills 'truly wonderful and beautiful'.[32] His drawings and paintings in Wales and in Scotland added a new dimension to the English understanding of the nature of the British landscape. That such assistance was frequently necessary may be illustrated by the remarks, also made in 1792, of a reviewer in the *Public Advertiser* of Raeburn's portrait of Sir John and Lady Clerk of Penicuik. The work was thought promising, but he objected to what he called 'gooseberry bushes' which had been painted on the left-hand side of the picture. More colour was also thought to be needed. These remarks suggest that the English critic had no knowledge of the stunted thorn bushes and low-toned landscape of the Pentland Hills.[33]

The mid-Victorian decades saw sustained attention to the

[30] R. M. Downs and D. Stea, *Maps in Minds: Reflections on Cognitive Mapping* (New York, 1977); P. Gould and R. White, *Mental Maps* (Harmondsworth, 1974).

[31] I was especially conscious of this difficulty in my own *The Eclipse of a Great Power: Modern Britain 1870–1975* (1983). See also my Raleigh Lecture, 'Core and Periphery in Modern British History', *Proceedings of the British Academy*, 70 (1984), 275–97.

[32] J. Gage (ed.), *Collected Correspondence of J. M. W. Turner . . .* (Oxford, 1980), 16. In general see G. Grigson, *Britain Observed: The Landscape through Artists' Eyes* (1975); J. Holloway and L. Errington, *The Discovery of Scotland: The Appreciation of Scottish Scenery through Two Centuries of Painting* (Edinburgh, 1978).

[33] D. Irwin and F. Irwin, *Scottish Painters at Home and Abroad, 1700–1900* (1975), 154.

Scottish scene. English painters, pre-eminent among them Landseer, took up residence in Scotland for lengthy periods. His
*Highland Valley* (1824) was his first true landscape painting. It was
followed, over the years, by the depiction of a steady succession of
mountain scenes or foaming rocky rivers. Above all, Landseer
stamped the proud form of the stag upon the Victorian consciousness: a shy, proud, gentle yet ferocious, creature whose ambiguous
qualities reflected Victorian ambivalence in the face of 'wild nature'.
The artist's 'best months and most successful themes' were found in
the Scottish Highlands. There was an unusual honesty in his
comment, made on his election to the Royal Scottish Academy in
1866, that Scotland was 'where I have spent the best years of my
life'.[34]

Many Scottish painters, on the other hand, felt that they spent
the best, or at least the most profitable, years of their lives in
England. In this instance, however, a different set of considerations
applied. For personal and professional reasons, a Landseer or a
Millais might habitually spend many months of each year in
Scotland, yet there was no doubt that they would return to England.
Scottish painters who moved south did not do so in order to bring
to the limited Scottish purchasing public the delights of English
landscape. 'When I was in Scotland,' wrote David Wilkie to his
father in 1806, the year after moving to London, 'I considered that
everything depended on my success in London; for this is the place
of encouragement for people of our profession, and if we fail here
we can never be great anywhere.'[35] Andrew Geddes found more
sitters prepared to pay for his services in London than he had in
Edinburgh, even if the result, in the eyes of one critic, was work
which retained 'a slightly east-windy quality'.[36] The Aberdonian,
William Dyce, lost little time in making his way to London and,
supported by the Prince Consort, could certainly not be said to have
'failed'.[37] The aspiring Scottish landscape painter in London could,
however, become a tragic figure. John Burnet's novel *The Progress of
a Painter in the Nineteenth Century* (1854) is modelled on the career of
his younger brother, who had died of consumption in England at an
early age. Wilkie himself, of course, rose to greatness in England,

[34] C. Lennie, *Landseer: The Victorian Paragon* (1976), 45-6, 182, 215.

[35] Irwin and Irwin, *Scottish Painters*, 169.

[36] I. Finlay, *Art in Scotland* (1948), 103.

[37] M. Pointon, *William Dyce 1806-1864: A Critical Biography* (Oxford, 1979).

but the Scottish *genre* painting which had brought him early recognition perhaps remains his best work. For better or worse it established images of Scottish domestic life and circumstances which were to endure in England throughout the nineteenth century.

Increasing numbers of mid- and late Victorians, however, no longer had to rely for their images of Scotland or anywhere else in Britain on the canvasses produced by others. The age of travel was dawning and on an ever-accelerating scale people could explore their own country for themselves. Maps became increasingly accessible and sophisticated throughout the Victorian age. Most modern techniques of non-topographic cartographic representation came into existence in the twenty years after 1835. Publishers argued that their maps were indispensable to those who sought 'to know the real condition of their country'. The diligent student could 'see' his land laid out before him more intimately than had ever previously been accomplished. Specialists could turn to such works as *The Fox-Hunter's Atlas* or the *Wesleyan Methodist Atlas* for detailed information on the distribution of foxes and Wesleyans throughout the country. In addition, map-makers helped children by various pictorial devices. It was possible, for example, to make the map of Scotland look like a kilted piper and turn North Wales into a portrait of 'Auntie Gwen'.[38] There was scope for the representation of psychic as well as physical space. The travellers who were thus equipped therefore experienced at first hand both the similarities and peculiarities of 'British' life. Two facets of that encounter merit special attention here since it had an immediate relevance for them: climate and food and drink. Was Britain really 'one' country?

The belief that climate played an important part in forming 'national character' was widely entertained. David Hume was by no means unique in speculating on this matter. However, he took the view that, compared with some other states, Britain did not experience major variations in climate. The differences that did occur had little explanatory value. Since other writers took a contrary view, it is worth reminding ourselves, in outline, of the

---

[38] D. Smith, *Victorian Maps of the British Isles* (1985), 110-13; J. B. Harley and G. Walters point out what great care was taken by the compilers of the Ordnance Survey in their treatment of Welsh orthography; 'Welsh Orthography and Ordnance Survey Mapping, 1820-1905', *Archaeologia Cambrensis*, 121 (1982), 120-1.

patterns that occur. Temperatures (in January and July respectively) can average approximately 8°C and 16°C in the Scilly Isles, 5°C and 17°C in London, and 3°C and 14°C in Aberdeen.[39] These are recent figures and weather is never constant; nevertheless there is no reason to believe that Victorian figures were significantly different. Such averages, however, can hide particular climatic features and disguise specific temperature peaks or troughs. They do not in themselves disclose the quality of the weather. It is apparent, in general terms, that the southern climate was preferable to the northern. Certainly, it was not uncommon to find that Englishmen brought north of the Border to work complained of the weather. The Duke of Sutherland, for example, employed men from his Staffordshire estates on a particular project in North-East Scotland, but had great difficulty in persuading them to remain because conditions were so much worse than they were used to in the Midlands.[40]

Of course, the British climate was much more varied than this simple picture of a steady deterioration in average temperatures as one moved from south to north would imply. The extraordinary diversity of the British landscape produced subtle local patterns in climate which could make particular areas attractive even if a region as a whole rated unfavourably. However, since the net air movements in the British latitude pass from west to east, and early encounter high ground after their journey across the ocean, the mean annual rainfall is naturally highest in the north and west of Britain. There could be as many as 250 rainy days a year on the west coast and fewer than 175 on some parts of the east coast.[41] In the nineteenth century, in industrial areas, rainfall and smog could combine to produce particularly disagreeable climates. Richard Lodge, the first Professor of History in the University of Glasgow, took a closed carriage to transport himself the one hundred yards from his house to his lecture-room in an attempt to preserve his health. He moved, in despair, to a Chair in Edinburgh.[42] There, however, other natural hazards attended him. He encountered what might be termed a 'bracing' climate. Although the term is not

[39] G. M. Howe, *Man, Environment and Disease in Britain: A Medical Geography through the Ages* (Newton Abbot, 1972), 17.

[40] E. Richards, *The Leviathan of Wealth: The Sutherland Fortune in the Industrial Revolution* (1973), 226–7.

[41] Howe, *Man, Environment and Disease*.

[42] M. Lodge, *Sir Richard Lodge* (Edinburgh and London, 1946), 88.

easy to define, climatologists distinguish five zones of 'bracingness' in Britain, ranging from 'very bracing' on the east coast of Scotland and the North-East of England to 'very relaxing' in the western part of the English south coast. A simple North/South division does not apply: the traveller would find Galloway almost as relaxing as Cornwall.

'Wet weather in Glasgow and my impressions of that den by no means pleasant,' wrote William Morris in 1884 concerning a particularly unsuccessful visit.[43] He was not alone. An official at the Ministry of Munitions acknowledged in 1917 that Englishmen were complaining at having to work on Clydeside. They did not like the climate and wanted to return south.[44] It was the absence of sun as much as the presence of rain that caused dismay. Indeed, in general terms, the average number of hours of bright sunshine per day in Britain does follow a North/South pattern. It is only along the English south coast and coastal East Anglia that the average is higher than four and a half hours. Nowhere in northern England or Scotland attains four hours and the average is closer to three hours. In the western Highlands of Scotland the average falls below three hours. The presence of sunshine undoubtedly causes marked changes in at least subjective sensations of health. The differences in the British climate were sufficiently marked to cause elderly Scotsmen to seek to end their days in Sussex by the sea if they had sufficient resources. They were helped by the availability of weather maps for the tourist, though these had not reached the sophistication obtainable today and which so usefully enable historians to plan their place of retirement with precision.

Late eighteenth-century travellers frequently remarked upon the eating habits of the people they visited and speculated, in an unscientific way, upon the implications of the diets they encountered. Interest in this topic never waned. In the early twentieth century, the writer on rural England, George Sturt, believed that the 'second sight' supposedly possessed by Scottish Highlanders could be explained by their high consumption of fish. It is clear that British identity could not be related to a common diet! Even allowing for the fact that patterns of consumption varied at different income levels, considerable regional variations in eating and drinking habits existed. In 1831, the young John Brown, later a

43 P. Henderson (ed.), *The Letters of William Morris* (1950), 218–19.
44 I. McLean, *The Legend of Red Clydeside* (Edinburgh, 1983), 248.

substantial literary figure, came to England to sojourn with a fellow-countryman who was a general practitioner in Chatham. Brown was delighted to find that supper remained 'as Scotch as can be, *porridge* and bread and cheese'. This fare in no way reflected poverty, for the doctor was reputedly making money fast. It did, however, reflect his control over his English wife.[45] Sir William Burrell, Glasgow millionaire art-collector, is believed to have asked for porridge when he breakfasted at Claridge's. Sir John Gladstone, on his deathbed, became more animated on the topic of porridge than on any other matter—somewhat to his son's dismay. Porridge and Scotland went together. Even though improved transport within Britain facilitated the creation of ever larger markets for food and drink, local tastes remained strongly entrenched. These tastes, in turn, reflected the local availability and prices of particular products as established over centuries. Even studies specifically devoted to diet, however, can frequently do little more than generalize about eating habits. All that is attempted here is to draw attention to certain details which relate to the broad theme of our enquiry. Taken in the round, despite continuing diversity, developments in agriculture, transport and the emergence of a 'food industry' all pointed in the direction of a 'British' diet.

From Sir Frederick Eden onwards, observers had perceived a clear difference between 'North' and 'South'. A basic diet of oatmeal, milk, and potatoes characterized the former, and one of white bread, a little meat, and peas and root vegetables, characterized the latter.[46] A Scottish contributor to the *Quarterly Journal of Agriculture* in 1836 noted that potatoes, which were preferred to bread by the children of the Scottish gentry, were scorned by labourers in the South of England. 'What an English labourer spends on his bacon, beer and white bread', the author smugly added, 'is in the hilly parts of Scotland spent by the Scottish labourer on the education of his children.'[47] Dr Edward Smith's pioneering food enquiry of 1863 confirmed that Northumberland, Durham, and Cumberland had particularly good nutritional records, while those of Wiltshire, Dorset, and Somerset were

[45] D. W. Forrest (ed.), *Letters of Dr John Brown* (1907), 11.

[46] J. Drummond and A. Wilbraham, *The Englishman's Food: Five Centuries of English Diet* (1957), 208–9.

[47] Cited by J. Burnett, *Plenty and Want: A Social History of Diet in England from 1815 to the Present Day* (1966), 22.

particularly bad. He further concluded, in general terms, that Welsh and Scottish diets were comfortably superior to English ones. In ten English counties, none of them northern, the nitrogenous content was below the minimum.[48] It would seem that Margaret (in *North and South*) was wise in urging the workman Higgins not to move to the South. 'You could not stand it,' she told him, 'You would have to be out in all weathers. It would kill you with rheumatism. The mere bodily work at your time of life would break you down. The fare is far different to what you have been accustomed to.'[49]

Even so, by the twentieth century, despite the continued existence of regional preferences, standardization was becoming steadily more prevalent. The contraction, and then virtual elimination, of home baking was accompanied by the emergence of the standard commercial loaf, though that delectable object had still to triumph completely. Across a wide range of food products, erstwhile 'local specialities' either lost ground before 'national' products or were themselves marketed beyond their former home territory. The result was some convergence of taste throughout the country. Milk, for example, became much more generally available is southern England than it had formerly been—being transported from as far away as Wales. Conversely, more Scotsmen began to eat green vegetables, though with caution. Previously, they had been in the habit of consuming vegetable broth, but this nutritious habit was neglected in the cities.[50]

There were many other points of contact between different parts of the country. Smithfield market in London became one of the best places to observe the diversity of types that went to make up Britain. One contemporary wrote in mid-century that 'here are all the country costumes that a man might find between South Wales and Northumberland or further north. The stubby, round-faced Welshman, the huge North Briton, the breeder from the fens, the London drover.'[51] The reference to the 'huge' North Briton is revealing. Preliminary work by Professor Floud suggests that in the

[48] Burnett, *Plenty and Want: A Social History of Diet in England from 1815 to the Present Day*, 122.

[49] Gaskell, *North and South*, 305–6.

[50] R. H. Campbell, 'Diet in Scotland: An Example of Regional Variation', in T. C. Barker, J. C. McKenzie, and J. Yudkin (eds.), *Our Changing Fare: Two Hundred Years of British Food Habits* (1966), 56–9.

[51] A contributor to *The Lady's Newspaper*, 20 Jan. 1849, cited by K. J. Bonser, *The Drovers . . .* (1970), 223.

nineteenth century 'the Welsh' were shorter than 'the English' who were in turn slightly shorter than 'the Scots'. Scottish-born recruits to the United States Army, for example, were on average 2 cm. taller than English-born recruits.[52] Scottish prowess in agricultural and horticultural matters was widely acknowledged. The Scottish potato, skilfully developed by William Paterson of Dundee and others, flooded on to the English market. Such varieties as 'British Queen' and 'Great Scot' became appropriately popular south of the Border. Scottish livestock also particularly impressed English judges. Scottish owners often carried off the main championship at the Royal Show in the 1880s and 1890s.[53] Scottish gardeners regularly found work in parks and on estates in England and Wales. In the person of 'Mr McGregor', Beatrix Potter gave such men a lasting literary memorial.

The advent of North American wheat and refrigerated meat from different parts of the world contributed further to eating uniformity. Such carcasses rendered local availability less significant. Even so, differences of preference and price remained. In Scottish cities, for example, the best meat was less expensive than in London, but the poorest was dearer. This was not a matter of egalitarianism. In southern England, roasted meat was preferred but in Edinburgh and the rest of Scotland broth and boiled meat was customary.[54] Subtle differences of taste were more apparent in roasted meat— and had to be paid for. The Scottish butcher—except that in Scotland and the North of England he was normally called a flesher—had different carving priorities from his English counterpart. Thus travel from one part of Britain to another could cause the purchaser of meat considerable difficulties. It could almost literally be the case that one man's meat was another man's poison. Diet indeed caused particular difficulties in the armed services. A medical officer to the Guards noted that, in his experience, Irishmen could appear strong and fit when they joined up, but they often found their health undermined by the military regimen of bread, meat, and potatoes. It was generally found that Scottish recruits, bred on oatmeal, milk and vegetable broths, were more hardy than their English counterparts.[55] It was, in short, no easy

[52] I am indebted for this information to Prof. R. Floud.

[53] J. H. McCulloch, *The Scot in England* (1934), 251-2, 257-8.

[54] R. Perren, *The Meat Trade in Britain, 1840-1914* (1978), 26.

[55] F. Buckland was discussing Smith's lecture on diet in *Journal of the Society of Arts*, 12 (1863), cited by Drummond and Wilbraham, *Englishman's Food*, 329.

matter for most of the century to provide British fare which could be described as standard.

It was equally plain that there was no uniformity in British drinking. It was a commonplace observation that 'the Scotch drink harder than the English or Irish.' 'In England,' one writer noted, 'I have observed sturdy Scotchmen fall into an atrophy in a manner unaccountable, who were never observed to be inebriated. The truth was, that day after day they touched on the verge of inebriety with their potent corn spirit ...'.[56] In fact, however, while such impressions were prevalent, deaths from alcoholism or cirrhosis of the liver were higher in England and Wales after the mid-1880s than in Scotland—though earlier in the century the position had been reversed.[57] Drinking habits were markedly different north and south of the Border. There was a disparity between the duty on spirits levied in Scotland and that levied in England. Whisky began to conquer the world beyond Scotland, and a significant proportion of the increased exports went to England. In 1877, six Lowland grain patent still distillers combined to form the Distillers Co. Ltd., and, by the end of the century, helped by disease in France which halted the production of cognac, blended Scotch whisky was firmly established on the sideboard of English gentlemen.[58] Scottish brewers also looked to the English market—as early as the 1820s 'Scotch Ale' was on sale in Bristol and elsewhere in southern England. By 1890, more than a third of William Younger's sales were taking place on Tyneside.[59] But, just as Scottish brewers and distillers would use some English grain if the price was right, so, as early as the 1820s, many Scottish breweries were either owned or managed by Englishmen.[60] Youngers told Scottish drinkers, tempted by the fashion for English porter, that they had 'engaged a London brewer of great professional ability' whose product was equal to anything imported from London.[61] Whatever they drank, however, travellers who visited a Scottish 'bar' knew that it was not the same institution as an English 'pub'. The 'tied house', which prevailed in England, scarcely existed in Scotland where retail licences were normally issued to individuals.[62]

[56] C. Redding, *Fifty Years' Recollections, Literary and Personal*, iii (1858), 49.

[57] G. B. Wilson, *Alcohol and the Nation* (1940), 424–7.

[58] D. Daiches, *Scotch Whisky: Its Past and Present* (1969), 62–6.

[59] I. Donnachie, *A History of the Brewing Industry in Scotland* (Edinburgh, 1979), 135, 216–17.

[60] Ibid. 42, 87.          [61] Ibid. 115.          [62] Ibid, 206–7.

The 'discovery of Britain' and the accompanying awareness of diversity only became a serious business at the end of the eighteenth century.[63] Men of means, especially when they were deprived of access to continental Europe by Napoleon, were increasingly excited by what their own country had to offer. The cult of the Romantic and the Picturesque now found exotic beauty to exist in what civilized metropolitan man had formerly regarded as barren wilderness. Ladies and gentlemen, sketchbook in hand, took summer driving tours through North Wales. They wrote diverting 'Letters from the Mountains' to their friends and relatives trapped in lowland England. So popular did this pursuit become that one visitor remarked that, while Wales contained many fine things, 'the "comeatability" of the place destroyed its beauty,'[64] William Hutton, for example, was one traveller who completed no fewer than sixteen tours through North Wales and on the strength of them felt able to publish certain *Remarks* for the benefit of the people of Birmingham. His Grace the Duke of Rutland kindly published in 1813 a journal of a tour he had undertaken to the 'Northern Part of Great Britain'. A Mr Walford published in 1818 his *The Scientific Tourist through England, Wales and Scotland*. Many other examples could be given. This extensive genre of travel-writing was not totally new, but its expansion created in England, at least among sophisticated circles, an increased awareness of the topographical complexity of *Britain*. There was the danger, however, that this kind of travel produced a sense of space which was defined by linear movement. As John Barrell puts it, the concern was always to be moving through a place and

to see it never primarily as a place-in-itself, but always as mediated by its connection to one place to the east, and another to the west . . . so that to stop at a place is still to be in a state of potential motion.[65]

Most travellers 'discovered' Britain by advancing from the South but it was, of course, equally possible to 'discover' it from the North.

---

[63] E. Moir, *The Discovery of Britain: The English Tourists 1540 to 1840* (1964). Unfortunately, reasons of space prevent this useful book from 'discovering' Scotland. See T. C. Smout, 'Tours in the Scottish Highlands from the Eighteenth to the Twentieth Centuries', *Northern Scotland*, vol. v (1983), 99–121; M. Lindsay, *The Eye is Delighted: Some Romantic Travellers in Scotland* (1971).

[64] Redding, *Fifty Years' Recollections*, iii. 40.

[65] J. Barrell, *The Idea of Landscape and the Sense of Place, 1730–1840* (Cambridge, 1972), 89.

John Gibson Lockhart's novel *Reginald Dalton* gives the author's own impressions on his journey south from Scotland to Oxford. Southern travellers were impressed by the grandeur of the North but what struck 'Dalton' was 'the boundless spread of beauty' which he encountered in England. The hedges and hedgerows seemed to be woven by distance into the semblance of one vast wood. He marvelled at 'the apparent ease—the wealth—the splendour—the limitless magnificence—the minute elaborate comfort—the pictur-esque villages—the busy towns—the embosomed spires—the stately halls—the ancestral groves—everything the assemblage of which stamps "England herself alone".'[66] The image of England as a country of lush and green opulence was not, however, the only one to strike Scottish visitors. In his *First Impressions of England and its People*, Hugh Miller was acutely conscious, as he moved south through the country, that it was extremely difficult to conceive of England as a single entity. His knowledge of geology made him more aware than most travellers of the distinctive features of the landscape and of the regional settlement patterns to which they gave rise. Miller sensed the existence of deep historic boundaries as he moved from place to place. That acute awareness may in turn derive from his own mixed ancestry and upbringing in Scotland, blending, as it did, Highland and Lowland elements.[67]

Crossing the Border, in whichever direction, was undoubtedly felt by travellers to be a significant step, pregnant with uncertain consequences. Murray's *Handbook for Travellers in Scotland*, which went through many editions, warned that in the West travellers would be subjected to 'an intolerable insect plague of "midges"—small gnats, scarcely visible, but covering the face with painful and enduring punctures.' Bonnie Prince Charlie, it was claimed, was nearly driven to distraction by them. Turpentine was said to be an antidote, though it was feared that the cure was almost as bad as the disease.[68] On his way back from touring Scotland with Thomas Telford in 1819, Robert Southey stopped at Longtown in Cumberland with some relief—'the cleanliness of the Inn there appearing to great advantage after the Inns of Scotland.'[69] In 1893, Walter Raleigh, the English critic, 'crossed the Kershope Burn on

[66] Cited by M. Lochhead, *John Gibson Lockhart* (1954), 12.

[67] G. Rosie, *Hugh Miller: Outrage and Order* (Edinburgh, 1981), 16–17.

[68] *Murray's Handbook for Travellers in Scotland* (1894 edn.), p. xxi.

[69] C. H. Herford (ed.), *Robert Southey, Journal of a Tour in Scotland in 1819* (1929), 268.

the Border at about 4.0 and met crowds of sheep and Scotchmen driving them. We knew we were in Scotland, for they scowled at us when we wished them good afternoon ...'. He soon espied 'a beastly Presbyterian church' and felt moved to hope that both the Established and Free Churches should be scraped off the face of the earth, since 'Their low ways, dirty pride, and animal cunning, blended with their scriptural texts, their maps unto my feet, rocks of ages—are a very nauseating combination ...'. It is perhaps a little surprising that this particular traveller accepted the Chair of English Literature at the University of Glasgow seven years later.[70]

Other travellers, however, were less conscious of the Anglo-Scottish Border as a great divide. The Revd Francis Trench, who lived in southern England and was a seasoned continental traveller, finally succumbed in 1835 to the desire to explore both the North of England and Scotland. He felt himself to be in 'foreign' territory the moment he left the North Midlands.[71] In certain respects Scotland was only a further extension of that 'foreign' feeling. Conversely, it was not until she was south of Durham, with 260 miles to go to London, that Walter Scott's Jeanie Deans felt herself to be in alien territory after leaving Scotland. At that point she became acutely conscious of her isolation. Her bare feet, dress, speech, and manners called forth sneers, taunts, and sarcasm couched, according to Scott, 'in a worse *patois* by far than her own.'[72] It is, of course, a common-place, that every traveller 'reads' a particular landscape or territory according to his own preconceptions. John Mason Neale, the hymnologist, whose hopes were firmly fixed on heaven, saw Swansea at night in 1850 and could not imagine any scene on earth more nearly resembling hell. The green flames of the copper furnaces created a 'ghastly effect' and the entire scene was 'awfully beautiful'.[73]

At the mid-century, the 'discovery of Britain' ceased to be the prerogative of the gentleman traveller. 'It was in Scotland', Thomas Cook later recalled, 'that I first began to combine tickets for railways, steamboats, and other conveyances under one system, in

[70] Lady Raleigh (ed.), *A Selection from the Letters of Sir Walter Raleigh 1880–1922* (1928), 57. Despite these remarks, Raleigh's mother was the sister of Lord Gifford, the Scottish judge (and founder of the lectureship), and although his father had become minister of Kensington Chapel, London, he came from a Kirkcudbrightshire Cameronian family.

[71] F. Trench, *Scotland, its Faith and its Features* (1846), 35.

[72] J. Reed, *Sir Walter Scott: Landscape and Locality* (1980), 111.

[73] *Letters of John Mason Neale*, selected and edited by his daughter (1910), 146.

order that passengers travelling under our arrangements might well be able to calculate the expense and foresee the engagements they would have to enter into.'[74] That first venture began in 1846 and business steadily expanded thereafter. By the 1860s, the Scottish railway companies collaborated (not with Cook but with the London and North-Western) in putting together a tourist programme. A decade later, the London and North-Western and the Caledonian railway companies began a night train from London to Greenock, enabling passengers to connect with a steamer for the Western Isles. It soon became known as 'The Tourist'. Meanwhile, the Scottish railway network was still expanding—from Perth to Inverness in 1863 and, by the end of the 1870s, lines reached Oban, Wick, and Thurso. Around the turn of the century, the railway companies evolved further schemes to attract additional visitors. Major hotels were constructed at coastal or inland sites, preferrably with a golf-course close by. Never before had Scotland been so accessible by land from the rest of Britain and so anxious to receive visitors.

Of course, as historians of the holiday have demonstrated, it was not only Scotland that was 'opened up'.[75] A highly variegated pattern of 'resorts' developed all round the coasts of Britain from Aberdeen to Penzance. They all differed from each other in tone and facility, catering with increasing sophistication for the needs and desires of the 'holidaymaker' who was anxious to cast off the cares of business or the atmosphere of the city. Such 'excursions' took hundreds of thousands of people away from their immediate environment and, in the process, increased their awareness of the diversity of their country. From the 1870s, they dispatched picture postcards in large numbers to their friends and relatives. Some resorts naturally served the needs of nearby towns and cities—Blackpool, Weston-super-Mare, Skegness, and the North Wales resorts are among those that spring to mind—but no resort was entirely regional in its appeal. Families travelled large distances in search of a 'complete change'. Areas hitherto considered inaccessible and mysterious—like the Lake District or Snowdonia—were now becoming relatively easy to reach from any part of Britain.[76]

[74] Cited by J. Simmons, 'Railways, Hotels and Tourism in Great Britain, 1839–1914', *Journal of Contemporary History*, 19 (1984), 206–12.

[75] J. K. Walton, *The English Seaside Resort: A Social History, 1750–1914* (Leicester, 1983).

[76] I am indebted to my son's 1986 BA dissertation at the University of York: P. J. G.

The 'incorporation' of Cornwall is a good example of this process. As Professor Simmons has pointed out, it became the last English county to be connected into the 'national' railway system—as late as 1859. He suggests that before that date few people visited such a 'remote' area. The journey by coach, or by coastal steamer to Falmouth, was lengthy and tedious. In any miscellaneous gathering in mid-Victorian England there would invariably be a greater number of people present who knew more about Paris at first hand than about Truro. Even with the advent of the railway, there was no immediate rapid expansion of passenger traffic. A sleeping-car between London and Penzance was put on in 1877, but it was not until the turn of the century that significant reductions in journey times were achieved. Then the number of passengers carried more than doubled as the phrase 'The Cornish Riviera' was given extensive publicity.

Thomas Cook was the first man—in 1859—to see the county's potential for 'tourism'. In that year he put on a special train to the south-west starting from Bristol. Significantly, his second tour, later that summer, attracted bookings from as far north as Kelso and Berwick.[77] Cornwall was no longer isolated. One London young lady tells us that she travelled from the county, where she was then holidaying, to Dovey Junction on the Cambrian coast. Mobility of this kind might still be exceptional, but she was not unique. Even so, Cornwall retained a sense of 'difference'. Its attraction for English painters, particularly for Stanhope Forbes and his friends at the end of the century, can be compared with the enthusiasm of French artists for Brittany during the same period. Anthony Smith comments that the latter had 'all turned their backs on the materialism of city life, on technological advance and commercialism, and on the ever-increasing complexity of a centralized, regulated state, and sought instead some antidote far from the capital.'[78] Cornwall served a similar purpose in England: it had to remain remote yet also become accessible in its remoteness.

It was the railway network which presented this paradox. All contemporaries were aware of the diminishing significance of

Robbins, *Llanfairfechan: The Development and Social Tone of a Victorian Seaside Resort, 1840–1900*.

[77] J. Simmons, 'The Railway in Victorian Cornwall', *Journal of the Royal Institution of Cornwall*, 14, no. 1 (1982), 11–24.

[78] A. D. Smith, *The Ethnic Revival* (Cambridge, 1981), pp. xi–xii.

distance brought about by the increased speed of travel. Stage-coaches had reached the technical limits of their speed by 1830 at around 10 m.p.h. At that juncture, Liverpool, Manchester, and the main Yorkshire cities were around thirty hours' distance from London. By 1845, Liverpool could be reached in about seven hours and York in nine. In 1852, the journey from Edinburgh or Glasgow to London took eleven or twelve hours. By the late 1880s, however, the railway companies were engaged in a fierce 'race to the North' and the journey time to Edinburgh was reduced to seven hours and forty-five minutes and it took eight hours to reach Glasgow. By 1895, the journey time to Aberdeen had come down to eight and a half hours. These dramatic changes were most apparent on the main North/South Anglo-Scottish routes. Travellers wishing to make their way criss-cross up and down Britain were by no means so fortunate. All substantial routes, however, led to London and it was the railway map, at any rate psychologically, which determined whether or not one felt close to the hub of the kingdom.[79]

The requirements of the railway timetable combined with the needs of industrial work discipline to undermine local fairs and holidays. By mid-century, for example, in Cornwall, only Christmas Day and Good Friday were universally observed as holidays in the mining districts—as compared with the many days devoted to wrestling-matches, pitched battles, and riotous revellings in earlier decades. Up and down the country, 'wakes' and 'fair holidays' with their rich but local rituals steadily yielded to a 'national' pattern of leisure and recreation.[80] 'The present generation', wrote one writer on English customs in 1896, 'has witnessed the extinction of many observances which our fathers practised and revered, and doubtless the progress of decay will continue.' Even so, bonfires continued to burn with a particular fury in Sussex on 5 November and, on its eve, 'Mischief Night' was observed in Yorkshire with an intensity which alarmed southern visitors who happened to be stranded in the county. English visitors to Scotland or Wales at Hallowe'en also had some surprising experiences. They would have been puzzled by the

---

[79] This information is derived from J. Simmons, *The Railways of Britain* (1986) and M. Freeman and D. Aldcroft, *The Atlas of British Railway History* (Beckenham, 1985).

[80] J. Rule, *The Labouring Classes in Early Industrial England, 1750–1850* (1986), 216–26. See also J. K. Walton and R. Poole, 'The Lancashire Wakes in the Nineteenth Century' in R. D. Storch (ed.), *Popular Culture and Custom in Nineteenth-Century England* (1982), 100–24; R. W. Malcolmson, *Popular Recreations in English Society, 1700–1850* (Cambridge, 1973).

headlong flight downhill to escape the dreaded *hwch ddu gwta* (black sow without a tail) in Wales or the spectacle of a ring of people ecstatically dancing around a bonfire, as was frequently the case in parts of Scotland.[81]

The advent of the railways, however, did have one further unanticipated consequence for the 'nationalization' of life. Time-tables could not function properly when 'local time' prevailed in different parts of the country. By the late 1840s, the companies had succeeded in enforcing a uniformity across Britain which Greenwich standard time offered. There were demonstrations at Stroud in Gloucestershire against this 'alien' yardstick. It was not until 1880 that an Act of Parliament officially standardized time throughout Britain. However unpopular in particular localities, especially in the West, this measure was an ever-present reminder, from John-O'Groat's to Lands End, that all communities belonged to Britain.[82]

It is difficult to assess the bearing of this accelerating pattern of travel on the 'identity of Britain'. By the end of the century a substantial (though unquantifiable) segment of the population was personally acquainted with Britain *as a whole*—a greater proportion than had ever previously been the case. The expansion in route miles and the better facilities for third-class travellers produced a major increase in passenger journeys, from some sixty million in 1850 to almost 300 million by 1870. Total route length in Britain continued to grow until 1912. Tourism was still in its infancy. Its great paradox—the erosion of that individuality which the visitor seeks by the very act of visiting—had not fully manifested itself, but the signs were there. Even the act of railway construction pointed to this dilemma, as English and Scottish engineers pressed deep into the heart of Wales. 'I felt like a foreigner,' wrote one of their number 'and indeed was looked upon as such by the natives of the district [*the Swansea Valley*]. I felt very lonely and almost shut out from verbal communication with anyone.' Welshmen were apparently more difficult to work with than other peoples he subsequently encountered in the Ottoman Empire and India.[83] Integration into a 'national' network served to emphasize how

---

[81] C. Hole, *British Folk Customs* (1976), 86, 140–1.

[82] D. Parkes and N. Thrift, 'Time Spacemakers and Entrainment', *Transactions of the Institute of British Geographers* (1979), 365–7.

[83] *1812–1899, John Brunton's Book: Being the Memoirs of John Brunton, Engineer* (Cambridge, 1939), 17–20.

much diversity remained in the nation. Significantly, the organization of the railway companies took no account of 'England', 'Scotland', or 'Wales', though by 1892 the broad gauge finally disappeared and there was a uniform track throughout Britain. Within England, the Great Western, the Great Eastern, and the Great Northern, amongst others, had all established their own 'territories'. Two English-based companies came to divide Wales between them, while the North British and the Caledonian companies, both Scottish-based, substantially divided Scotland between them.

This 'railway blending' could be welcomed or feared. An Anglican parson from Denbighshire recognized the dilemma in some verses he addressed to Snowdon in 1864:

> All-conquering English rushes on apace,
> Railways already drive it to thy base:
> Soon shall 'Dim Saesneg' be a sound gone by,
> And, like the echoes of the breezes, die.
> 'Tis well 'twere so! the people now are one,
> Need but one tongue to work in unison.[84]

When Lord Rosebery addressed Edinburgh students in 1882 he told them that their generation might be critical for the survival of Scottish traditions and character. 'Much of that character', he thought, 'has been taken away from us by the swift amalgamating power of railways, by the centralisation of Anglicizing empire, by the compassionate sneer of the higher civilisation.' There were, however, limits even to the 'swift amalgamating power of railways'. Their ability to integrate depended, at a deeper level, on the vitality of diversity in the other important sectors of British life to which we shall turn in successive chapters.

[84] T. Hughes, cited by R. Garlick, *An Introduction to Anglo-Welsh Literature* (Cardiff, 1972), 56.

## 2

# Language, Literature, and Music
# Links and Barriers

The forces of language and literature can be either cohesive or disruptive. Every European state in the nineteenth century wrestled with the issues they provoked. Language was at once a link and a barrier. In Central Europe in particular there was a close association between the revival of language and the re-emergence of national aspirations. Conflict mostly centred upon the relationship between a 'master' language used administratively—French, German, or Russian—and the claims of 'minority' languages to parity. However, from Scandinavia to Spain and Italy, there was also dispute between 'high' and 'low' forms of the same language, and rivalry for supremacy between closely related languages or 'dialects'. In less acute fashion, all these forms of conflict were present in nineteenth-century Britain.

The English language was such an exceptional instrument that most Victorians supposed that it was destined to be the language of Britain: indeed, most supposed that it already was. In his *History of the Inductive Sciences*, Whewell described it as:

a conglomerate of Latin words, bound together in a Saxon cement, the fragments of the Latin being partly portions introduced directly from the parent quarry, with all their sharp edges, and partly pebbles of the same material, obscured and shaped by long rolling in a Norman or some other channel.[1]

In other words, there was little that was 'pure' about English. The language itself was the product of a blending of the various elements in the English past. It was the expression of the diversity that was England. For many writers, as on the continent, the native language had come to have an almost sacred character. According to Dean Trench, language was 'the embodiment, the incarnation . . .

---

[1] Cited by H. Aarsleff, 'The Early History of the Oxford English Dictionary', *Bulletin of the New York Public Library* (Sept. 1962), 421. See also J. W. Burrow, 'The Uses of Philology in Victorian England', in R. Robson (ed.), *Ideas and Institutions of Victorian Britain* (1967), 180–204.

of the feelings and thoughts and experiences of a nation . . . and of all which through long centuries they have attained to and won.'[2] 'Englishness', by definition, could only be expressed through the English language.

Mid-Victorians, however, were aware that there was a problem. Thomas Watts addressed himself to it in a paper given to the Philological Society of London in 1850 'On the probable future position of the English language'. The circumstances of its evolution meant that English was a 'medium' language, uniting as no other did Romanic and Teutonic stocks. Its vocabulary was, accordingly, marvellously rich. He concluded that English might become the most widely spoken language on earth: a state of affairs which would be an equal blessing to religion and literature.[3] English was already the language of the United States and of the colonies of settlement throughout the world. Macaulay's minute had ensured that it was becoming a language of the Indian élite. Such expansion was no doubt admirable but it did mean that the exclusive bond between the English language and the English nation was being broken. This was not a new phenomenon, but its implications were becoming more apparent. Englishmen might soon become a minority among English-speakers. Their version of the language might cease to be 'standard'. This incipient globalism had important consequences. It gave Britain a 'world identity' quite unlike any other European state. As the nineteenth century developed, the status of the English language in its standard form waxed enormously. This world role added another dimension to the discussion of language and literature within Britain itself where, in this area also, the apparently competing claims of integration and diversity had still to be resolved.

The link between the English language and the English nation had long ceased to be exclusive, even within Britain. Ever since the Acts of Union of 1536 and 1543, when Welsh had been proscribed as an official medium, English had been steadily replacing Welsh in the principality—for most public purposes. Only in the sphere of religion, in both established and Nonconformist churches, did the Welsh language, at the beginning of the nineteenth century, still

[2] R. C. Trench, *On the Study of Words (1864)* 21.
[3] Cited by H. Aarsleff, *The Study of Language in England, 1780–1860* (Princeton, 1967), 222–3.

hold a prominent, even dominant, place in public discourse. Yet, such bald statements do not do justice to the continued vitality of Welsh. In large measure, however, language use was a reflection of social position. The Welsh gentry had, for several centuries, adopted English as their habitual medium, even if, in some cases, patronage was still extended to some Welsh-language activities. Welsh might still be necessary for converse with 'inferior persons'. Precision in this matter is impossible, but in 1840 perhaps more than two-thirds of the total population of Wales still spoke Welsh, more than half of whom spoke no English. The 1844 Commissioners noted that South Wales exhibited the 'phenomenon of a peculiar language isolating the mass from the upper portion of society.' There were also, however, clear signs of a steady geographical erosion of the language, extending beyond areas such as the Gower peninsula, the Vale of Glamorgan, and South Pembrokeshire, where English had long been in the ascendancy. Reporting on competence in English and Welsh in a large number of schools, the Commissioners in 1858 found that in South Wales 63 per cent of children over 10 had good English, 32 per cent imperfect English, and 5 per cent Welsh only: in North Wales, however, the corresponding figures were 43 per cent, 44 per cent, and 13 per cent.[4]

English visitors to Wales had long conceded that, scattered among waterspouts and crags, there were people who spoke Welsh. Lady Crewe, for example, thought in 1795 that there was 'a sort of gutteral uncouthness' about the language, but admitted with approval the existence of words so full of vowels that the Welsh mouth opened frequently.[5] Public men who lived along the Border, however, were less impressed, even by vowel sounds. Sir Edmund Head, writing from Hereford in 1837, was not enamoured of the 'Celtic savages' nearby. 'The gradual action of Boards of Guardians, railroads, and other opportunities of intercourse', he supposed, 'may civilize them in about three centuries.' Sir George Cornewall Lewis concurred in his reply and added, 'how that intelligence is to be raised, while they retain their villainous Celtic language, it is not

[4] E. G. Lewis, *Bilingualism and Bilingual Education* (Oxford, 1981), 100–1.

[5] Moir, *Discovery of Britain*, 132–3: Thomas Roberts obligingly compiled *The Welsh Interpreter: Consisting of a Concise Vocabulary, and a Collection of Useful and Familiar Phrases, with the Exact Mode of Pronunciation*; *Adapted for Tourists who May Wish to Make Themselves Understood by the Peasantry During Their Rambles through Wales* (South Leigh, 1831).

easy to see.'⁶ The *Eclectic Review* put matters more solemnly: 'the retention of the language obstructs the progress of the inhabitants of the Principality in all the higher developments of civilisation.'⁷ It was a verdict which increasing numbers of Welsh speakers also came to accept. David Davies of Llandinam, who was to make his fortune in the coal-carrying trade, put the matter (in Welsh) graphically: 'If you wish to continue to eat black bread and to lie in straw beds carry on shouting "Long live the Welsh language". But if you wish to eat white bread and roast beef you must learn English.'⁸

In the last half of the nineteenth century, therefore, the place of the two languages in the life of Wales was fraught with ambiguity. If we take 'Anglicization' simply to mean a steady advance in familiarity with the English language, then it was certainly happening. It is difficult, however, to capture the manifold subtleties in this evolving situation. Statements about an ability to speak two languages are not very helpful as a guide to actual use. The *proportion* of Welsh speakers dropped, but in absolute numbers there were more Welsh speakers in 1901 than there were in 1801. Zones of linguistic comprehension or incomprehension existed throughout the principality: the ability to understand English or Welsh did not necessarily imply an ability to speak or read one or other of the languages. English, as the language of 'modernity', was expanding. For the same reason, however, not particularly liking the world that was evolving, or feeling excluded from its benefits, many Welshmen clung to Welsh. On many occasions, therefore, language use could lead to acrimonious discussion. Organizations emanating from England, not being certain where the linguistic land lay, sometimes decided that their interests would be best served by appointing Welsh-speaking agents and sometimes translated material into Welsh. The Anti-Corn-Law League did both while the Fabians contented themselves with the latter.⁹

---

⁶ Sir Gilbert Lewis (ed.), *Letters of the Rt. Hon. Sir George Cornewall Lewis* (1870), 79. Sir Edmund, the Assistant Poor Law Commissioner, compared the South Wales coalfield in 1839 to a penal colony inhabited by 'bad characters' and 'runaway vagrants'. D. J. V. Jones in Emsley and Walvin (eds.), *Artisans*, 82.
⁷ Cited by I. G. Jones, 'Language and Community in Nineteenth Century Wales', in D. Smith (ed.), *A People and a Proletariat: Essays in the History of Wales, 1780–1980* (1980), 48.
⁸ Ibid. 62.
⁹ I. G. Jones, 'The Anti-Corn Law letters of Walter Griffith', *Bulletin of the Board of Celtic Studies*, 28 (1978) 95–128; R. Wallace, 'The Anti-Corn Law League in Wales', *Welsh History Review*, 13 (1986), 1–23.

Such bilingualism can be seen merely as a transitional stage along the road to complete 'Anglicization' but, if so, that condition had not been reached in our period. The culture that was emerging, evanescent though it might prove, was a unique *British* blend. Works of English literature or technical instruction appeared alongside a vigorous Welsh literature. They did not replace them. Thousands of people in Wales had become, or were becoming, neither Welsh (if to be Welsh was to be without English) nor English (if to be English was to abandon all links with another language and culture). The relative speed of the mass diffusion of English did mean, however, that, in general, the English used in Wales was 'standard'. At the point of linguistic cross-over, bastard forms of English might appear, but they were largely ephemeral. Certain patterns of word order might be carried over from Welsh into English, but there was virtually no word transfer. English was spoken with a distinct Welsh intonation, but there was no single 'Welsh' accent. The interaction of the two languages was accompanied at times by some ostentatious public events designed, at least in intention, to give a historical foundation to the contemporary linguistic pluralism. The principal prize at the 1865 National Eisteddfod, held at Aberystwyth, was for an essay on the origins of the English nation, with a particular view to bringing out the links between the English Nation and the Ancient Britons. The adjudicator was no less a person than Prince Lucien Bonaparte. Sadly, he felt unable to make an award.[10]

The census first attempted to establish the linguistic position in Wales in 1891. It revealed that 54 per cent of the population could speak Welsh; twenty years later that figure had dropped to 44 per cent. Of the thirteen Welsh counties in 1891, five had more than 90 per cent Welsh speakers (Cardigan, Anglesey, Carmarthen, Merioneth, and Caernarfon); four between 51 per cent and 68 per cent (Flint, Denbigh, Montgomery, and Glamorgan); four between 10 per cent and 5 per cent (Brecon, Pembroke, Monmouth, and Radnor).[11] The 'coverage' of Welsh still looked impressive on a linguistic map, though a high intensity of Welsh-speakers frequently corresponded with a low population density. The swiftly changing pattern of language made it increasingly difficult to think of Wales as a single *Kulturgebiet*, if indeed it ever had been.

[10] B. Davies, 'Empire and Identity: the "Case" of Dr. William Price', in Smith (ed.) *People and Proletariat*, 87.   [11] Lewis, *Bilingualism*, 119.

The possibility of living in an entirely Welsh world was a privilege increasingly only possessed by those living in geographically remote areas. A major segment of the population was switching, with greater or lesser facility, between two languages; sometimes with each language possessing its own mental territory, sometimes not.[12] The working-man poet John Jones captures the atmosphere of mid-century Holywell (Clwyd) in these lines:

> 'Tis market day, loud dealers strain their lungs,
> And High-street echoes with two different tongues.
> The Welsh and English there alternate cry
> 'Rhai'n, rhai'n, yw pethau rhad'—'Come buy, come buy'.[13]

An increasing proportion of the population could not speak Welsh at all. In part, it was made up of English-speakers in areas where Welsh had long since died; in part, it stemmed from a failure in linguistic transmission between the generations, by design or accident; in part, increasingly the case in the early twentieth century, it arose from substantial English settlement in Wales.[14]

That process was most dramatic in Glamorgan which registered a fivefold growth, from a population of 232,000 in the sixty years after 1851. Immigration, largely from England, accounted for more than half of this increase. In the decade ending in 1911, for example, over 85,000 people entered the county from England, mostly to work in the coalfields. In the Rhondda and Merthyr, Welsh in-migration was sufficient, for a time, to maintain the Welsh language, but such a concentration may have been at the expense of non-coalfield areas where it collapsed rapidly.[15] In Cardiff in 1911 only 6 per cent spoke Welsh, though in Merthyr, the Rhondda, and Swansea the figures were 50 per cent, 54 per cent, and 27 per cent respectively. Few incomers learnt Welsh and therefore they further

---

[12] K. Roberts, *Feet in Chains*, translated by John Idris Jones (1980), 63, gives an example of a school prize-giving in North Wales. The schoolboy wanted his mother to come but she said that she had no English and no nice clothes. The reply came 'You don't need English . . . Everyone will be talking Welsh except those on the stage'; See also G. A. Williams, *The Merthyr Rising* (1978) 26–7.

[13] Cited by Garlick, *Anglo-Welsh Literature*, 56.

[14] G. Williams, *Religion, Language and Nationality in Wales* (Cardiff, 1979); P. T. J. Morgan, 'From a Death to a View: The Hunt for a Welsh Past in the Romantic Period', in E. J. Hobsbawm and T. O. Ranger (eds.), *The Invention of Tradition* (Cambridge, 1983), 43–100; P. T. J. Morgan and D. Thomas, *Wales: The Shaping of a Nation* (Newton Abbot, 1984), 46–55.

[15] P. N. Jones, 'Aspects of Internal Migration to the Glamorganshire Coalfield, 1881–1911', *Transactions of the Honourable Society of Cymmrodorion* (1969), 90–5.

accelerated 'Anglicization', yet they were not impervious to their new surroundings. Some degree of residential segregation was initially observable, but it was not maintained with any rigour. Intermarriage was not infrequent. It was the 'English/Welsh' who were often in the van when it came to industrial or political activity—the names of A. J. Cook and Frank Hodges may be mentioned. Out of this vigorous and occasionally violent society emerged a new kind of 'Anglo-Welshness'. It was a society which began to write about itself with an unmistakable prose style. It was only in the early nineteenth century that the novel came of age in Wales and, at its end, there emerged a 'regional' writing which, one suspects, could only have emerged in a mixed society which was neither thoroughly Welsh in speech nor thoroughly English.[16] Such a blending was not confined to Glamorgan. It also occurred in the industrialized North-East.[17] The English language also lapped steadily against the sea-shore in such places as Barry, Aberdyfi, and Prestatyn.

Population also left Wales. Professor Brinley Thomas has long stressed the fact that migrants from the rural West and Mid-Wales could find work in industrial Glamorgan but he is probably wrong to suggest that Wales was a discrete economy with its own migration pattern which was largely unrelated to the pattern of English migration.[18] Recent work suggests that in 1861, two-thirds of the 190,000 persons who had left rural Wales (and not emigrated) were living in England and only about a quarter were in Glamorgan. Baines argues that the position was much the same at the end of the century. The main destination of migrants from Central Wales was the West Midlands and those from North Wales went to Merseyside.[19] That pattern of lateral movement clearly

[16] T. J. Ll. Pritchard's *The Adventures of Twm Shon Catti* (1828) has been described as 'the first Anglo-Welsh novel'. Morgan and Thomas, *Wales*, 188.

[17] Daniel Owen, a Mold tailor, wrote about his area in short stories in Welsh. See W. T. R. Pryce, 'Migration and the Evolution of Cultural Areas: Cultural and Linguistic Frontiers in North-East Wales, 1750–1851', *Transactions of the Institute of British Geographers*, 65 (1975), 79–107.

[18] B. Thomas, 'Wales and the Atlantic Economy', *Scottish Journal of Political Economy* (1959), 169–92, was a pioneering study.

[19] D. Baines, *Migration in a Mature Economy: Emigration and Internal Migration in England and Wales, 1861–1900* (Cambridge, 1986), 277–8. Professor Thomas's latest reflections, 'The Industrial Revolution and the Welsh language', in C. Baber and L. J. Williams (eds.), *Modern South Wales: Essays in Economic History* (Cardiff, 1986), 6–21 were written before Baines's book was published.

emerges when the Welsh-born population of Liverpool is contrasted, for its county origins, with that of Bristol or Birmingham.
The Welsh-born population of mid-century Liverpool reached
5 per cent of the total (under 2 per cent of Manchester, under 1 per
cent of Birmingham, over 3 per cent of Bristol, and under 1 per cent
of London). However, it was only London that attracted Welshmen
from all over the principality. No single Welsh county provided
more than around 11 per cent of the Welsh population of London.[20]
There were also identifiable Welsh communities outside the big
English cities—in such places as Sunderland and Middlesbrough on
the one hand, or Bath and Brighton on the other. There were more
males in the former and more females in the latter.

The Welsh 'community' in England was, of course, bigger than
the Welsh-born population settled there, but is the term appropriate? Was there scope for the maintenance of linguistic identity?
Certainly, for a time. Areas of Liverpool, particularly Everton, were
known Welsh strongholds. Welsh was still frequently used by
Liverpool-born Welsh people into the twentieth century. There was
much Welsh-language publishing. In the nineteenth century, the
city received the National Eisteddfod on three occasions. Sixty per
cent of married male Welsh heads of households in Liverpool in
1871 were married to Welsh-born women. However, where they
did not marry Welshwomen, they were more likely to choose a
migrant English partner rather than a local-born Liverpudlian or
migrants from Scotland or Ireland.[21] The proximity of North Wales
meant that cultural replenishment was relatively easy. Welshness
may have been preserved because mixing with the local middle
class was socially difficult at the same time as Welsh educational
enthusiasm marked them off from the local working class. By the
end of the century, however, as new migration decreased, and
the second and third generations of Liverpool Welsh easily used the
English language, Merseyside Welshness lost ground, though it was
still readily discernible.[22] The same process happened elsewhere,
but it could happen that in the next generation 'secret Welshmen'
were overcome by unaccountable *hiraeth* (nostalgia/longing) for

[20] C. G. Pooley, 'Welsh Migration to England in the Mid-Nineteenth Century',
*Journal of Historical Geography*, 9 (1983), 293.

[21] Ibid. 299–301.

[22] Id., 'The Residential Segregation of Migrant Communities in Mid-Victorian
Liverpool', *Transactions of the Institute of British Geographers* (1977), 364–82; J. G.
Davies, *Nationalism as a Social Phenomenon* (Liverpool, 1965), 22–51.

the land of their fathers which they had never known. The father of David Jones, the London-born artist and writer, moved to London in the 1880s from Wales—his own parents, both Welsh-speakers, had discouraged him from using Welsh. He married an English-woman. In a not uncharacteristic twist, David Jones bitterly regretted that he was an English monoglot.[23] Likewise, the young Edward Thomas, an undergraduate at Lincoln College in 1897–8, and pupil there of O. M. Edwards, felt increasingly drawn to the Wales of his cousins. He visited them in Wales during the Long Vacation. His *Beautiful Wales* (1905) was the fruit of his grappling with a mysterious aspect of his own identity—Englishman though he outwardly seemed to be.[24]

It appeared indeed as though literary England was full of secret Welshmen. On the eve of the First World War, therefore, the condition of the languages and literatures of Wales appeared to be ambiguous. The advance of English appeared inexorable. Both 'push' and 'pull' factors operated in its advance. Those factors varied in their impact from individual to individual and from community to community. The passport to a wider world, not only in Britain but beyond, offered by fluency in English, was irresistible. Linguistic integration in nineteenth-century Wales was not only perceived as advantageous, it seemed in the circumstances inescapable. The penetration of English could only perhaps be avoided by leaving Britain altogether—the course taken by Michael D. Jones and his followers when they established a *gwladfa* (homeland) in Patagonia in 1865. There, however, they had to swim in a Spanish sea.

Two fundamental issues remained: the survival of the Welsh language and the expression of 'Welshness' in English. Acceptance of the onward march of English did not have as an inevitable corollary the abandonment of Welsh. There was no conflict between integration and diversity. Welsh could flourish alongside English in congenial harmony. Such an aspiration was easier to state than to achieve. A perception that one language is 'in decline' is apt to accelerate that decline. Yet, in the late nineteenth century, it was not clear that Welsh was in decline—which perhaps accounts for a certain complacency amongst Welsh speakers. Since the drop in the proportion of Welsh-speakers was accompanied by an increase in the total number it was difficult to assess the vitality of

---

[23] H. Grisewood (ed.), *David Jones: The Dying Gaul and Other Writings* (1978), 35.
[24] R. G. Thomas, *Edward Thomas: A Portrait* (Oxford, 1985), 66–81, 120–3.

the language. The speed of its post-war decline was to shock those who believed that the diversity of Wales was self-sustaining. However, in the Wales of 1914, there were an increasing number of people who had lacked Welsh for generations. They resented suggestions either from Welsh-speaking Welshmen or from Englishmen that their 'Welshness' had therefore evaporated. From their perspective, cultural diversity did not depend upon the maintenance of linguistic diversity.

In his *Letters from England* (1807), Robert Southey has his supposed Iberian traveller write thus on the subject of 'Scotch' dialect:

It differs far more from English than Portuguese from Castillian, nearly as much as the Catalan, though the articles and auxiliars are the same. Very many words are radically different, still more so differently pronounced as to retain no distinguishable similarity; and as this difference is not systematic it is the more difficult to acquire. No Englishman reads Scotch with fluency, unless he has long resided in the country . . .[25]

A recent writer on language in Britain confesses to have changed his mind four times on whether he should have a separate chapter on Scots. Was it a language or was it a dialect?[26] This highly ambivalent position adopted by students of language in the present had been anticipated in nineteenth-century Scotland itself. Prior to 1800, sophisticated men in Edinburgh and Glasgow had become uncomfortably aware of 'Scoticisms'. Societies and books advised on how they might be eradicated.[27] When Francis Jeffrey left Edinburgh for Oxford in September 1791 he was bent on ridding himself of the national inconvenience by associating with the 'pedants, coxcombs and strangers' of Queen's.[28] However, he soon reported that he felt more a Scotchman than when he had lived in Scotland: 'My opinions, ideas, prejudices and systems are all Scotch. The only part of a Scotchman I mean to abandon is the language; and language is all I expect to learn in England.'[29] Cockburn, his biographer, commented sadly on this remark 'Our mere speech was

[25] R. Southey, *Letters from England* (Gloucester, 1984), 462.
[26] G. Price, *The Languages of Britain* (1984), 186. See also M. Robinson (ed.), *The Concise Scots Dictionary* (Aberdeen, 1985), pp. xi–xiii.
[27] J. Beattie, *Scoticisms, Arranged in Alphabetical Order, Designed to Correct Improprieties of Speech and Writing* (Edinburgh, 1779), is but one example.
[28] Lord Cockburn, *Life of Lord Jeffrey*, vol. i (Edinburgh, 1852), 34–5.
[29] Ibid. i. 46–8.

doomed to recede, to a certain extent, before the foreign wave, and it was natural for a young man to anticipate what was coming.'[30] He also commented on another occasion:

English has made no encroachment on me; yet, though I speak more Scotch than English throughout the day and read Burns aloud, and recommend him, I cannot even get my own children to pick up a queer word of him here and there. Scotch has ceased to be the vernacular language of the upper classes.[31]

Spotting Scoticisms was one of Sydney Smith's favourite occupations.[32]

Such concern among an élite is comprehensible. To attempt to enshrine 'Doric' speech in a written language would cut Scotland off from the wider English-speaking world. It would handicap Scots in playing a role within Britain. For the time being, Scotch speech could simply be switched on and off as the occasion and company required. Jeffrey, we are told, could still speak it as correctly 'as when the Doric of the Lawnmarket of Edinburgh had only been improved by that of Rottenrow of Glasgow . . .'.[33] A feeling also remained that if the spoken language had to be abandoned 'our native *literature* was better fixed'. Jeffrey indeed continued to relish 'classic Scotch' writers such as Gavin Douglas, Burns, Scott, Wilson, Hogg, and Galt.

What was one to make of Burns? Southey's purported Iberian visitor had 'looked into the poems of Burns, which are very famous, and found them almost wholly unintelligible; a new dictionary and a new grammar were wanted and on inquiring for such I found that none were in existence.'[34] Charles Kingsley, however, considered that Burns succeeded in substantial measure in welding the 'Norse Scotch' and the 'Romanesque English':

a happy union, in the opinion of those who, as we do, look on the vernacular Norse Scotch as no barbaric dialect, but as an independent tongue, possessing a choiceness, melody, terseness, and picturesqueness which makes it, both in prose and verse, a far better vehicle than the popular English for many forms of thought.[35]

---

[30] Ibid. i. 48.
[31] Cited and discussed by K. Miller, *Cockburn's Millenium* (1975), 262–4.
[32] A. Bell, *Sydney Smith* (Oxford, 1980), 67.
[33] Cockburn, *Jeffrey*, i. 47.
[34] Southey, *Letters from England*, 462.
[35] C. Kingsley, 'Burns and his School', in *Literary and General Lectures and Essays* (1890), 158.

In general, however, Englishmen did not easily raise their glasses to the immortal memory of Burns or adopt him as a full-blown British poet, though James Murray of the Oxford English Dictionary told the ever-inquisitive Prince Lucien Bonaparte that 'The spelling of Burns . . . is *simply English*, partly disguised by the fact that he uses a considerable percentage of *words not British.*' Bonaparte, who was seeking the Gospel of St Matthew in Scots, was told that many of these words could not be pressed into service for the purpose he had in mind. It was extremely difficult, Murray continued, to find an orthography which conveyed what 'an actual living thing' a Scotch dialect was and 'its utter difference from English sounds.'[36] Gerard Manley Hopkins took the view that Burns's poems 'lost prodigiously by translation. I have never read them since my undergraduate days . . .'.[37] Thus, however central to a certain conception of Scottish culture, Burns remained at the margin of British, though a Lancashire weaver, Benjamin Brierley, records in his autobiography that it was only when he joined the companionship of Burns and Byron that he felt the 'God within me'.

Lord Byron was 8 years old when Burns died. His career, too, can be taken to exemplify the tensions of a double inheritance. His English father was worthless and until the age of 10 he was brought up in some poverty in Aberdeen by his mother, the Gordon heiress. In the celebrated passage in his *Don Juan*, Byron described himself as 'half a Scot by birth and bred / A whole one.' He had 'scotched, not killed' the Scotsman in his blood and had come to love the land of mountain and flood. His subsequent education at Harrow and Cambridge left him with conflicting feelings about the land of his boyhood and it seems an overstatement to describe him as a 'Scottish genius' 'finding itself as best it may in the alien medium of English, which he writes like a brilliant foreigner.'[38]

Movement between various 'speech-zones' was part of the everyday experience of nineteenth-century Scots, be they aristocrats or working women like Christian Watt from Buchan. Meeting a party of Highland women, she was impressed by their looks and their intelligence 'but what I saw wrong was they should have printed school books in the Gaelic.' She noted of herself 'I could

---

[36] K. M. E. Murray, *Caught in the Web of Words: James A. H. Murray and the Oxford English Dictionary* (1977), 81.

[37] C. C. Abbott, *The Letters of Gerard Manley Hopkins to Robert Bridges* (1935), 87.

[38] A. Bold (ed.) *Byron: Wrath and Rhyme* (1983), 21.

always think much quicker in Buchan doric rather than English, a language I had to always learn' and in forcing Highlanders to learn English 'Education was suppressing their self-respect.' When she sold fish in the Grampian glens few understood English and communication took place in a mixture of Doric and Gaelic. Christian did spend some time in London in the service of the Duchess of Leeds but it is noteworthy that she met few English people. She attended the Scots Kirk on Sundays and danced late on Saturday nights 'where all the Aberdeen folk gathered in a close off the Strand.' By the end of the century, however, she noted that the reverse was happening. English folk were pouring into Aberdeen to man the steam trawlers and there were constant fights between the locals and the incomers, a breach which never healed 'until almost all the sons of both laid down their lives in the war.'[39]

As for Gaelic, recent studies have mapped in detail its erosion in nineteenth-century Scotland, though the transition to a kind of English was neither complete nor speedy.[40] 'The common language of the people is Gaelic' stated the minister of Comrie parish in Perthshire in 1794. All the natives understood it, but many, especially the old, had little English. All the young people could speak English, though in order to acquire it they had gone to service 'in the Low Country'. Forty years later in Comrie the English language was generally spoken, and only a limited number attended the afternoon Gaelic church service. In many parts of the Highlands and Islands, however, the two languages existed side by side with some vitality. As in Wales, it was context—be it church, shop, business, or home—that determined which language was used. In the outer *Gaidhealtachd*, the loss of the Gaelic was most discernible in the South and East, though a Gaelic accent in the pronunciation of English survived. In the inner *Gaidhealtachd*, Gaelic was still preferred, though English was increasingly understood and spoken. There was a shift in the intensity of Gaelic rather than a complete change from Gaelic to English.

This steady 'Anglicization', however, was not imposed from England. The view expressed by one anonymous contributor in the *Edinburgh Journal* in 1877 that Gaelic was 'a NUISANCE which everyone should aid in removing with all reasonable speed' may have been particularly blunt but it was not unique. An editorial in

[39] D. Fraser (ed.), *The Christian Watt Papers* (Edinburgh, 1983), 28, 30–4, 127.
[40] V. E. Durkacz, *The Decline of the Celtic Languages* (Edinburgh, 1983).

the *Glasgow Herald* in June 1908 suggested that 'the first requisite for a Highlander is such a knowledge of English as will open up to him the lucrative employment from which ignorance of English must shut him out.' The Registrar-General's Report in 1871 declared:

The Gaelic language may be what it likes, both as to antiquity and beauty but it decidedly stands in the way of the civilization of the natives making use of it, and shuts them out from the paths open to their fellow-countrymen who speak the English tongue. It ought, therefore, to cease to be taught in all our national schools; and as we are one people we should have but ONE language.[41]

There could be no clearer declaration of principle, though the particular prescription was not applied.

Such sentiments reflected the fact that, in previous centuries, the divergencies between levels of illiteracy in the Highlands and Lowlands of Scotland were much greater than those between areas of England. This has prompted the suggestion that Lowland Scotland and the four northern counties of England can be looked upon as a distinct *Kulturgebiet*, despite the formal existence of the Border.[42] R. K. Webb takes the view that in England, although there were 'astounding' variations, a greater consciousness of the value of education seemed prevalent in the North of the country.[43] When James Murray was five, he was taken up a road where a little burn in a deep ditch marked the Anglo-Scottish border. A 'wee Scot' himself, the future editor of the Oxford English Dictionary could not understand how one piece of land could be called 'England' and another 'Scotland'. He then met an English farmer who wore knee breeches and wooden clogs with bright brass mountings. Murray apparently concluded that such attire distinguished Englishmen from Scotsmen! In later life, his linguistic studies seemed to confirm that there was little difference between his own native Border speech and that of Northumberland.[44]

[41] C. W. J. Withers, *Gaelic in Scotland, 1698–1981* (Edinburgh, 1984), 87, 98–9.

[42] R. A. Houston, *Scottish Literacy and Scottish Identity: Illiteracy and Society in Scotland and Northern England, 1600–1800* (Cambridge, 1985), 264–5.

[43] R. K. Webb, *The British Working-Class Reader, 1790–1848* (New York, 1971), 21–2.

[44] Murray, *Murray*, 12–13; one enduring source of irritation and confusion lay in the use of shall/will. Sir Edmund Head turned from the problems of South Wales to publish an essay on this topic in 1854. See Lewis, *Letters*, 275 and C. C. Abbott, *Further Letters of Gerard Manley Hopkins* (1956), 169.

At the end of the nineteenth century, therefore, the languages of Scotland were in a precarious position. Apart from pockets of speakers in the major cities, Gaelic was in full retreat, destined only to survive on the periphery in the Highlands and Islands. Since, in the modern era, Gaelic had never been the language of Scotland its further geographical concentration was less ominous than the comparable, if less complete, regionalization of Welsh. The eventual loss of Gaelic, supposing that occurred, would spell the end of Gaeldom but would not in itself prove fatal to a Scottish identity. The consequence of the loss of Scots was more problematic. As in Wales, 'push' and 'pull' factors had been operative in the attempts over more than a century to remove 'awkward' features in Scots. Once again, integration, not only into Britain but into 'world-English', appeared to require such a course. The professional classes had largely made this transition. They wrote, and largely spoke, a language which caused no difficulty south of the Border. The bulk of the population, however, still retained elements of vocabulary and occasional patterns of word-order which could be difficult to interpret 'outwith' Scotland. The incursion of Irish/English patterns, particularly into the speech of the West of Scotland, added to the mixture. The diversity which survived seemed more classifiable as a strongly accented speech (which did survive high up in the social scale) rather than a Scots language which could stand in relation to English in a condition analogous to the relationship between Catalan and Castilian. There is something a little odd in the fact that, as late as 1904, the *English Dialect Dictionary* believed that *taxman* was a Scottish word![45]

What was the 'English' of England itself? At the academic level, it is sometimes said—'especially', Professor Palmer naughtily notes, by Scotsmen—that the study of English began in Scotland. However, he observes that there were Professors of English in London and Manchester 'for some time' before the Regius Chair of English Language and Literature was established in the University of Glasgow in 1862. At Edinburgh the Chair of Rhetoric and Belles Lettres was redesignated the Chair of Rhetoric and English Literature in 1865 when David Masson, from University College, London, was appointed. When Chairs were established at Aberdeen and

---

[45] Cited by P. Wright, *The Language of British Industry* (1974), 27.

St Andrews in the 1890s, Palmer points out, there was no longer any novelty in such developments.[46] Such a corrective is necessary, but Scotsmen do seem to have been disproportionately heavily involved in the evolution of English as a discipline. Masson was himself a returning Scot and the subject at Manchester owed a good deal to the impetus provided by A. J. Scott, the first Principal of Owen's College. Scott, an early associate of Edward Irving and Erskine of Linlathen, had been deposed from the ministry of the Church of Scotland in 1831 for heresy. Moving to London, he developed close friendships with, among others, Carlyle, Thackeray, Kingsley, and Ruskin. Becoming Professor of English Literature at University College, London, he was the personal link between some of the leading theological reformers of Scotland and England. He performed the same role in Manchester.[47] John Nichol, who was appointed to the Glasgow English Chair, was a graduate of the university who had then gone to Balliol where he became a leading light in that Anglo-Scottish 'Old Mortality' circle which included T. H. Green and James Bryce.[48] He had strong aesthetic interests but also lectured on the history of the English language, that is to say the language of England.[49] Perhaps the phrase 'our English poets' tripped more easily from the lips of his friend Lord Lytton than from his own. It is perhaps significant that Nichol wrote a small, though successful, book on *English Composition* in 1879. His biographer remarks that it helped students 'to avoid the pitfalls of provincialism and inaccuracy'.[50] It is not entirely fanciful to suggest that concern for 'good English' derived from Nichol's awareness of teaching across a linguistic frontier. On his retirement, Nichol moved to London. He was gratified to learn that A. C. Bradley was to be his successor: 'Our "nature's raw material"', he wrote, 'is very fair, but wants refining, and wants purging of its provincial dross, its love of rhetoric, and admiration of bad models . . .'.[51]

The English Association was formed in 1907 to promote, amongst other matters, the recognition of English as 'an essential

[46] D. J. Palmer, *The Rise of English Studies* (1965), 171.

[47] J. P. Newell, 'A Nestor of Nonconformist Heretics: A. J. Scott (1805-1866)', *Journal of the United Reformed Church History Society*, 3, no. 1 (1983), 16.

[48] C. Harvie, *The Lights of Liberalism: University Liberals and the Challenge of Democracy, 1860-1886* (1976).

[49] W. Knight, *Memoir of John Nichol* (Glasgow, 1896), 184.

[50] Ibid. 241.

[51] Ibid. 225.

element in the national education' and to promote 'the correct use of English, spoken and written'. It was the outcome of thirty years during which 'English Studies', in some form or other, had received increased attention. Linguistic uniformity and a shared literary awareness would serve the needs both of 'national enlightenment' and 'national efficiency'. Yet what was the 'standard' English to be promulgated? In the Bulletin of the Association in 1909, S. K. Ratcliffe was alarmed at the 'rapid degeneration' which he detected in spoken English: 'a debased dialect of the Cockney ... is spreading from our schools and training colleges all over the country. In ten years' time the English language will not be worth speaking.'[52]

It was, of course, a matter of opinion what English was 'worth speaking'. In 1869 the philologist A. J. Ellis spoke of a 'received pronunciation' emanating from 'the educated pronunciation of the metropolis, of the court, the pulpit and the bar' though there remained 'a varied thread of provincial utterance running through the whole.'[53] He noted that teachers were sent into remote districts 'to convey the required sounds more or less correctly' and this effort, combined with the rapid communication of individuals 'such as rail roads now effect' did much 'to produce uniformity of speech'. But he stressed that even in 'small, educated and locomotive England' different regions still had their burrs or brogues.[54] The generalization may be risked that there was more variety of accent in the House of Commons in the half century after 1850 than before it. There even remained traces of Lancashire and Liverpool in the speech of Mr Gladstone.[55]

It is likely, too, that pleasant/unpleasant indices, as identified by students of language in our own time, can be pushed back into the past—with London, Birmingham, Liverpool, and Glasgow coming at the bottom of the scale.[56] Visiting Liverpool in 1813, for example, Maria Edgeworth could not understand the answers to her questions, so rich was the dialect. Mr Roscoe of Allerton Hall spoke excellent language 'but with a strong provincial accent which destroys all idea of elegance.' In North Wales, too, her father had

[52] Cited by B. Doyle, 'The Invention of English', in R. Colls and P. Dodd (eds.), *Englishness: Politics and Culture, 1880-1920* (1986), 108.

[53] A. J. Ellis, *On Early English Pronunciation* ... (1869), 23.

[54] Ibid. 19.

[55] R. T. Shannon, *Gladstone* vol. i (1982), 93.

[56] P. Trudgill, *On Dialect: Social and Geographical Perspectives* (Oxford, 1983), 222.

not been able to understand their Welsh postillion, or at least had disagreed about the proper pronunciation of quarry.[57] Nearly a century later, the chairman of the examination board of the National Union of Teachers remarked of Manchester children that 'they spoke the perverted Lancashire dialect of the towns, had a narrow vocabulary, and could not understand diction.'[58] Elizabeth Gaskell's minister husband William had analysed Lancashire dialect in less severe terms in the 1850s.[59] The appropriately named Mr York, in Charlotte Brontë's *Shirley*, was forthright in affirming that 'A Yorkshire burr was as much better than a Cockney's lisp, as a bull's bellow than a ratton's squeak.'[60]

The choice, of course, was not simply between 'the North' and 'London'. The speech of East Anglia could not be mistaken for that of Dorset. Some cities, like Bristol, contained peculiarities of speech which set them apart even from surrounding counties. Distance alone, however, did not determine the vitality (or impenetrability) of English dialect. In West Cornwall, where, two hundred years earlier, Cornish was spoken, a mid-nineteenth-century writer noted that Cornish speech was more pure—more like Standard English than the dialect of neighbouring 'Anglo-Saxon' Devon.[61] A Tyneside shipworker and a Somerset farm-labourer, if they had come into frequent contact, would have found mutual understanding difficult. Normally, of course, such extremes would not meet: encounters tended to take place between speakers of Standard English and speakers of particular dialects. Where this happened, as when a Commission of Enquiry took evidence from Tyneside miners, an 'interpreter' had to be present.[62] Technical terms, even in the same industry, varied widely and 'glosses' were required.

In general, however, it appeared to contemporaries that dialectical 'aberrations' from Standard English, like the non-English languages, were in irreversible decline. T. E. Brown, the 'Manx'

[57] C. Colvin (ed.), *Maria Edgeworth: Letters from England, 1813–1844* (Oxford, 1971), 7, 10–11.

[58] Cited by Doyle in Colls and Dodd (eds.), *Englishness*, 85.

[59] W. Gaskell, *Two Lectures on the Lancashire Dialect* (1854).

[60] Cited by A. Briggs, 'Private and Social Themes in *Shirley*', in his *Collected Essays*, vol. ii, *Images, Problems, Standpoints, Forecasts* (Brighton, 1985), 69.

[61] M. F. Wakelin, *Language and History in Cornwall* (Leicester, 1975), 99–100.

[62] B. H. Harrison, *Peaceable Kingdom: Stability and Change in Modern Britain* (Oxford, 1982), 292.

poet, noted that, at least in comparison with the Ayrshire dialect used by Burns, 'our dialects are apologetic things, half-ashamed, half-insolent.' And, of Brown's own verse, a friend remarked that it was 'a courageous and loving attempt to enshrine the spirit of a dying age'. It attempted 'to catch an accent that was doomed to fade.'[63] The English Dialect Society was started in Cambridge in 1873—it later moved to Manchester—but it was wound up in 1896. During this period, however, Joseph Wright compiled his major dialect dictionary. He had left school in Bradford at the age of 13 and had to acquire much of the vocabulary and sound-system of standard English later in life. He managed to include in his dictionary the term *Throssen-up*, meaning 'stuffy' or 'stuck up', used by his mother to describe ladies from the South. It is interesting to note that Wright found that his most enthusiastic helpers in the work of compilation were from the North and West of England. People from Kent and Surrey apparently had little interest in preserving the folk-speech which the nineteenth century had inherited from the past. In his old age, Wright (who had become an Oxford professor) reverted to some of his boyhood pronunication. He startled a well-bred young lady from Kingston-upon-Hull by accusing her of 'cooming from 'ooll'.[64]

It is not difficult to understand why the decline of dialect seemed unavoidable to many observers in the late nineteenth century. It was linked to mobility and the transport revolution, on the one hand, and formal education, on the other. It was commonly believed that the maintenance of dialect required the continued existence of self-contained compact communities. Such communities were ceasing to exist and, in consequence, the pool of local speech peculiarity was running dry. There was no place, either, for dialect in formal school instruction. No doubt this frequently meant that there was a gap between the language of the teacher and the language of the pupil. Even where this was acknowledged, however, the solution could not lie in granting some formal status to prevailing local speech codes. Inevitably, the resulting structure of language in England blended regional and class conventions. 'Standard English' can be seen as a hegemonic device, but it also offered a way of escape for those who felt themselves to be

---

[63] *Thomas Edward Brown: A Memorial Volume 1830–1930* (Cambridge, 1930), 152–3.

[64] E. M. Wright, *The Life of Joseph Wright* (1932), i. 20–1; ii. 358, 677.

restricted by the limitations of a provincial *patois*. Accents remained strongly entrenched, but differences of vocabulary began to disappear as the language of 'Standard Authors' advanced. The social integration of England on a national basis was also apparent in the fact that, unlike the position in some continental countries, it was rare for dialect or even accented speech to come forth from the lips of the highest social classes. A short examination of certain contemporary literature confirms this general impression.

The literary presentation of the diversity of Britain was itself diverse. 'There grows in the North Country', runs the opening sentence in Arnold Bennett's *A Man from the North*, 'a certain kind of youth of whom it may be said that he is born to be a Londoner. The metropolis, and everything that appertains to it, that comes down from it, that goes up into it, has for him an impervious fascination.'[65] Although Bennett's 'North' stopped at Stoke-on-Trent, the sentence could be taken to refer to almost any ambitious writer. For some the place of their origin was little more than a temporary starting-point, for others it left a permanent mark, for yet others it had scarcely any significance either way. Some writers came to know their Britain well; others scarcely shifted from their (normally) southern residences. Some ignored regional peculiarities of speech in their dialogue passages, others attempted a more or less accurate representation of it. Some contented themselves with little more than standard stereotypes of 'Northerners' or 'Scotsmen'. It was, of course, inescapable that books were written to be read.[66] Publishers in London and elsewhere knew that chunks of dialect could prove unacceptable to readers even if veracity might have gained by its inclusion. Toleration of *couleur locale* had its limits. Authors knew this too. 'The present author', Scott stated in his 1830 introduction to *Ivanhoe*, 'felt that in confining himself to subjects purely Scottish, he was not only likely to weary out the indulgence of his readers, but also greatly to limit his power of affording them pleasure.'[67]

Charles Dickens described his children as 'half-bred English and

[65] A. Bennett, *A Man From the North* (1898), 1.

[66] D. C. D. Pocock, 'The Novelist's Image of the North', *Transactions of the Institute of British Geographers* (1979), 62–76; A. H. Paul and P. Simpson-Housley, 'The Novelist's Image of the North: A Discussion', ibid. (1980), 383–7.

[67] Cited by J. Reed, *Sir Walter Scott: Landscape and Locality* (1980), 135–6.

Scotch' and, in the early flush of his marriage, he was prepared to obtain from Scotland a little Toddy-water kettle to console his wife.[68] As a journalist, he had covered the reception given in Edinburgh to Earl Grey in 1834. The Edinburgh Pickwick Club set a fine example and Dickens wrote to congratulate the officers on their foresight in forming so useful a body.[69] The city of Edinburgh became the first British city to bestow its freedom upon the writer. Six years later, in 1847, the gorgeous state-lunch he received in Glasgow filled the humble Englishman with amazement.[70] The Lord Provost, and thousands of his fellow citizens, gave him a more hearty reception than he had received anywhere. In his speech—it was Christmastide—Dickens boldly referred to 'the English emblem of this period of the year, the holly tree.'[71] *A Christmas Carol* may have softened some Scottish hearts which were otherwise not disposed to notice the festival. Dickens's enthusiasm for Scotland diminished with the passage of time, and with the failure of his marriage, but the 'enthoosymoozy' among the Scots for his own writing did not diminish. His audience was truly British. In his novels, however, we only encounter Scotsmen as teachers or doctors, and then not very flatteringly. In *Bleak House*, the doctor at once discloses his nationality by asking one penetrating question: 'Air you in the maydickle profession?' Dickens used, after a fashion, three English regional dialects: East Anglian in *David Copperfield*, Yorkshire in *Nicholas Nickleby*, and Lancashire in *Hard Times*. It was the speech of London, however, to which his ear was most closely attuned.[72]

Alfred Tennyson (and his brothers) from time to time wrote poems in the Lincolnshire dialect that surrounded them in their boyhood. In 1832–4, however, he produced his first set of Arthurian poems and became steadily more engrossed with the mysterious lands of the West. Coleridge had declared in conversation that 'As to Arthur, you could not by any means make a poem on him national to Englishmen. What have we to do with him?'[73] Tennyson disagreed. The *Idylls of the King* demonstrated that Arthur could

[68] M. House and G. Storey (eds.), *The Letters of Charles Dickens* (Oxford, 1965), i. 135.

[69] Ibid. 346.

[70] House and Storey, *Letters of Dickens*, iv. 216.

[71] K. J. Fielding (ed.), *The Speeches of Charles Dickens* (Oxford, 1960), 85–92.

[72] G. L. Brooke, *The Language of Dickens* (1970), 117.

[73] T. M. Raysor (ed.), *Miscellaneous Criticism of Samuel Taylor Coleridge* (1936), 429.

again become a British hero. Tennyson took Wales seriously, making a trip through Mid- and North Wales in 1839 and undertaking subsequent tours in 1856, 1868, and 1871 to different parts of the principality.[74] In 1856 he began to study Welsh in a modest way. He had a copy of Thomas Price's *Hanes Cymru* (History of Wales) and solemnly made a list of common Welsh words and their English meanings.[75] Visitors to Aldworth were often puzzled to find a tiled motto in a strange language on the floor of the entrance hall. Translated from the Welsh, it read: 'The truth against the world'.[76] It testified to the unexpected fusion accomplished by such an eminent product of the Danelaw.

Sir Walter Scott's unchallengeable achievement, despite his preface to *Ivanhoe*, was to have stamped an enduring image of Scotland beyond its borders. His own sense of landscape and locality was disconcertingly precise.[77] It was made all the more poignant by his knowledge that the Scotland he portrayed was passing away before his eyes. Lockhart described his father-in-law as writing in 'what is all over Scotland Scotch National' but, arguably, his massive *œuvre* left both his Scottish contemporaries and successors with a problem of language which they never solved.[78] John Galt's *Annals of the Parish* (1821) was written in a strong West-of-Scotland dialect—in Lockhart's eyes Galt and Hogg were using 'too much the dialects of particular districts' to which the alternative was not 'Scotch National' but standard English.[79] In fact, Galt's own subsequent career, in London and Canada, was almost a parody of a Scotsman 'on the make'. Crabb Robinson, however, found him 'neither rude nor servile, though a Scotchman.'[80] In *Sir Andrew Wylie of that Ilk* the formal theme of the novel was indeed 'the progress of a Scotchman in London', and in one of his last stories he follows a former Lord Mayor of London on a triumphal trip back to Glasgow. 'Everybody kens it as natural for a

[74] H. G. Wright, 'Tennyson and Wales', *Essays and Studies by Members of the English Association*, 14 (1929), 71–3.

[75] J. P. Eggers, *King Arthur's Laureate: A Study of Tennyson's 'Idylls of the King'* (New York, 1971), 225.

[76] F. B. Pinion, *A Tennyson Companion* (1984), 47.

[77] J. H. Paterson, 'The Novelist and his Region: Scotland through the Eyes of Sir Walter Scott', *Scottish Geographical Magazine*, 81 (1965) 146–52.

[78] G. Tulloch, *The Language of Sir Walter Scott: A Study of his Scottish and Period language* (1980).

[79] Cited by Hart, *Lockhart*, 96.

[80] I. Gordon, *John Galt: The Life of a Writer* (Edinburgh, 1972).

Scotchman, who has done well in the world, to show his testi-
monies among his kith and kin when he grows old, as it is for him to
eat parritch for his breakfast, and to go about barefooted when
young.'[81]

The career and writing of George MacDonald exemplifies
another Scottish pattern. He moved from Aberdeen, via London, to
a pastorate in Sussex. Disagreement with his congregation on
theological issues led him to depart for Manchester, where he
received the patronage of A. J. Scott. MacDonald's *Robert Falconer*,
and some of his other early novels, were 'Scottish', but in his later
works, which brought him enduring fame, he moved away from his
Scottish origins, both in subject matter and the language he
employed. It was not until 1855 that this English-based Scot visited
Edinburgh and found living-conditions there incredible 'after our
orderly clean commonplace well-behaved Manchester.'[82] The
paradoxes in which such Scots found themselves could not be
better expressed than by the jingle which Greenock-born James
Thomson learnt as a child:

> I thank the goodness and the grace
> Which on my birth have smiled;
> And made me in these Christian days
> A happy English child.[83]

Perhaps the 'city of dreadful night' could not be located in any
particular country. The perspective of William Sharp, who wrote
under the name Fiona Macleod, was different again. He brooded
long on the fate of the Celts but, unlike some of his friends, he had
little patience with political or racial Celticism. 'I am not English',
he declared, 'and have not the English mind or the English temper,
and in many things do not share the English ideals', but that did not
mean that, as a Scot, he was 'irreconcilably hostile' to them. He
would do his best, while seeking to preserve his own heritage, 'to
understand, sympathise, fall into line with them as far as may be,
since we all have a common bond and a common destiny.'[84]

At another level, there was a market for 'Scotch stories' in

[81] Cited by Gordon, *Galt*, 136.
[82] G. MacDonald, *George MacDonald and his Wife* (1924), 229; K. Triggs, *The Stars and the Stillness: A Portrait of George MacDonald* (Cambridge, 1986).
[83] W. D. Schaefer, *James Thomson (B.V.): Beyond 'The City'* (Los Angeles, 1965), 38.
[84] F. Alaya, *William Sharp—'Fiona Macleod', 1855–1905* (Cambridge, Mass., 1970), 169.

England, as Mrs Oliphant proved with her *Margaret Maitland*, though her own background was Liverpool Scots. Paradoxically, her *Salem Chapel*, which described the life of English Dissent, drew on her memories of the Free Church of Scotland in that city.[85] Her somewhat intermediary role made her a suitable biographer for Edward Irving. Another supplier of the market was George Gilfillan. From Dundee, he launched himself on lecturing tours amongst the English, publicizing his own writing too.[86] In 1889 Mrs Oliphant told her publisher that, while there was a touch of genius about J. M. Barrie's *Auld Licht Idylls*, the Scotch speech was 'much too provincial'.[87] Barrie survived this verdict and gave the English a picture of his mother *Margaret Ogilvie*; but he had concluded that Scotland was best contemplated from London.[88] It was from this position of voluntary exile that he discussed the significance of *Kidnapped* with that other exiled purveyor of Scotland to the outside world—Robert Louis Stevenson. That story, too, had been about two different worlds but, despite what 'Anglo-Saxon' theory supposed, Alan and David did not stand for Celt and Saxon. Stevenson, in any event, denied that 'there exists such a thing as pure Saxon, and I think it more than questionable if there be such a thing as a pure Celt.'[89] The more one considered them, the more elusive 'boundaries' became. The literary invasion of England continued with the remarkable success of 'Ian Maclaren''s *Beside the Bonnie Brier Bush*, from which derived the so-called 'Kailyard' school, much-criticized in a later Scotland for allegedly misrepresenting Scots for the amusement of English readers and theatre audiences.[90] 'Maclaren' and other writers were able to appeal to a wide Anglo-American readership.[91] He was himself a Presbyterian minister in Liverpool,

[85] *The Autobiography and Letters of Mrs M. O. W. Oliphant* (Edinburgh and London, 1899), 84; M. Williams, *Margaret Oliphant: A Critical Biography* (1986).
[86] Gilfillan was a little disconcerted that his works were better known in Bristol than in his own Dundee. R. A. Watson and E. S. Watson, *George Gilfillan: Letters and Journals with a Memoir* (1892), 26–7, 211.
[87] Oliphant, *Autobiography*, 364.
[88] In general, see I. Campbell (ed.), *Nineteenth-Century Scottish Fiction: Critical Essays* (Manchester, 1979).
[89] Cited by J. Dunbar, *J. M. Barrie: The Man Behind the Image* (1970), 84. See also J. M. Robertson, *The Saxon and the Celt: A Study in Sociology* (1897).
[90] G. Blake, *Barrie and the Kailyard School* (1951); C. Harvie, 'Drumtochty Revisited: The Kailyard', *The Scottish Review*, 27 (1982).
[91] T. D. Knowles, *Ideology, Art and Commerce: Aspects of Literary Sociology in the Late Victorian Scottish Kailyard* (Göteborg, 1983), 63–4.

though he drew on his earlier experience of a Perthshire parish near the Highland Line.[92]

In England, Mrs Gaskell is sometimes thought to have been more sensitive than Disraeli in demonstrating the existence of two nations within the same island.[93] However, as with Charlotte Brontë, the 'nations' of which she was aware were more than two. 'North' and 'South' were, at best, shorthand. In the Brontë background was the North of Ireland—and Mrs Gaskell thought that father Brontë spoke 'with a strong Scotch accent'.[94] She had an ear for such an accent since she thought her husband had a slight one— though a native of Warrington he had gone to Glasgow University—and her own father had come from Berwick-on-Tweed and had initially worked in Scotland. Holidays in Wales from her Cheshire home as a girl had given her another dimension. She honeymooned in Wales before settling down to Manchester life.[95] The 'North' of her experience was, therefore, complex: the 'South' and 'the ways down there' was not simple either. 'The beauty of Helstone', one commentator writes, 'is contrasted to the ugliness of Milton, but the values of both are contrasted to the idle luxury of London.'[96] Manchester men saw the citizens of the capital 'ruining good English' yet despising provincial society themselves.[97] Charlotte Brontë in *Shirley* defended her characterization by pointing out that while 'the people of the South object to my

---

[92] W. R. Nicoll, *Ian Maclaren: The Life of the Rev. John Watson* (1908); 'Maclaren' was born in England of Highland Scots parentage (his mother was Gaelic-speaking). His uncle was Sir Samuel Ferguson who, amongst other achievements, may have invented the term 'Anglo-Irish'. F. S. L. Lyons, *Culture and Anarchy in Ireland, 1890–1939* (Oxford, 1979), 28–33. John Buchan also wrote about Scotland for a British audience and latterly came to do so, to the dismay of some of his countrymen, from the quiet of the Oxfordshire countryside. W. Buchan, *John Buchan: A Memoir* (1982), 50; George Douglas Brown's *House with Green Shutters* (1901) presented a different picture of Scottish community life. He too, though for different reasons, could only write about Scotland from England.

[93] Briggs, *Collected Essays*, ii. 70.

[94] J. A. V. Chapple and A. Pollard (eds.), *The letters of Mrs Gaskell* (Manchester, 1966), 245.

[95] W. Gérin, *Elizabeth Gaskell* (Oxford, 1976), 1–49. A number of her husband's friends had also been educated at Glasgow University. In *North and South* she daringly permitted herself to observe that it was widely felt that a young man sent 'to even the Scotch Universities' came back unsettled for commercial pursuits. E. Gaskell, *North and South* (1973 edn.), 68; B. Brill, *William Gaskell, 1805–1884: A Portrait* (Manchester, 1985).

[96] E. Wright, *Mrs Gaskell: The Basis for Reassessment* (1965), 134–5.

[97] E. Gaskell, *My Lady Ludlow* (1906), 492–3.

delineation of Northern life and manners, the people of Yorkshire and Lancashire approve. They say it is precisely the contrast of rough nature with highly artificial cultivation which forms one of their own characteristics . . .'.[98] North and South, concluded Higgins in Mrs Gaskell's novel:

have each getten their own troubles. If work's sure and steady there, labour's paid at starvation prices; while here we'n rucks o'money coming in one quarter, and ne'er a farthing th' next. For sure, th' world is in a confusion that passes me or any other man to understand . . .[99]

Defenders of the 'South Country' had to be on their guard simultaneously against London and 'the North'. Here, for them, was the heart of England. George Gissing could think of no lovelier musing place than the leafy walk beside the Palace Moat at Wells.[1] 'I was born and bred a west-countryman, thank God!' declared young Tom Brown, 'a Wessex man, a citizen of the noblest Saxon kingdom. . . . There's nothing like the old countryside for me, and no music like the twang of the real old Saxon tongue, as one gets it fresh from the veritable in the White Horse Vale.'[2] W. H. Hudson and George Sturt seldom strayed north of the Thames or west of the Exe in their descriptions of the natural world.[3] It was Gissing, however, who had been in Manchester and was Wakefield-born, who was most direct. The typical inhabitant of Sussex or Somerset belonged to the ancient order of things, wheras the rude man of the North was, by comparison, but lately emerged from barbarism. It was his misfortune, in addition, to have succumbed to that scientific industrialism which had encouraged rather than mitigated his 'frank brutality'. The northerner's fierce shyness and arrogant self-regard were, Gissing thought, 'notes of a primitive state'. However, the sound of the traction-engine coming along the road was an indication that the idyllic isolation of the rural South might not endure.[4] Thomas Hardy, however, was there to capture 'Wessex' in his novels of 'character and environment'. Throughout his work,

[98]   Cited by Briggs, *Collected Essays*, ii. 70.

[99]   Gaskell, *North and South*, 307.

[1]   G. Gissing, *The Private Papers of Henry Ryecroft* (1902), 81.

[2]   T. Hughes, *Tom Brown's School Days* (Cambridge, 1857), 18. Hughes usually refers to 'the British nation'.

[3]   A. Howkins, 'The Discovery of Rural England', in Colls and Dodd, *Englishness*, 74.

[4]   Gissing, *Ryecroft*, 258–9.

Hardy showed a keen awareness of the social registers of language. The sounds, grammar, words, and phrases of Dorsetshire had been familiar to him since his childhood, and he attempted to indicate pronunciations by appropriate spellings so that they could be imitated beyond 'Wessex'.[5] Not for him the merely local resonance of William Barnes's Dorset dialect poems.[6] The eager students and staff of the University of Aberdeen could understand and, in April 1905, he travelled 700 miles from Dorchester to receive an honorary degree and join in 'Auld Lang Syne' and other customs of the region.

It was when he purported to be living in the Midlands—'They are sodden and unkind'—that the great hills of the 'South Country' came into Belloc's mind. Inevitably, the more a contrast between the 'North' and the 'South' was attempted, the more the Midlands faced both ways. George Eliot, who used the dialect of the North-West Midlands in her *Adam Bede*, knew Britain well by the time of its publication in 1859. Fourteen years earlier she was reported to have been 'in ecstasies ... beyond everything' after a visit to Scotland. Fervent admirer of Walter Scott though she was, however, she preferred to stay at home reading an article on the atomic theory of Lucretius rather than attend the Edinburgh celebrations marking the centenary of Scott's birth.[7] Awareness of the characteristics of her own native region, however, did not turn her into a 'regional novelist'. The Nottinghamshire of the young D. H. Lawrence was quintessentially 'in between'. Eastwood itself had a 'northern' mining ethos, but beautiful countryside was near at hand so that, as he put it, 'the mines were an accident in the landscape and Robin Hood and his merry men were not very far away.'[8] The world of Bennett's Five Towns was different again, and equally neither 'North' nor 'South'.

---

[5] R. W. E. Elliott, *Thomas Hardy's English* (Oxford, 1984), 338–9.

[6] Gerard Manley Hopkins believed that 'the use of dialect to a man like Barnes is to tie him down to the things that he or another Dorset man has said or might say, which though it narrows his field, heightens his effects. C. Abbott, *The Letters of Gerard Manley Hopkins to Robert Bridges* (1935), 87.

[7] G. S. Haight, *George Eliot: A Biography* (Oxford, 1968), 57–8, 439.

[8] D. H. Lawrence, 'Nottingham and the Mining Countryside', in D. Trilling (ed.), *The Portable D. H. Lawrence* (Harmondsworth, 1977), 613; L. Spolton, 'The Spirit of Place: D. H. Lawrence and the East Midlands', *East Midlands Geographer* 5 (1970), 88–96.

Language and literature in nineteenth-century Britain served, on balance, as a link rather than a barrier to communication and a shared culture. Scottish literature, in whatever language or combination of languages it was written, remained distinct. It could only have arisen from Scotland, yet it could not be contained within Scotland. It functioned, as Scotland functioned, within the context of Britain. Scott became a 'British' author. Conversely, English literature could not be confined within England. Moving in the opposite direction, Dickens too became a 'British' author with an appeal and standing in Scotland as great as it was in England. Such British stars outshone any writers, whether in Scotland or England, who attempted to work through a more restricted linguistic medium. The interaction, however, was largely Anglo-Scottish. Literature in Welsh remained inevitably at the margin of British literary consciousness, although Lady Charlotte Guest's translation of the *Mabinogion* attained a certain popularity. Welsh literature in English was slow to make an impact—there were a number of unsuccessful aspirants for the role played by Scott.

In conclusion, two illustrations, both drawn from the world of the railways, point both to accelerating integration and the tension it generated. Shortly after the railway reached Aberdeen, George MacDonald wrote to his relatives in the city commenting on how strange the fields would look with the 'iron nerves' running through them. It was a magnificent development which made 'the dear, rugged North one body with the warm, rich, more indolent South.'[9] Differences certainly remained and, as a writer who had lived in both countries, he was sensitive to them, but isolation had ended. A new Britain was emerging. 'Good-bye, Harrow-on-the-Hill', said the dying Scotsman to his wife as they left Euston on his last journey back to Scotland. R. B. Cunninghame Graham's character liked Harrow but 'ye can scarcely ca' yon wee bit mound a hill, Jean.' His wife had always pronounced her name 'Jayne' and smarted inwardly at the Scotch variant her husband had habitually used. He was a 'hard, unyielding, yet humorous and sentimental Lowland Scot'. She was a Londoner who had loved her husband, yet an intangible veil of misconception had arisen between them. 'Each saw the other's failings, or, perhaps, thought the good qualities which each possessed were faults, for usually men judge each other by their

[9] MacDonald, *MacDonald*, 177.

good points, which, seen through the prejudice of race, religion and surroundings, appear to them defects.'[10] This personal relationship symbolizes the subtle tensions which nineteenth-century British writers felt as they explored both the unity and the diversity of their country.

Music also separated and linked the people of Britain. It would be difficult, however, to say precisely what might be meant, in the nineteenth century, by 'British' music. There was a kind of English tradition, a kind of Scottish, and a kind of Welsh. Up to a point, it could be separately identified but music was also composed and played in a British context. While there is an element of artificiality in seeking to identify the distinct strands, it is not fruitless to do so since both the substance and status of music was not the same throughout Britain despite the common elements.

In Scotland, for the fifty years up to Scott's death in 1832, antiquarians had been busy copying down songs and selling them as 'authentically Scottish' to the Scottish aristocracy. About this time, however, the upper classes seem to have concluded that the idea was futile and that 'they were trying to glue dead leaves back on to a tree.'[11] Ballads and songs were still sung by the lower orders but more sophisticated persons ceased to find in this music a specific national tradition. Coincidentally, Scottish 'classical' musical composition, which had modestly existed in the eighteenth century, virtually came to an end. The result, at least according to Professor Blackie, was that when 'you ask a Scottish young lady in a Scottish West-End drawing room to fill with a little sweet vocalism the void which nature abhors, she will sing a German or an Italian song, or a light French ariette, but she will not sing a Scotch song. . . .'[12] By late in the century the passion of German composers for Scotch airs was largely spent. Earlier, Beethoven had confessed to 'a very great liking for Scottish airs' and had readily agreed to write piano sonatas based upon them. It is significant, however, that his Scottish correspondent replied in the following terms: 'It would be quite desirable if you wrote the variations in a style that

[10] A. Knight (ed.), *Beattock for Moffat and the Best of R. B. Cunninghame Graham* (Edinburgh, 1979), 12–13.

[11] D. J. Johnson, *Music and Society in Lowland Scotland in the Eighteenth Century* (1972), 198.

[12] J. S. Blackie, *Scottish Song: Its wealth, Wisdom and Social Significance* (Edinburgh, 1889), 15.

is *familiar* and *easy* and a bit brilliant, so that the majority of our ladies may play them and relish them. And please remember that the ladies of Scotland are not so strong as those of your country, where music is extensively cultivated.' Mendelssohn's *Scotch Symphony* was given its first performance in Leipzig in 1842. Queen Victoria graciously accepted the dedication, though on this occasion it is a pity that it described her as Königin Victoria von *England*.[13]

The musical life of Scotland, as that term would have been understood in continental Europe, was, in short, undistinguished. Scotland only received any special attention because of the distinct tradition of pipe music. Pipe bands became popular way beyond their Highland home. In the country as a whole, Presbyterians gave no particular encouragement to music-making. It was not until 1844, for example, that Handel's *Messiah* was performed north of the Border. Twenty years later, however, the social and religious climate was changing. A Glasgow Music Festival aimed to rival that of Leeds.[14] However, it was not until the last decade of the century that the forerunner of the Royal Scottish Academy of Music and Drama was established, in Glasgow. Demand from students increased, compelling the Professor of Music at Edinburgh at length to attend to their needs.

There was talk, by the end of the century, of a Scottish musical renaissance, though would-be Scottish composers found it hard to gain support in their own country. Hamish MacCunn made his name with his youthful overture *The Land of the Mountain and Flood* (1887), which is still played a century later, but exile from that land to London shortened his life. Alexander Campbell Mackenzie wrote *Scotch Rhapsodies* and a *Scottish Piano Concerto*, but he likewise moved away from Scotland, becoming Principal of the Royal Academy of Music in London.[15] There is a nice irony in the fact that, just before 1914, Oscar Hammerstein announced that *Fionn and Tera* was to be the second 'English opera' to be performed at the London Opera House on Kingsway. It was in fact written by the Scottish composer, Learmont Drysdale, with a libretto by no less a person than the Duke of Argyll: a Scottish opera, though performed

[13] R. Fiske, *Scotland in Music: A European Enthusiasm* (Cambridge, 1983), 72–5.
[14] C. Ehrlich, *The Music Profession in Britain Since the Eighteenth Century: A Social History* (Oxford, 1985), 69.
[15] K. Elliott and F. Rimmer, *A History of Scottish Music* (1973), 60–9.

in England.[16] It was sadly the case that Scottish composers, even when they wrote tone-poems with titles as illustrious as *William Wallace* or *Tam O'Shanter*, could not flourish, or even subsist, in Scotland itself. It appeared that they could only exist in England.

The musical life of Wales was rather different. The principality, pleased to be thought 'The Land of Song', went its own musical way. Handel's works, in contrast to Scotland, had been early and enthusiastically welcomed there. Many infant Welshmen found themselves christened with that composer's surname as their first name—a fate which also befell children whose parents admired Haydn. It could not be disputed that, by mid-century, enthusiasm in Wales for choral singing was widespread, generously helped by instruction provided by the London Tonic Sol-fa College. Many chapels had their *Ysgol gân* (singing school) and *cymanfa ganu* (singing festival) and it became commonplace elsewhere in Britain to believe that the Welsh possessed 'a strong love of music'.[17] Welsh choirs came regularly to London to sing, and those who came to listen to them were by no means all Welsh. Welsh hymn tunes, either newly minted or adaptations of older tunes, came to be associated with particular hymns throughout the English-speaking world. 'Anyone who has not heard a Welsh nonconformist gathering sing a hymn', wrote one English visitor to Wales, 'has really no idea what a hymn should be.'[18] By 1870, Wales had become 'the land of the great choirs.' The victories obtained at the Crystal Palace musical festivals of 1872 and 1873 by the great choir of the conductor Caradog of Aberdare ( *Côr Mawr Caradog*, *Aberdâr* ) firmly embedded this image of Wales amongst metropolitan audiences.[19] This Welsh choral enthusiasm was also reflected in the work of Welsh composers, most of whom were amateur and, with the possible exception of Joseph Parry, were unknown to the English musical world. English choral composers found a ready response in Wales. Elgar, for example, conducted his oratorio *The Kingdom* at the 1907 Cardiff Festival. He particularly admired the singing of David Ffrangcon Davies. In the early twentieth century, therefore, the English and Welsh musical worlds penetrated each other in various ways. The links were close, as indeed they had been

[16] E. W. White, *A History of English Opera* (1983), 377.
[17] Morgan and Thomas, *Wales*, 198–9.
[18] Hughes, *A London Family*, 361.
[19] Morgan and Thomas, *Wales*, 198–9.

since the mid-eighteenth century when William Williams, Panty-celyn, directed his first book of Welsh hymns to be sung to the English tunes which were popular in the principality at the time.

It is well known that England in the nineteenth century was described as the 'Land without Music'. It is equally well known that continental Europeans rarely made any distinction between England and Britain. In the particular sense, much effort has gone into establishing that this notion is overdrawn. There were composers at work in Victorian England, though some of them, like Stanford, were not English. The operas of Gilbert and Sullivan had a popularity throughout the country. Nevertheless, as that term was understood around the turn of the century by protagonists of an 'English revival', the nineteenth century had made no contribution to 'national music' in England. Cecil Sharp and others rediscovered the existence of English folk-songs and collected them assiduously. The young, part-Welsh Ralph Vaughan Williams arranged them enthusiastically. Henry Purcell was rediscovered. So were the Tudor composers. It was possible for Englishmen to write excellent music and in due course they might be able to conduct it themselves. Mr von Holst, as he was then known, joined in the fun. England was back on the musical map.

Curiously, however, particularly in the decade before the war, other English composers could not seem to exist without the inspiration of Celtic myth and legend. It was not 'England' that caught their imaginations, but an earlier 'Britain'. Rutland Boughton launched his Glastonbury Festival in the same month as the Great War broke out and for this reason the singers had to rest content with only piano accompaniment. He had a further group of Arthurian music dramas in prospect. Josef Holbrooke was another contemporary English composer walking round with an operatic trilogy on Welsh themes in his head.[20] Arnold Bax went even further. Although in fact born in Streatham, South London, Bax let it be known to enquirers that at some rather unspecific point in time he might have emerged into consciousness from a bog-lake in County Mayo, Ireland. He certainly journeyed to County Donegal and adopted, for his literary purposes, the name 'Dermot O'Byrne'.[21] Granville Bantock was another Edwardian irresistibly drawn to music with Celtic connotations. And it was perhaps a

20   White, *English Opera*, 394.
21   C. Scott-Sutherland, *Arnold Bax* (1973), 4.

cosmopolitanism stemming from his birth in the Savoy Hotel, London, that led 'Peter Warlock' to confess that he had 'never understood the sentiment of patriotism'. In the summer of 1917, indeed, he left England for Ireland. He became a particular enthusiast for the revival of the Cornish language. 'What more effective protest', he wrote, 'against imperialism (in art as in other matters) could you or I make than by adopting, as pure ritual, a speech, a nationality, that no longer exists?'[22] It is indeed not easy to explain this musical flight from 'Englishness' in any other terms.

The man whom Ernest Newman described in the *Musical Times* for September 1914 as still the only impressive figure in English music took a different view of his wartime responsibilities from 'Peter Warlock'. On the outbreak of war, Sir Edward Elgar was in fact stranded in North-West Scotland and unable to get to London. He found himself in a strange Highland world where English five-pound notes would not be accepted. It was, indeed, a somewhat distant vantage-point from which to be contemplating his native England in her hour of need.[23] Elgar had not been ashamed in the past to wave the *Banner of St George* (1897) and he would not shirk his musical duty now.

Elgar was indubitably an Englishman from the West Midlands. He assessed the English past from the vantage-point of the Malvern Hills—described by the Cambridge Public Orator on the occasion of Elgar's honorary degree as 'the cradle of British arts'.[24] He had travelled on a number of occasions to Scotland and had embarked on, though he did not complete, a 'Scotish [*sic*] Overture'. A deeper influence, however, was the land behind the Malvern Hills. Welsh tunes lingered fruitfully in his mind for years. Stanley Baldwin, another Worcestershire man, had once confessed 'a kind of affection for Welshmen' that even extended to Lloyd George.[25] So did Elgar. Even so, these links and experiences did not substantially dent his 'Englishness'. What turned him into the musical voice of Britain was something he did in the early months of 1902. He fitted his new *Pomp and Circumstance March No. 1* to the words *Land of Hope and Glory* which Arthur Benson had written for Edward VII's coronation. 'I like to look on the composer's vocation', Elgar wrote

[22] I. A. Copley, *The Music of Peter Warlock* (1979), 7–8, 13.
[23] Cited by J. N. Moore, *Edward Elgar: A Creative Life* (Oxford, 1984), 668–9.
[24] Ibid. 337.
[25] S. Baldwin, *On England* (Harmondsworth, 1937), 20.

in 1904, 'as the old troubadours or bards did. In those days it was no disgrace to a man to be turned on to step in front of an army and inspire the people with a song.'[26] By 1914, *Land of Hope and Glory*, to Elgar's music, had sufficiently permeated the national consciousness for crowds outside Buckingham Palace to join in spontaneously when a military band struck up. 'I saw across the channel', wrote one private from the front in France, 'a picture of home, and knew that England depended on us; and the knowledge set me aglow with pride. I wanted to sing Land of Hope and Glory.'[27] So did many other Britons. During the war itself, Sir Edward set Laurence Binyon's war poems to music, most notably *For the Fallen*. Elgar's *The Spirit of England*, one writer suggested, a decade later, made him 'our national minstrel in a finer way than the *Land of Hope and Glory* song did.'[28] Elgar's greatness was, of course, particularly emphasized during the war when throughout the British Empire there were campaigns against recent German music and the use of German musical instruments. In Sydney, for example, Dame Nellie Melba was admonished for singing *Land of Hope and Glory* to the accompaniment of a Bechstein grand.[29] After the war was over, Elgar was appointed Master of the King's Musick. *The Times* described him as 'one who is to the nation at large the personification of British music.'[30] In a fundamental sense, perhaps, 'British music' still did not exist but Sir Edward had forged links and cut through barriers throughout Britain in a way never before achieved. Even in Presbyterian Glasgow there was an early successful performance of *The Dream of Gerontius*. It was well received. There could be no greater tribute.

[26] Moore, *Elgar*, 339.
[27] Cited by J. Crump, 'The Identity of English Music: The Reception of Elgar 1898–1915' in Colls and Dodd, *Englishness*, 176–7.
[28] Sheldon, cited by Crump, 'Identity of English Music', 176–7.
[29] C. Ehrlich, *The Piano: A History* (1976), 161.
[30] Crump, 'Identity of English Music', 178.

# 3
## Church, Chapel, and the Fragmentation of Faith

The splintered condition of nineteenth-century British Christianity was in itself a further testimony to the difficulty the Church has always experienced in reconciling a theoretical commitment to unity with the remorseless disposition of believers to reject uniformity in worship, doctrine, and government. It follows that a common Christianity underpinned the integrity of the State however much individuals or particular social groups might distance themselves from formal Christian belief. At another level, however, the fractured condition of Christianity meant that the churches expressed or reinforced a diversity within the nation which was far from being straightforwardly theological in substance. 'British Christianity' was an artificial construct without institutional foundations. Consciously or not, the various churches of England, Scotland, and Wales were all 'carriers' of traditions which they believed to be deeply embedded in the spiritual life of their peoples. Even the Roman Catholic Church, when it came to re-establish an ecclesiastical structure in the mid-nineteenth century, knew that it could not do so on a British basis. It was not until 1878 that the Scottish hierarchy was restored—twenty seven years after it had been restored in 'England and Wales'. All the main ecclesiastical families—Roman Catholic, Episcopalian/Anglican, Presbyterian, Methodist, Baptist, Congregationalist/Independent, Unitarian, Quaker—were present in all parts of Britain. To that extent there was homogeneity, but the distribution was far from uniform and the strength of particular denominations varied widely from one part of Britain to another. Above all, the Act of Union had enshrined the establishment of one church in Scotland (Presbyterian) and one church in England and Wales (Anglican). It is not surprising, therefore, that Anglo-Scottish issues were at the heart of 'British' Christianity. Yet there was also a distinctive place for Wales in these relationships. At least in the eyes of some contemporary observers, the Welsh were peculiarly religious. The balance of denominational strength in Wales placed the principality in a

unique position in Britain. As a result, by 1914, when the disestablishment of the Church of England in Wales was on the
statute-book, Britain possessed two different religious establishments, while in one part of the country there would be no
establishment at all. Indeed, in no sphere was the plurality of Britain
more apparent than in religion. Additionally, in Scotland and Wales
particularly, churches attracted a degree of 'non-religious' support
precisely to the extent that, in the absence of separate political
institutions, they constituted bulwarks of distinctive identity. On
the other hand, particularly by the end of the century when 'non-
church-going' had been identified as a significant phenomenon
even in Scotland and Wales, a more ecumenical disposition began
to dawn. For some, their membership of a particular ecclesiastical
family was more important, within a British context, than their
'Englishness' or 'Scottishness'. Minority churches in one part of
Britain looked for support, on terms, from majority churches in
another part. Majority churches 'intervened' elsewhere, even
though they were not always welcome. These complicated patterns
of interaction form the substance of this chapter.

In 1916 Baron von Hügel turned his attention to analysing *The
German Soul* in not altogether dispassionate circumstances. Despite
having a Scottish (originally Presbyterian) mother, however, he was
not tempted to discover its British counterpart.[1] It is, perhaps, an
impossible task. 'In spite of a mutual aversion, as bitter as ever
separated one people from another,' Macaulay wrote in his 1839
review of 'Gladstone on Church and State', 'the two kingdoms
which compose our island have been indissolubly joined together.'
Enough ancient national feeling remained to be 'ornamental and
useful', but for the ends of government the two nations were one.
How had that happened? The answer was simple. 'The nations are
one for all the ends of government because in their union the true
ends of government alone were kept in sight. The nations are one
because the Churches are two.'[2]

Macaulay's forthright judgement, made in the *Edinburgh Review*
several months before his election as MP for the city, stemmed
from knowledge that was 'in the blood'. Thoroughly English by

---

[1] Baron von Hügel, *The German Soul* (1916); L. F. Barmann, *Baron von Hügel and
the Modernist Crisis* (Cambridge, 1972), 1–2.

[2] Lord Macaulay, *Essays and Lays of Ancient Rome* (1889), 510.

birth and education—though Carlyle thought his face rather resembled a bowl of porridge—his personal knowledge of Scotland only derived from his lately deceased father, Zachary, the son of a Presbyterian minister but who had himself long since diluted his Scottish past. Thomas's perception that religion held the key to the success of the union was shortly to be put to practical tests and indeed it would make his own political position uncomfortable. In June 1841, he reported to his sister Frances that he was surrounded 'by the din of a sort of controversy which is most distasteful to me.' It was not easy to answer a constituent who wanted to hear his views on the headship of Christ over the Church.[3] A year later he wrote to Macvey Napier that he would not visit Edinburgh 'while your meeting of fanatical priests is sitting'.[4] Subsequently, he feared that his willingness to permit the payment of Catholic priests in Ireland would lead to 'a violent explosion of public feeling'.[5] In 1847, he met electoral defeat, though after 1852 he served for a further four years. He remained, however, an outsider. In October 1852, for example, he reported that he had attended Guthrie's church on Sacrament Sunday, witnessing the Presbyterian administration of the Eucharist, which he had not seen for thirty-five years. The town was as still as if it were midnight. Any person who opposed himself to the 'fanatical humour' on this subject ran a great risk of being affronted.[6]

The enthusiasm for Sabbath observance in Scotland and the indifference to the festivals of the Christian Year constantly surprised English visitors. Of course, Sabbatarianism had a long history in England, too, and the 'Victorian Sunday' was to some extent a British phenomenon. Nevertheless, at a meeting of the Evangelical Alliance in mid-century, the English Dissenter Thomas Binney described the Sabbath as 'very much a Scotch question' and it did indeed seem that all the varying viewpoints common in England were expressed with particular vehemence north of the Border. Governments in the 1850s and 1860s were believed to have been persuaded by the strength of Scottish feeling to block attempts to attach passenger coaches to Sunday mail-trains.[7] The

---

[3] T. Pinney (ed.), *The Selected Letters of Thomas Babington Macaulay* (Cambridge, 1982), 178.
[4] Ibid. 193.    [5] Ibid. 204.    [6] Ibid. 258.
[7] J. Wigley, *The Rise and Fall of the Victorian Sunday* (Manchester, 1980), 65, 201; The Lord's Day Observance Society, however, drew most of its support from the area south of a line from Boston to Gloucester. See B. H. Harrison, *Peaceable Kingdom* (Oxford, 1982), 129.

non-observance of Christmas in Scotland was a source of some bewilderment even to English Nonconformists whose Puritan ancestors had once shown a similar attitude. Lloyd George, whose observance of the Christian Year was otherwise not complete, celebrated Christmas in high style on the train back to London after addressing Clydeside workers on Christmas Day 1915—which was not a holiday for his audience.[8] And, earlier, Principal John Shairp, Presbyterian though he was, reflected concerning Good Friday that his church might have cut itself off 'from an enormous fountain of spiritual life, by having turned our back on this day'. The Church of England had done right to retain Holy Week.[9] His, however, was a minority view.

Such contrasting attitudes to sacraments and festivals in her two kingdoms could cause problems for the sovereign. Could Queen Victoria cement the souls of her two peoples by her actions? The first occasion on which Her Majesty was present at a Communion service according to the rite of the Church of Scotland was in November 1871. She recorded that she 'longed to join in it'. It was very striking to see 'simple good people in their nice plain dresses', but she refrained. Two years later, however, much to the displeasure of the Scotsman in Lambeth Palace, the Queen became the first British monarch to partake of the Sacrament in a Presbyterian Church. She continued to do so every autumn in Crathie church in defiance of the Archbishop of Canterbury.[10]

Macaulay's personal reactions seem to confirm that a sophisticated southern mind, even of Evangelical provenance, could not attune itself to Scottish religious modes and moods. The southern sense of smell complicated the problem. Southey's visit to Glasgow Cathedral led him to observe that the seats were so closely packed 'that any person who could remain there during the time of service in warm weather, must have an invincible nose.'[11] In general, indeed, there was no sphere apparently more resistant to blending

[8] A. J. P. Taylor (ed.) *Lloyd George: A Diary by Frances Stevenson* (1971), 87.

[9] W. A. Knight, *Principal Shairp and his Friends* (1888), 293.

[10] G. B. Burnet, *The Holy Communion in the Reformed Church of Scotland, 1560–1960* (Edinburgh and London, 1960). The oath in Queen Victoria's Coronation Service had little relation to Scotland since the oath relating to the position of the Church of Scotland was taken before the Privy Council. F. C. Eeles, *The Coronation Service: Its Meaning and History* (1952), 37.

[11] Herford, *Southey's Journal*, 255.

than the ecclesiastical. In the early decades of the century, at least, it did seem that the identity of England and Scotland was most firmly encapsulated in the respective established churches, though historians have often had little to say about British religion. Professor Christie, for example, in his Ford Lectures, discusses the widespread assumption that 'the Christian Churches in Britain in the eighteenth century formed one of the bulwarks of political and social stability', but does not himself, in this connection, make a reference to the Scottish churches.[12] Another writer argues that in the early nineteenth century British society 'was also a religious organization, or rather a set of interlocking organizations', but gives no space to Scottish 'religious organizations' and to what extent they therefore interlocked with those south of the Border.[13]

It was, once again, those who travelled who became most aware of differences and tensions. In his assessment of *Scotland, its Faith and its Features*, the Revd Francis Trench found himself confirmed in the merits of the liturgy of the Church of England. 'The very small proportion of Scripture read in the Scotch Church is', he wrote, 'a very great deficiency and loss ...'.[14] If he had been travelling in the Marquis of Bute's yacht *Ladybird* off northern Scotland on a Sunday thirty years later, he would have had less reason for complaint. In the absence of a minister, the marquess proposed 'instead of a sermon, some immense bit of Scripture, e.g. the whole Epistle to the Romans.'[15] Two years later, he converted to the Church of Rome. Trench's general view, that the Book of Common Prayer ensured that Anglicans were *secure* of sound and effective doctrine through a large portion of the services while Presbyterians were too much exposed to the whims of individuals, was common.[16] An Evangelical himself, however, he felt that the Episcopal Church in Scotland, at least judged by the newly opened chapel at Jedburgh, was indulging in excessive pomp and parade. To adopt such measures in England was objectionable enough: 'To introduce them in Scotland is still more mischievous, as a country where the feelings and opinions are so exceedingly

[12] I. R. Christie, *Stress and Stability in Late Eighteenth-Century Britain: Reflections on the British Avoidance of Revolution* (Oxford, 1984), 183.

[13] A. D. Harvey, *Britain in the Early Nineteenth Century* (1978), 64.

[14] Trench, *Scotland*, 121.

[15] D. Hunter Blair, *John Patrick, Third Marquis of Bute KT (1847–1900): A Memoir* (1921), 48.

[16] Trench, *Scotland*, 121.

sensitive and keen as to any display of the kind.'[17] Hugh Miller, descending south of the Border in late 1845, felt that 'The growing Tractarianism of the National Church threatens to work greater changes than the bad potatoes ...'. Visiting York Minster, his Presbyterian education had led him so little to 'associate the not unelevated impulses of the feeling with the devotional spirit' that he had failed to uncover his head. He did so when asked, and apologized for his ignorance. 'Ah, a Scotchman', came the reply, 'I thought as much.'[18]

Such general observations, revealing though they are, merely touch the surface. Differences of custom and practice are also apparent in marking birth, marriage, and death. When Dean Stanley travelled to Broomhall by Dunfermline to take part in the funeral of General Bruce he encountered what he described as 'a little knot of ecclesiastical difficulties which I had not anticipated.' Where was the service to be held?—a compromise was reached whereby the first part was to be in the house and the rest at the grave. After prayer and Bible-reading within the house, first wine and then cake were handed round. Somewhat amazed, Stanley was led to understand that this was the relic of a past practice, which had long existed, of a feast given to the friends, which for many years was the only service at a Scotch funeral, the clergyman merely being asked to say grace before and after.[19] Attending the burial of the Duchess of Argyll in 1878, Gladstone described as 'an odd hash' the prayer in the nature of an eloquent sermon delivered by Dr Macgregor.[20] A little later, an American visitor to Skye found that those arriving for a funeral were provided with a sup of whisky and light refreshments. After a short service at the house, the men then formed in procession to the grave, bearing the bier between them in rotation. Women were not to be seen.[21] One funeral bill contains the following expenses: 17*s.* 6*d.* for the coffin and morth cloth, £3 10*s.* 2*d.* for bread, and £4 4*s.* 2¾*d.* for wines, rum, whisky,

[17] Trench, *Scotland*, 250.

[18] H. Miller, *First Impressions of England and its People* (1847), 22.

[19] R. E. Prothero and G. G. Bradley, *The Life and Correspondence of Arthur Penrhyn Stanley*, vol. ii (1894), 94-5.

[20] H. C. G. Matthew (ed.), *The Gladstone Diaries, vol. ix, January 1875–December 1880* (Oxford, 1986), 320; A. Gordon, *Death is for the Living* (Edinburgh, 1984) has useful material on death in Scotland.

[21] Cited by D. Cooper, *Road to the Isles: Travellers in the Hebrides, 1770–1914* (1979), 183.

and beer.[22] For his part, Hugh Miller was startled by a funeral he happened to witness in England. He was 'a good deal struck with its dissimilarity, in various points, to our Scotch funerals of the same class.'[23] Whilst it is not precisely clear what caused him most amazement, it is likely to have come from the small number of mourners present (and, possibly, among them, some women?). A more modest source of his disquiet was the fact that coffins were carried by the handles, rather than being supported on staves or on the shoulders. English visitors were also surprised to find that, in most cases, weddings took place in the manse rather than in church and that the function of a clergyman was minimal. These habits, however, were subject to changes as the century wore on. A Presbyterian told Stanley that 'they are now [*1862*] accustomed to funerals with the English service, even in their churches.'[24] Alterations in practice, however, should not be too simply attributed to 'Anglicization'. They may derive more from the altered rhythms and demands of an urban society in Central Scotland, though it is worth noting that until the First World War (and beyond) relatively few Scottish weddings took place in a church.

When Macaulay wrote in 1839 of the nations being one because the churches were two, he over-simplified the ecclesiastical structures of Britain. Even at the time he wrote, neither the Church of England nor the Church of Scotland could be said to be fully 'national'. They were the established churches, but they were not comprehensive. They also contained within themselves—it scarcely needs to be said—factions and groupings to the extent that it is not easy to envisage a single relationship between the two churches. Certainly, no formal mechanism of contact or collaboration existed between them. Even if the Church of England could be considered Protestant, the weight of the past appeared to point Episcopalian and Presbyterian along different paths. And, in the first half of the century, it seemed that both churches were subject to such internal pressures that their cohesion was in jeopardy. Significantly, however, it was only in Scotland that the Great Disruption actually occurred—in 1843. The drama of that year was the culmination of a

[22] Cited by T. Ferguson, *The Dawn of Scottish Social Welfare* (1948), 184. I owe these last two references to Dr J. McCaffrey.

[23] Miller, *First Impressions*, 226-7.

[24] Prothero and Bradley, *Life*. For a short discussion of the emergence of a 'Scottish' funeral service see D. Forrester and D. Murray (eds.), *Studies in the History of Worship in Scotland* (Edinburgh, 1984), 91.

long dispute about rights of patronage. Up and down Scotland, ministers and congregations had to decide whether to 'go out' or 'stay in'. The consequences in Scotland were momentous. The Established Church looked momentarily as if it might collapse—as the secessionists hoped. Nearly 40 per cent of ministers and a third of congregations were prepared to shoulder the enormous burden of attempting to parallel the Established Church throughout Scotland. Inevitably, for the remainder of the century, the Church of Scotland lost its comprehensive character, but it did recover its nerve, while the Free Church proved unable to sustain its initial momentum. Additionally, the United Presbyterian Church (a union of two eighteenth-century seceding groups) came into being in 1847, with a membership roughly equal to that of the two halves of the old church.[25] Disraeli's Monsignore in *Lothair* noted the invention of this new church and argued, implausibly, that it would 'render Scotland simply impossible to live in' and drive millions to seek refuge in the bosom of their only mother.[26] In the event, that remained the Scottish ecclesiastical pattern until 1900 when most of the Free Church joined with the United Presbyterians to form the United Free Church.

The disruption affected all of Scotland, but not uniformly. The highest percentage of those 'going out' occurred in the northern synod of Ross (75.8 per cent) and the lowest along the Border (22.5 per cent in Galloway, for example). It has been speculated that, in this latter area, parishes were generally well-endowed and 'English attitudes regarding the nature of Church–State relations had greater influence.'[27] If we substitute 'Anglican' for 'English', that remark may have substance for, south of the Border, there was no unanimity about how to react to these Scottish church crises. Inescapably, they were a matter of concern for the British government and, to a degree, for the churches of England and Wales. Prominent Scottish preachers had, from time to time, taken London by storm. The most conspicuous example in the first half of the century was Edward Irving.[28] The 'hero' of 1843, Thomas

[25] For general information see A. L. Drummond and J. Bulloch, *The Scottish Church, 1688–1843* (Edinburgh, 1973); *The Church in Victorian Scotland, 1843–1874* (Edinburgh, 1975); *The Church in Late Victorian Scotland, 1874–1900* (Edinburgh, 1978); also A. C. Cheyne, *The Transforming of the Kirk: Victorian Scotland's Religious Revolution* (Edinburgh, 1983).   [26] B. Disraeli, *Lothair* (1975), 32.
[27] S. J. Brown, *Thomas Chalmers and the Godly Commonwealth* (Oxford, 1982), 335.
[28] A. L. Drummond, *Edward Irving and his Circle* (1937).

Chalmers, was, however, a well-known name in England. Scottish by birth, ancestry, and education, he had early revealed a sturdy British patriotism: 'May that day in which Buonaparte ascends the throne of Britain be the last of my existence.'[29] His first visit to London as a young man in 1807 produced this not untypical reaction: 'Oh London, artful as a serpent in the dark and tortuous paths of iniquity, but simple and credulous as a child in the higher fields of the intellect.'[30] The English, it seemed, were ripe for instruction and, a decade later, we find London congregations impressed by his words: 'The Tartan beats us all,' George Canning declared. Chalmers rapidly became a 'British' phenomenon, though he preferred to stay in Scotland rather than accept the London University Chair that he was offered. He delivered the first of the Bridgewater lectures on natural theology and received a DD from Oxford University in 1835. Much of his fame also derived from his views on social questions. In 1838 the Church Influence Society in England brought him down to deliver his celebrated lectures on *The Establishment and Extension of National Churches*. As Chalmers was at pains to point out in the ensuing crisis, he and his friends were 'the advocates for a national recognition and national support of religion—and we are not Voluntaries.'[31] English Nonconformists, in turn, brought down the Glasgow Congregational minister, Ralph Wardlaw, to deliver a rejoinder.[32] In the defence of, or assault upon, 'Establishment' Presbyterians and Anglicans united against Secessionists and Dissenters the issue had a British dimension.[33]

Despite the excellence of his London contacts, however, and the lobbying of the Melbourne government, the 1838 Royal Commission had not advocated the additional grants for church extension that Chalmers and his friends desired. In 1842 he made a plea to 'the Capital of the empire' so that its inhabitants should be informed of 'a case of gross, and grievous, and multiplied oppression, which

---

[29] Cited by Brown, *Chalmers*, 31.

[30] Ibid. 33.

[31] W. Hanna, *Memoirs of the Life and Writings of Thomas Chalmers* (Edinburgh, 1852), iv. 348. Dr McCaffrey has drawn my attention to the fact that from an early point Chalmers was 'sighing' to be 'fairly introduced to the public in London': ibid. i. 132–3.

[32] D. M. Thompson, 'Scottish Influences on the English Churches in the Nineteenth Century', *Journal of the United Reformed Church History Society*, 2/2 (1978).

[33] G. I. T. Machin, *Politics and the Churches in Great Britain, 1832–1868* (Oxford, 1977).

is now going on in one of the provinces—an oppression which, if not remedied, will have the effect of trampling down the Church of Scotland into utter insignificance.'[34] It went unheeded. It was clear that no British government was going to permit the Church of Scotland to reassert its former authority over Scottish society. The rights of Dissenters would be defended.[35] It is arguable, further, that the Scottish crisis gave the spur to anti-establishment activity amongst English Dissenters. Voluntary Church Societies, on the Scottish model, began to appear. Edward Miall formed the Anti-State Church Association in 1842.[36] The title of his subsequent book—*The British Churches in Relation to the British People*—demonstrated that he was well aware of the wide dimensions of the problem. There is a certain irony in the fact that it was the use in Scotland of the term 'Free Church' which led to its increasing use in England, even though the Free Church was not, in intention, Voluntarist. In general, however, it was not possible for the broad body of English and Welsh dissent to react to Scottish developments straightforwardly, because circumstances were not precisely like their own, though sympathy for the Free Church was widespread. 'We intend', Lewis Edwards of Bala wrote to Chalmers, 'to collect from eight to nine hundred pounds without putting the Free Church to any expense in sending deputations to Wales.' He had no doubt that every Welsh Calvinistic congregation would contribute something.[37] However, Hugh Miller had been 'a good deal impressed by the marked difference which obtains between the types of English and Scotch Dissent.' They indicated 'the very opposite characters of the two countries.' No form of Dissent, he argued, ever flourished in Scotland that was not of the Presbyterian type, whereas in England there were two fundamental forms, episcopacy and independency, 'and both flourish to the exclusion of almost every other.'[38] He regarded Wesleyanism as an offshoot of Episcopacy. There was, in other words, no such thing as *British* religious Dissent.

It was, indeed, not an easy matter for English Baptists, Congrega-

[34] Cited by Brown, *Chalmers*, 248.
[35] Ibid. 373.
[36] D. M. Thompson, 'The Liberation Society, 1844–1868', in P. Hollis (ed.), *Pressure from Without* (1974), 213.
[37] Cited by Machin, *Politics and the Churches*, 144.
[38] Miller, *First Impressions*, 356.

tionalists and Methodists to identify with any form of Scottish Presbyterianism without causing difficulties for their own counterparts in Scotland. Although small in number, the history of these bodies throws further light on the conflicting pressures operating within the two countries. Baptists and Congregationalists looked strongly to England, although they also had Scottish roots. The activity of the Haldane brothers in particular gave both denominations a Scottish flavour. The Evangelical Union, which developed from the followers of James Morison, was entirely Scottish in origin, deriving its appeal from its rejection of certain prevailing types of Calvinism.[39] Scottish Baptists and Congregationalists were tardy in forming national 'Unions', in both instances decades after the comparable bodies in England and Wales.[40] It proved difficult, also, to formalize relationships with their southern equivalents. Both Scottish denominations wished to protect themselves against charges that they were merely alien 'English outposts', though English ministers occupied prominent pulpits in Edinburgh and Glasgow. The influence of Charles Haddon Spurgeon among Scottish Baptists was strong, and it is not surprising to find a 'Spurgeon Memorial Temple' opened in South Leith in 1894.[41]

On the whole, however, it was not the excessive penetration of English influences which was a cause for concern in these small denominations but the loss of many of their own members, particularly their ministers, to the South. Many candidates sent to Baptist Colleges in England never returned to Scotland. Dr Kenneth Brown has noted a particular influx in the third quarter of the century. English Congregationalism, too, at various levels owed a good deal to Scots. He has calculated that for most of the century approximately 10 per cent of the intake into their main English colleges came from Scotland.[42] In Lancashire, in the absence of adequate Presbyterian provision (English Presbyterianism having frequently turned into Unitarianism), many Scottish incomers turned to Congregationalism. One historian of the time described

[39] H. Escott, *A History of Scottish Congregationalism* (Glasgow, 1960).

[40] E. A. Payne, *The Baptist Union: A Short History* (1959).

[41] D. B. Murray, *The First Hundred Years: The Baptist Union of Scotland* (Glasgow, n.d.)

[42] Dr Kenneth Brown of Queen's University, Belfast is preparing a study of the recruitment of the British Nonconformist ministry and I am grateful to him for supplying figures which have been cited here and elsewhere in this section.

Manchester Congregationalism as 'enveloped in a Scotch mist'.[43]
Manchester Nonconformists could 'sit under' Drs McLaren,
Thomas, Macfadyen or Finlayson or, if they really wanted an exotic
combination, they could plump for Dr Alexander Mackennal who,
unlike the others, was a Cornish Scot.[44] At another level, two of the
foremost minds in English Congregationalism at the end of the
century—A. M. Fairbairn and P. T. Forsyth—had both come from
Scotland.[45] Fairbairn resisted attempts to persuade him to return,
though he thought his native country 'so without the ecclesiastical
shadows that make England so sad a land to the man who loves
religious freedom and spiritual brotherhood.'[46] He took the struggle
to the heart of enemy territory by becoming the first Principal of
Mansfield College. He believed that the Dissent of England and
Scotland should grow closer together and he spoke of 'British
Congregationalists'. A joint meeting of the English and Scottish
Congregational Unions was indeed held in Manchester in 1901,
with an assembly in Glasgow the following year. Such gatherings, it
was stated, constituted 'the realisation of a dream', though no closer
integration was even attempted.

'British' Methodism had some comparable problems. In comparison with England, Scottish Methodism (substantially Wesleyan)
had been statistically unimpressive. After Wesley's death, there was
some controversy over whether he had intended to set up a
Scottish Methodist Conference. By the early 1820s, membership
was falling and an over-ambitious building programme was causing
grave financial problems. Jabez Bunting, the 'Pope' of English
Methodism, was scathing: 'I think if Methodism in Scotland were
put up to auction, it would be the best thing that could be done with
it, except Glasgow, Edinburgh, Dundee, Perth, and perhaps Ayr.
We have spent more money in Scotland than we can account for to
God, or to our people . . .'.[47] The auction did not take place, but
there was much soul-searching about the *raison d'être* of Scottish

[43] J. Waddington, *Congregational History: Continuation to 1850* (1878), 51.
[44] D. Macfadyen, *Alexander Mackennal, BA, DD: Life and Letters* (1915).
[45] W. B. Selbie, *The Life of Andrew Martin Fairbairn* (1914); W. L. Bradley, *P. T. Forsyth: The Man and His Work* (1952); J. B. Paton was another Scot who became prominent in English Congregationalism. See J. L. Paton, *John Brown Paton: A Biography* (1914).
[46] Selbie, *Fairbairn* 98.
[47] A. J. Hayes and D. A. Gowland (eds.), *Scottish Methodism in the Early Victorian Period* (Edinburgh, 1981), 5.

Methodism. The Edinburgh superintendent noted in 1832 many persons who were 'heartily sick of Calvinism' but who would not 'come over' without the certainty of a permanent Methodist church.[48] Some Methodist customs were modified to conform to Scottish habits—a quarterly rather than a monthly communion service, for example. Some Scottish Methodists believed that the formation of the Free Church removed their own role, but that was not a universal view. Scottish Methodists could still:

keep up to its proper height the standard of experimental Godliness, abate the severity of Calvinism, moderate hostility to the residuary church & from our known friendship for the Church of England . . . we are a sort of breakwater to the ferocity of their anti-episcopal wrath.[49]

The ecclesiastical and national dilemmas could not be more neatly put.

By mid-century Wesleyanism in Scotland was described as 'hovering between life and death', but it survived, even initiating in major cities the Central Halls that had started south of the Border. The polity of Wesleyanism, however, ensured that ministers were sent rather than called to Scotland and many of its most prominent ministerial figures there were Englishmen.[50] Methodists other than Wesleyan made little impact. 'Halls, lofts, shops and other places may do as a starting place', confessed one sad writer in the *Primitive Methodist World*, 'but never as a permanent abode for God's people, and will never be considered (especially in Scotland) as churches.'[51] Paradoxically, the greatest Methodist success north of the Border was in the Shetland Isles—furthest away from England. One London Methodist MP helped in the work against the 'dog in manger wretches' of the local Calvinist churches by sending by sea the glass required for a manse and three chapels there—thus avoiding contamination from Scotland altogether!

[48] Ibid. 65.

[49] Ibid. 110.

[50] The minister who built up the Methodist Central Hall in Edinburgh was a Grimsby man. A. Jackson, *George Jackson: A Commemorative Volume* (1949), 15–22. H. N. Brailsford, the radical journalist, whose father was a Wesleyan minister in Edinburgh and who was himself a student at Glasgow University, had some difficulty in establishing that he was not a Scot. F. M. Leventhal, *The Last Dissenter: H. N. Brailsford and his World* (Oxford, 1985), 9–10.

[51] Cited by A. Skevington Wood, 'Methodism in Scotland', in R. Davies, A. R. George, and E. G. Rupp (eds.), *A History of the Methodist Church in Great Britain*, vol. iii (1983), 274.

Inevitably, as Scottish families settled in England throughout the century, the Presbyterian churches which were formed in all major English cities had to wrestle with the problem of allegiance. Was it their function to help maintain 'Little Scotlands' in England, or should they align themselves with mainstream English religious life?[52] The circumstances of particular congregations necessarily differed. In York, for example, the Presbyterian congregation was growing rapidly around the turn of the century, largely because Scottish regiments stationed in the city preferred it to the Anglican chapel in their barracks.[53] In other places, as the century passed, congregations became very mixed—consisting of recent arrivals, second or third generation 'Scots', English wives, 'British' children, and Englishmen who liked Presbyterian preaching—and the 'Scottish' imperative diminished. It was not easy to set out how these churches related to the Church of Scotland. Should they be bound to it in a fixed constitution? Was the Church of Scotland entitled to exercise jurisdiction in what the General Assembly referred to as 'a foreign country'? In the late 1830s, steps were taken to establish a synod embracing the English presbyteries. Such a body was to be 'in connection with' the Church of Scotland, but it was made clear from Scotland itself that all Presbyterian congregations who placed themselves under the care of this synod had no right of appeal to the General Assembly or other Church Courts in Scotland. Naturally, the events in Scotland in 1843 had their repercussions in England. Feeling in the London Presbyterian churches was strongly in favour of the Seceders and, as a result, London was reduced to a Presbytery of four congregations. In speaking of their efforts to maintain the 'loyalty' of one church its elders claimed that without such work 'it had been added to others in London wrenched from lawful connection and illegally and forcibly held by the Free Seceders or English Presbyterians.'[54]

Mid-century, therefore, was a time when individuals and congregations were in confusion. The basic division was between those who wanted to tend the 'scattered sheep' of Scotland and those who wanted to shed the Scottish cloak and emerge as the

[52] K. M. Black, *The Scots Churches in England* (1906); R. Buick Knox, 'The Relationship between English and Scottish Presbyterians, 1836–1876', *Records of the Scottish Church History Society*, 21 (1981–3), 43–66.

[53] E. Royle, 'Religion in York', in C. H. Feinstein (ed.), *York, 1831–1981* (York, 1981).

[54] G. G. Cameron, *The Scots Kirk in London* (Oxford, 1979), 133–4.

English Presbyterian denomination. Signs of tension were everywhere, and were most acutely felt by ministers, many of whom were still recruited from Scotland. In 1849, for example, the Revd George Young, minister of an Islington Presbyterian church, was asked to leave after only six months in his charge. A 'defect of adequate adaptation' had been detected.[55] The minister had come from Paisley. As it happens, he had a subsequent distinguished career in Canada, but there was a certain feeling that the ministers sent to England 'had been the refuse of the Church of Scotland'. On the other hand, there was a certain arrogance among many of the incomers. James Hamilton, minister of the prominent Regent Square church, took the view that '. . . the usual ministrations of English pulpits are in doctrine very meagre and jejeune. English piety is too moluscous' but he thought that with a 'tonic to English theology' provided by the Presbyterian Church in England 'southern piety would stand on its own feet exceeding strong and fair.'[56] It had to be conceded, however, that the English often interpreted a minister's gestures with his fist as a threat to knock his congregation down rather than an attempt to knock the truth into them.

The problems of allegiance and organization in England were further complicated by the growth of the United Presbyterian Church in England. It had four English presbyteries. However, since it was strongly voluntarist in outlook, the Border had little significance and the English churches were firmly integrated into the Scottish parent body. This arrangement naturally added to the difficulties when moves started to bring about a union between the Presbyterian Church in England and the English presbyteries of the United Presbyterian Church. An additional problem was that in Scotland itself there were discussions between the United Presbyterians and the Free Church, and the English tail was in no position to wag the dog. It was the Revd John Cairns, judiciously positioned as a minister in Berwick on Tweed, who advocated union in England.[57] One idea, initially canvassed by the Lancashire presbytery of the Presbyterian Church in England, was that there should

[55] D. Cornick, '"Catch a Scotsman Becoming an Englishman": Nationalism, Theology and Ecumenism in the Presbyterian Church in England, 1845–1876', *Journal of the United Reformed Church History Society* (1985), 203.

[56] Ibid. 207; also R. Buick Knox, 'James Hamilton and English Presbyterianism', *Journal of the United Reformed Church History Society*, (1982), 286–307.

[57] A. R. MacEwen, *Life and Letters of John Cairns* (1898), 494.

be a Presbyterian Church of Britain, consisting of the Free Church, the United Presbyterian Church, and the Presbyterian Church in England. In addition to other factors, however, by this juncture English Presbyterians did not relish becoming simply a small segment of a British church which would be Scottish dominated. And in Scotland itself, fears of splits within both the United Presbyterian Church and the Free Church, largely on the issue of establishment, still prevented union in the 1870s. In England, however, after much debate, a union was agreed in 1876 between the Presbyterian Church in England and the English synod of the United Presbyterian Church. It is perhaps appropriate that a church with such a complex national background should be indebted to one of its members who was a converted Italian Jew for its history.[58] This new body became the Presbyterian Church of England. Its links with the English Free Churches strengthened, but there remained substantial differences of ethos. Between 1876 and 1925, with the exception of two Irishmen, all the moderators of the Presbyterian Church of England were Scots. Union with English Congregationalists (which did take place in 1972) was mooted at this time, but had few supporters. It is not surprising, therefore, that English Presbyterians were uncertain whether they should join English Free Churchmen in campaigning against the 1902 Education Act—which, of course, did not apply to Scotland. Adam Rolland, however, member of the Marylebone Church and later Liberal MP for the Kilmarnock Burghs, had no hesitation. He told the 1903 synod that Scots, Irish, and Welsh came into England 'to take our share in the burdens and problems of English life. To sit apart and shirk responsibility will surely mark us as something alien . . .'.[59] In this connection it has been noted that the (Scottish) Crown Court Church in London looked in all respects like an English Dissenting Chapel, apart from the fact that there were thistle-shaped glass shades round the gas lamps.

A speaker at the 1866 Assembly of the Presbyterian Church in England feared that if Scots prospered in England, and were not adequately shepherded into Presbyterian Churches, they might join the Church of England. That was bad enough, but many of them would later return to Scotland and buy estates on which they would

---

[58] L. Levi, *Digest of the Actings and Proceedings of the Synod of the Presbyterian Church in England, 1836–1876* (1877).

[59] A. Rainy, *Life of Adam Rolland Rainy* (Glasgow, 1914), 143.

build 'little episcopalian chapels'.[60] That was the other side of the
British ecclesiastical coin. Scottish Presbyterianism in England, it
seemed, was reluctantly having to accommodate itself to English
religious realities. It was another thing, however, to acquiesce in any
development which might encourage the growth of episcopalianism in Scotland. A genuine 'British Presbyterianism' appeared to
be a non-starter but 'British episcopalianism' might have brighter
prospects. The dilemmas confronting Scottish Episcopalians
mirrored those confronting most English Presbyterians.[61] English
Presbyterians, however, for the most part recognized that they were
not likely to subvert the Church of England and turn England into a
Presbyterian country. The situation in Scotland was more fluid. The
Episcopal Church in Scotland could be thought of as a Trojan
horse. It was attractive to those Scots who were simultaneously
attracted to English ways in general and who were becoming
dissatisfied with the kirk of their fathers.[62] The movement in this
direction was strongest amongst landed families, who frequently
sent their children to English (Anglican) public schools, but it was
not confined to them. In 1848, for example, the Duke of Argyll
warned his fellow-members of the Church of Scotland that the loss
of support from members of his class could only be stemmed if its
defective worship could be reformed.[63] The Episcopal Church in
Scotland looked for, and to an extent received, financial and moral
support from south of the Border. The involvement of the
Gladstone family in the establishment of Trinity College, Glenalmond, is a case in point.[64] There were always a certain number of
English clergy who rejoiced that in Scotland it was possible to be
both poor and a bishop. Oxford dons were regularly canvassed for
subscriptions to Glenalmond in the belief that it would advance the

---

[60] Cameron, *Scots Kirk*, 136.

[61] M. Lochhead, *Episcopal Scotland in the Nineteenth Century* (1966).

[62] W. Ruddick (ed.), *J. G. Lockhart: Peter's Letters to his Kinsfolk*, (Edinburgh, 1977).

[63] Duke of Argyll, *Presbytery Examined* (1848), 302–3. The worship of the Church
of Scotland did receive some attention in the last decades of the century, even
though critics of the changes attributed them to malign English influences.
Surprisingly quickly, and with comparatively little controversy, all the main
Scottish churches admitted an organ to their premises. Initially, however,
Englishmen, particularly Yorkshiremen, had to be imported to play them. The
hymn-books that began to appear in Scotland contained many non-Scottish hymns.
J. Kerr, *The Renascence of Worship* (Edinburgh, 1909) and D. Murray, 'From
Disruption to Union', in Forrester and Murray, *Studies*.

[64] H. C. G. Matthew, *Gladstone, 1809–1874* (Oxford, 1986), 97, 100.

cause of episcopalianism among the Scottish gentry. Lord Forbes was particularly anxious to touch Oxford pockets to support his new cathedral in Perth.[65]

On the other hand, whatever Presbyterian critics might say, the Scottish Episcopal Church was an authentic element in Scottish church life. It had suffered. It had its own internal divisions. The influence of the Oxford movement was strong, though not without opposition.[66] English episcopal congregations—frequently, para- doxically, with a strong Irish element—were available as alternatives in the large Scottish cities for those who did not like this influence. In general, throughout the century, the Episcopal Church moved closer to the Church of England and abandoned practices which it had formerly shared with Presbyterians. Disputes frequently centred on the future of the Scottish Communion Office, which differed somewhat from that of the Church of England. In 1863 it was enacted that while existing episcopalian congregations might continue to use the Scottish Office, the Book of Common Prayer should be adopted in any new congregations. It was also at this time that the obstacles were removed which had hitherto prevented full recognition being extended in England to clergy who had been ordained by Scottish bishops.

The theological and liturgical implications of these matters naturally received the fullest attention, but lying behind them were issues of identity.[67] Bishop Ewing wrote to Bishop Wordsworth in 1861 that he thought 'one Church for England, Ireland, and Scotland is worth even the sacrifice of the office in question.'[68] He had earlier declared that he 'always looked to union with the Church of England as the only hope of our own . . .', but others by no means agreed.[69] Bishop Wordsworth himself was prepared to advocate a union on a wider basis. He did not object to a union between the established churches of England and Scotland and, indeed, addressed English Dissenters in 1862 on the theme of 'Reunion of the Church in Great Britain'.[70] His ecumenical disposi-

[65] A. Mozley, *The Letters of the Rev J. B. Mozley* (1884), 194.

[66] W. Perry, *The Oxford Movement in Scotland* (Cambridge 1933).

[67] K. G. Robbins, 'Religion and Identity in Modern British History', in S. Mews (ed.), *Religion and National Identity: Studies in Church History*, 18 (Oxford, 1982), 465–87.

[68] A. J. Ross, *Memoir of Alexander Ewing* (1877), 312–13.

[69] Ibid. 279.

[70] J. Wordsworth, *The Episcopate of Charles Wordsworth: A Memoir* (1899), 154–7.

tion added to his not inconsiderable difficulties in his diocese—he was particularly embattled in Perth with a certain Canon Humble. More generally, informal discussions between individual Episcopalians and Presbyterians in Scotland took place, but there was no real prospect at this time of a 'Church of Great Britain'.[71] The decision by the Archbishop of Canterbury to lay the foundation-stone of the Episcopalian cathedral in Inverness in 1866 caused some controversy and was interpreted as an act of English ecclesiastical imperialism. Wordsworth himself was an Englishman and English bishops in Scottish sees had to move with care. One had to think twice before coming north. Dean Liddon happened to be in Constantinople in 1886 when he received a telegram announcing that he had been elected Bishop of Edinburgh. It was a surprise. He declined. Bishops, he thought, should be Scotchmen for 'so long as they are Englishmen that Church will always wear the appearance of an English importation in the eyes of the Presbyterian majority, whose conversion will thus be rendered more difficult by a sense of slighted national feeling.' He was, however, attracted by the fact that Scottish bishops lacked 'the unmeaning trappings of feudalism' which still hung around English sees.'[72]

On the other hand, it is perhaps not unfair to suggest that to certain Scotsmen, either of Episcopalian or Presbyterian background, inadequate prelatical prospects in their native country helped to lift their eyes away from the hills. There were the conspicuous examples of Archibald Campbell Tait and Randall Davidson who became Archbishops of Canterbury.[73] And, in 1881, a young son of the manse, Cosmo Gordon Lang, crossed into England for the first time and fell in love with her universities and her Church. He made his name with a stirring speech at the Oxford Union in 1883 in defence of the established Church of Scotland: only twenty-six years later, the Scottish undergraduate had become Archbishop of York.[74] Thus, on the eve of the Great War, the two

[71] M. Oliphant, *A Memoir of the Life of John Tulloch* (Edinburgh and London, 1889), 214–17.
[72] J. O. Johnston, *The Life and Letters of Henry Parry Liddon* (1904), 327–8.
[73] R. T. Davidson and W. Benham, *The Life of Archibald Campbell Tait* (1891); G. K. A. Bell, *Randall Davidson, Archbishop of Canterbury* (1935); F. W. Robertson 'of Brighton', the 'Prince of Preachers', was also a Scotsman, though this is not discussed in the assessment in M. J. Kitch (ed.), *Studies in Sussex Church History* (1981), 157–71.
[74] J. G. Lockhart, *Cosmo Gordon Lang* (1949), 19–23, 33.

highest clergy of the Church of England were Scotsmen. But, 'English' though he had become, Lang could never entirely throw off his Scottish past, and he remained interested in the ecclesiastical relationhsip between North and South Britain. One of his brothers followed him into the English episcopate and another became a minister of the Kirk: the Lang family circle epitomized the divisions of 'British' Christianity.

In a more general sense 'minister/manse' and 'parson/vicarage' stood in a British relationship which was (like the Langs themselves) 'familial' yet also 'distant'. Clustered around 'manse' and 'vicarage' were images and associations which still, to many, encapsulated an important difference between Scotland and England. Perhaps predictably, it was a Scottish minister who took the trouble to discover that, of all clergy sons with entries in the *DNB*, 1 out of 6.497 was the product of a Scottish manse rather than the 1 out of 9.7 that might have been expected from the proportion of Scots in Britain.[75] The 'minister' and the 'clergyman' were different types. 'I am partial to English clergymen,' Thomas Chalmers's daughter wrote in her diary in 1830, 'They are very agreeable, though generally of short stature. They have such amiable smiles.'[76] Of course, the contrast between Highland manse and a Dorset parsonage represented one extreme. There were many different forms of clerical life within both Scotland and England. There was no doubt, for example, that the diocese of Oxford was much more attractive to clergymen than the diocese of Ripon.[77] Samuel Wilberforce's well-known reluctance to go to Leeds in 1837 is at least matched by that of his son, who wrote to his wife, prior to accepting the new See of Newcastle in 1882: 'I cannot bear the thought of the black, black north—the separating from all the old ties of the south.' On being appointed Archdeacon of the East Riding in 1841, Robert Wilberforce had written: 'You can hardly fancy such louts as many of the clergy here.'[78] 'After two years' probation', Archbishop Thomson of York noted in 1870, 'it is common for Curates to seek a charge in the south, where the nearness of London, or of the family roof, or the smaller amount of

[75] A. W. Fergusson, *Sons of the Manse* (Dundee, 1923), 140–2; R. S. Blakey, *The Man in the Manse* (Edinburgh, 1978); B. Collins, *Victorian Country Parsons* (1977).

[76] Cited by D. L. Keir, *The House of Collins* (1952), 53n.

[77] A. Haig, *The Victorian Clergy* (1984), 118–21.

[78] A. Russell, *The Clerical Profession* (1980), 240.

dissent, or the more agreeable climate, or the more liberal stipend, or the less independent demeanour of the people may seem to tempt him.'[79]

At the level of theology and biblical scholarship, there was no sustained dialogue between Scotland and England. Scottish scholars liked to believe themselves far more closely attuned to continental developments than their English colleagues. The tradition of study in Europe, largely in Germany, was solidly maintained in Scotland. Scottish divines frequently felt more at home in Protestant Europe than they did in Anglican England.[80] Thomas Chalmers, for example, took great satisfaction from his address to the Royal Institute of Paris. Recent histories of nineteenth-century biblical scholarship confirm that it can scarcely be described as 'British'.[81] The point must not be exaggerated, but it is important.

A strong sense of a national theological tradition continued in Scotland. Addressing the students of the University of St Andrews in 1876, Dean Stanley mentioned such men as Caird, Tulloch, Shairp, Knight, McLeod Campbell, and Erskine of Linlathen. He urged the undergraduates to immerse themselves in the thoughts 'which have been enkindled, not by Germans, not by Anglicans, but by your own pastors and teachers.'[82] These authors were not unknown in England, but they were not assiduously studied there.[83] It is significant, too, that Tulloch's *Movements of Religious Thought in Britain during the Nineteenth Century* has long held the field as the only genuinely British survey. It is the work of a German-educated Scot, well-versed in English thought, but properly able to include his own countrymen as well.

The conclusion of our discussion should be clear. The English

[79] Haig, *Clergy*, 118–21.

[80] A. L. Drummond, *The Kirk and the Continent* (Edinburgh, 1956).

[81] J. Rogerson, *Old Testament Criticism in the Nineteenth Century: England and Germany* (1984), 5, explicitly states that Scottish scholarship must be separately evaluated. This has been attempted by R. A. Riesen, *Criticism and Faith in Late Victorian Scotland* (1985). Pusey's predecessor in the Regius Chair of Hebrew at Oxford was the brilliant but short-lived Aberdonian Episcopalian Alexander Nicoll. See also J. S. Black and G. W. Chrystal (eds.), *William Robertson Smith* (1912).

[82] W. Knight (ed.), *Rectorial Addresses Delivered at the University of St Andrews, 1863–1893* (1894), 232.

[83] F. D. Maurice and Dean Stanley knew and corresponded with Erskine, but outside Scotland his chief contacts were with continental Europe. W. Hanna (ed.), *Letters of Thomas Erskine of Linlathen* (Edinburgh, 1878); G. M. Tuttle, *John McLeod Campbell on Christian Atonement: So Rich a Soil* (Edinburgh, 1985).

and Scottish churches encountered each other in many different contexts but there was little disposition to unite. The 'high' Scottish Presbyterian did advocate *A United Church for the British Empire* in 1902 but his voice was a lonely one. He believed, a little later, that the First World War placed on the two national churches an obligation to agree. In a sermon delivered in St Paul's Cathedral in 1918 he argued that ecclesiastical union would in turn 'seal and consecrate the union of the British Empire'.[84] That was one vision destined never to be achieved.

'The Welch are a very religious people,' wrote one American visitor in 1834, 'more so than the Scotch, or the people of New England. There is perhaps no other Christian people in the world who manifest so much religious susceptibility, or who can, as a body, be brought so much under its power.'[85] The vigour of that piety was widely identified with Nonconformity. It was Nonconformity, in turn, that was the embodiment of a certain kind of Welshness—in the eyes of its supporters the most important kind.

At the beginning of the nineteenth century, however, such an identification could not have been made. 'Revival' had begun in the 1730s. It shared many characteristics with contemporary movements in Europe, elsewhere in Britain, and in the United States. 'Old-style' Dissent (Baptists, Independents, Quakers) existed in clusters in Wales but it was not notably more numerous than in England to which, particularly to Bristol, it looked for ministerial training. Both George Whitefield and John Wesley brought a somewhat different version of the Gospel from England. The 'stirring' was to this degree Anglo-Welsh. It was Howell Harris, for a time Whitefield's deputy, but indubitably Welsh, whose organizing capacity laid the foundations (still within the established church) of the denomination which, on its secession in 1811, became the Calvinistic Methodists. Fissiparous though their congregations tended to be, Baptists and Congregationalists shared in this growth. Even so, at the date when the Calvinistic Methodists 'came out', Nonconformity, old and new, amounted to probably no more than 20 per cent of the Welsh population.

[84] J. Cooper, *A United Church for the British Empire* (1902) and *Reunion: A Voice from Scotland* (1918).
[85] R. Carwardine, 'The Welsh Evangelical Community and "Finney's Revival"', *Journal of Ecclesiastical History*, 29 (1978), 465.

The expansion of all the sects over the next few decades was remarkable. In 1800 there were 967 Anglican places of worship and 402 Nonconformist. Fifty years later the figures were 1,110 and 2,695 respectively.[86] The religious census of 1851 is not easy to interpret but on the relevant Sunday Nonconformity claimed 87 per cent of the total number of worshippers at all services. The provision of places of worship in the principality comfortably exceeded the English proportion. Nonconformist spokesmen claimed thereafter that the balance of support was continuing to tilt firmly in their favour. Of course, this transfer of allegiance was somewhat misleading. Almost by definition, Dissent was divided, except in opposition to the established church which was frequently stigmatized as the 'English Church'. Competition between the Dissenting denominations was as frequent as collaboration. Doctrinal argument could be fierce. Diversity abounded. In addition, denominational strength was strongly localized within Wales. The Calvinistic Methodists came to be particularly strong in the North-West, for example, and the Baptists in the South-East. Unitarians had a mysterious hold on parts of South Cardiganshire. Although it is important to stress that 'Welsh Nonconformity' was far from monolithic, collectively Dissenters in Wales had achieved what their English counterparts had failed to achieve; numerical superiority over the established church. Their success begat a problem. Was an 'Anglo-Welsh' partnership about to break up?

A major issue was language. Dissent had struck its deepest roots in Welsh-speaking communities. The Calvinistic Methodists were overwhelmingly organized in Welsh-speaking congregations, as were the Congregationalists/Independents. Most Baptist congregations used Welsh in worship and even a majority of Wesleyans belonged to Welsh-speaking circuits. This consideration alone argued in favour of an 'all-Wales' ecclesiastical structure. In the case of the largest denomination, the Calvinistic Methodists, there was no problem. They had no English counterpart and their Welshness was therefore beyond question. Even the hint that they might establish English-speaking churches for the benefit of monoglot English speakers was sufficient to cause an internal crisis. In the case of the Baptists and Congregationalists, however, the issue was more complicated since when both bodies, despite their

---

[86] I. G. Jones, *Explorations and Explanations* (Llandysul, 1981), 36.

independent polity, established 'Unions' in the early 1830s they did so for 'England and Wales.' They inevitably functioned through the medium of the English language. What normally happened, therefore, was that the English-speaking congregations in Wales were affiliated to these London-based 'Unions' whereas the Welsh-speaking congregations were affiliated to the Union of Welsh Independents and the Baptist Union of Wales. In the last half of the century these Welsh-speaking denominations (for that, in effect, is what they were) developed their own magazines and papers and their ministers were trained in Wales in their own theological colleges. English, Scottish, and German theology was discussed in such periodicals as *Y Traethodydd* but the flavour of debate was Welsh. A Welsh chapel community had an ethos of its own—as the celebrated Birmingham Congregationalist, R. W. Dale, found when he stayed in Wales. English Nonconformity had its great preachers but the style and status of such men as Christmas Evans or John Elias, amongst many others, put them in a distinctively Welsh category. The poetic fervour of a Welsh Calvinist minister marked him off from his Scottish counterpart. Throughout the nineteenth century a steady trickle of Welshmen availed themselves of Dr Williams's bequest to obtain a theological education at a Scottish university but they were not invariably impressed by their exposure to Scottish life. They also sometimes found that Scottish church historians were not disposed to regard the Calvinistic Methodists (even though they subsequently adopted the name Presbyterian Church of Wales) as members of an authentic Reformed Church in the sense that the Church of Scotland was. The Welsh-speaking denominations in their late nineteenth-century 'golden age' therefore can scarcely be said to be integrated into the world of Anglo-Welsh religion.

The tension between 'England and Wales' and 'Wales' was most commonly experienced among Baptists and Congregationalists. Chapels of what were in name the same denomination in particular localities could be differently 'aligned'. A shift in language use was also a shift into a different network of relationships. The observation in a letter in 1836 from mid-Wales to the English Wesleyan leader Jabez Bunting that 'language is a perpetual subject of contention' has a more general validity.[87] More generally, English

Nonconformists rejoiced at the spectacular growth of Welsh Nonconformity but were perplexed as to why they did not share, to the same degree, in this expansion. The Welsh Revival of 1904–5 was a particular case in point. The inspired preaching of Evan Roberts, the youthful blacksmith, and his associates, reputely added approaching 100,000 fresh adherents in little more than a year. 'Is it too much for us to seek that tens of thousands may be converted to God in London, as has been the experience in Wales through the great outpouring of the Holy Spirit?' asked the London Baptist, the Revd J. H. Shakespeare.[88] He was a disappointed man. The fact that Nonconformists were in a majority in Wales but had failed to achieve this position in England complicated the struggle of the Liberation Society and other groups seeking to end the establishment of the Church of England.[89] By the end of the century it seemed clear that the argument in favour of that course in Wales was both just and politically feasible. This put English Nonconformists in a quandary. The combined strength of 'Anglo-Welsh' Nonconformity might conceivably achieve disestablishment in 'England and Wales'. If the Welsh campaigned on their own and were successful, the Church of England would remain the established church in England. In the end, it was that fate to which English Nonconformists had to resign themselves.

Despite the tension which this particular problem engendered, it would be wrong to exaggerate the gulf between 'Welsh' and 'English' Nonconformity. There were, of course, flourishing Welsh-speaking congregations in London and other major English cities. It seemed natural for Welsh miners in County Durham to set up their own chapel. The links between English-speaking Nonconformist denominations in Wales and their English counterparts were multifarious. Although no precise figures are possible, English-born members of English-speaking chapels in Wales were probably balanced by Welsh-born members of English-speaking chapels in England. Figures being compiled by Dr Kenneth Brown make it

---

[88] S. Koss, *Nonconformity in Modern British Politics* (1975), 43.

[89] I. G. Jones's excellent article 'The Liberation Society and Welsh Politics, 1844 to 1868' is reprinted in his *Explorations and Explanations*, 236–68. Despite the prominent position in the Liberation Society in England held by the London Welshman, John Carvell Williams, opinion in Wales was not willing to leave the issue in the hands of London for resolution in a British context. 'We *must* be free in Wales', wrote Stuart Rendel to Thomas Gee, 'to make it a Welsh question pure and simple ...'. Cited by D. W. Bebbington, *The Nonconformist Conscience* (1982), 33.

plain that English Baptist and Congregational chapels would have been hard-pressed to man their pulpits without the aid of men born in Wales. There was a vigorous export trade in Welsh ministers, though many of them, at least initially, had difficulties in communication. The grounds for dismissing a Welsh applicant for the Congregational College at Highbury in 1837 were that the man had 'so bad an articulation' that he was unfit for ministerial training and it was 'very difficult' to converse with him.[90] In all probability, this was not merely a matter of personal inadequacy. Behind the difficulty lay the Welsh language. In the half century after 1850, the proportion of Welshmen in English Free Church pulpits reached approximately one-third. Wesleyans also relied heavily upon Welsh reinforcements. Hugh Price Hughes, the London-based embodiment of the 'Nonconformist Conscience', came from Carmarthenshire. We read that he owed many of his political and social beliefs to a certain Alderman Rees, a Welsh Methodist prominent in the public life of Dover!

This influx of Welsh Nonconformist influence in England was not invariably welcomed. It was a Scots-born, English-domiciled Professor at the Presbyterian Westminster College, newly removed to Cambridge, who wrote in 1909 of a certain Welsh Baptist that he did not come up to his idea of an English gentleman. The Chancellor of the Exchequer was extremely inaccurate with regard to facts: 'one does not like to see the finance of England in the hands of a man who cannot be trusted to give an exact statement of anything.'[91] The Scotsman in residence at Bishopthorpe, York, has comparable reservations about Welshmen.[92] It is, perhaps, dangerous to proceed to any generalization about British religion which stems from meditating upon Mr Lloyd George. Nevertheless, by the early twentieth century, English Nonconformity, through the

[90] Dr K. Brown will be dealing with these matters more fully, but see his article, 'The Congregational Ministry in the First Half of the Nineteenth Century: A Preliminary Survey', *Journal of the United Reformed Church History Society* 3 no. 1 (1986), 334.

[91] Cited by R. Buick Knox, 'Professor John Gibb and Westminster College, Cambridge', *Journal of the United Reformed Church History Society*, 3 no. 8 (1986), 334.

[92] Lang was suspicious of 'that mysterious possession affecting the Celtic temperament which is called "hwyl" which makes the speaker say he knows not what and excites the audience they know not why.' Cited by J. H. Edwards, *Life of David Lloyd George*, vol. iv (1913), 126. Walter Raleigh wrote in Mar. 1912, 'If L. George is not found out soon I shall be puzzled. The worst of it is I have Celt enough in me to understand him.' Raleigh, *Letters*, 153.

considerable presence of Welsh verbal fluency and Scottish intellectual precision, could be said to come closer to being fully British in its composition than any other branch of the Christian church in Britain.

The growth of religious Dissent in Wales naturally caused acute problems for Anglicans in England and Wales. We have seen that John Mason Neale found Swansea somewhat hellish and the fact that Dissenters were rampant there and elsewhere in the principality did not improve matters. He declared of the 'brave old Church of England':

> Dissenters are like mushrooms,
> That flourish but a day;
> Twelve hundred years through smiles and tears
> She hath lasted on alway! . . .
>
> The true old Church of England
> She alone hath pow'r to teach;
> 'Tis presumption in Dissenters
> When they pretend to preach . . .[93]

The condition of the Church of England in Wales did not, at first sight, suggest that it was well-equipped to clear the mushrooms. It had not adapted well to a burgeoning industrial society, though it would be too simple to explain its difficulties solely in these terms. It is well known that no bishop since the reign of Queen Anne had been able to speak Welsh at the time of his appointment. Since 'England and Wales' was the ecclesiastical unit, there seemed no necessity even to appoint Welshmen to Welsh sees. The most distinguished Englishman to be appointed in the first half century was Connop Thirlwall who became bishop of St Davids in 1840 and stayed there for thirty years. A considerable scholar, Thirlwall found it easier to learn Welsh than his clergy did to absorb his scholarship.[94] St David's College, Lampeter, established in the 1820s, was an indication that Anglicans did have a commitment to higher education in the principality.[95] By mid-century, the influence

---

[93] Cited by S. W. Sykes and S. Gilley in their article, '"No Bishop, No Church!": The Tractarian Impact on Anglicanism', in G. Rowell (ed.), *Tradition Renewed: The Oxford Movement Conference Papers* (1986), 128.

[94] See J. C. Thirlwall, *Connop Thirlwall, Historian and Theologian* (1936).

[95] D. T. W. Price, *A History of St David's College Lampeter* (Cardiff, 1977).

of the Oxford movement was evident in both North and South Wales. The Church began to revive yet the Anglican dilemma became more acute. English Anglicans were reluctant to allow their Welsh brethren to be thrown to the Nonconformist wolves. The campaign to save the establishment enlisted some unexpected crusaders—such as F. E. Smith. Many Welsh Anglicans welcomed this outside support and were firmly committed to an integrated 'Anglo-Welsh' church. One of Thirlwall's successors at St Davids, Basil Jones, himself a Welshman, reiterated in 1886 that in his view 'Wales' was a geographical expression.[96] A 'Welsh Church' was quite unnecessary. On the other hand, there was another stream of Welsh Anglican opinion which held that the Church would never make progress in Welsh life unless it shook off the taint of 'Englishness'. The Dean of Bangor wrote an open letter to Gladstone in 1870 arguing that regaining the attachment of 'the religious Cymric masses' would depend upon a 'native' episcopate and clergy.[97] In that same year a Welsh-speaker was appointed to the see of St Asaph. Certainly, in a heavily Welsh-speaking diocese like Bangor, it could not be said that the Church catered merely for the English, or for English-speakers. Inevitably, there were conflicting opinions. Some clergy argued strongly that the Church did have a special responsibility to further the Welsh language in its life; others argued that it was no business of the Church of Christ to link its work to the fate of any language. The debate lasted until Disestablishment was imposed—and beyond. The ambiguities were confirmed by the fact that Welsh Anglicans neither described themselves as 'the Church of Wales' (on the Irish model) nor 'the Church of England in Wales' but 'the Church in Wales'.

By 1914, therefore, 'Anglicanism' in the United Kingdom (and in Britain) had come to have a rather different character from its condition at the beginning of the nineteenth century. Episcopalianism in Scotland had come nearer to the Church of England but still asserted that it was a Scottish church. Anglicanism in Wales (as earlier in Ireland) had come, with reluctance for the most part, to accept constitutional separation. Only in England did the State continue to recognize the Church of England as the established church. The belief that it was still the Church of the English nation was one to which Anglican writers firmly clung. 'The English

---

[96]  G. E. Jones, *Modern Wales* (Cambridge, 1984), 276.

[97]  H. T. Edwards, *A Letter to W. E. Gladstone* (1870), 49.

Church', wrote Mandell Creighton, historian and Bishop of London, 'must be the religious organ of the English people.' That no doubt remained the wish of millions but, at the turn of the century, it was as spurious a claim as the comparable one made on behalf of the Church of Scotland. The problem of how to maintain unity and diversity was about to tax the 'Anglican Communion' in new ways. Despite Creighton's claim that 'The Church of England has before it the conquest of the world', it appeared to have suffered a defeat in Britain.[98]

Finally, the study of integration and diversity in the sphere of religion cannot be limited to the formal denominational relationships across Britain. There were numerous other contacts between individuals. Examination of a number of societies and organizations discloses that the tensions seen at the denominational level were repeated in their affairs too.

In 1812, Thomas Chalmers affirmed that the great value of the British and Foreign Bible Society (founded eight years earlier) lay in 'its capacity to unite the entire British nation for a shared world mission ideal.' Its purpose transcended differences between the Protestant denominations on the one hand and the 'national groups within the British state' on the other.[99] The role of Welsh Evangelicals in the founding of the Society so that bibles in Welsh might be provided for Mary Jones and her contemporaries is well known. Between 1804 and 1830, nearly 300,000 Welsh Bibles and Testaments were published by the Society. It might be said that Mary Jones became the best-known Welsh girl in nineteenth-century Britain. Her story was familiar to any child brought up in an evangelical home.[1] The British and Foreign Bible Society was apparently able to provide for the needs of Wales relatively harmoniously. Anglo-Scottish relations, however, were stormy. There were various causes of contention. In the first place, there was much vexation stemming from a ruling in the House of Lords in the early 1820s that it was against the law for bibles printed in Scotland to be sold in England. By way of retaliation, the King's Printer in Scotland was successful in 1824 in obtaining an interdict

[98] L. Creighton, *Life and Letters of Mandell Creighton*, vol. ii (1913), 301–2.
[99] Cited by Brown, *Chalmers*, 64.
[1] R. M. Davies, 'Mary Jones, 1784–1964', *Transactions of the Calvinistic Methodist Historical Society* (1967).

which prevented the selling of English-printed bibles in Scotland. Much litigation followed until the 1840s when the respective monopolies in both countries were abandoned.[2] The issue had not been conducive to good feeling. The second problem was the great controversy concerning the status of the Apocrypha, on which radically different positions were taken in Scotland from those adopted in England. The powerful Glasgow and Edinburgh Bible Societies, which had agreed to work 'in concert' with the London-based BFBS, withdrew their collaboration in 1825 in protest against the London decision to print the Apocrypha in copies of the bible intended for continental distribution. Before the crisis, receipts from Scotland in London had been averaging some £5,000 per annum; afterwards, they collapsed to £235.[3] The BFBS retaliated by endeavouring to establish its own auxiliary network north of the Tweed. No doubt the status of the Apocrypha genuinely troubled minds, but it is also tempting to see the problem of control lurking behind the ostensible issue in contention. In 1861, most of the individual Bible Societies in Scotland came together in Glasgow to form the National Bible Society—a body which left scant room for the 'British' society in Scotland. It had not taken long for Chalmers's hopes for a society which would transcend the national groups to be dashed.

Comparable tensions within the same evangelical world can be seen in the attempt in the 1840s to establish an Evangelical Alliance—embracing British, European, and American churches. On this occasion, the tension existed between London and the English provinces rather more than between England, Scotland, and Wales. It is noteworthy, however, that when the proposed 'Articles' of the Alliance were being discussed a prominent English Congregationalist commented that the questions before the conference seemed to be 'English', 'Scottish', 'Irish', or 'American' rather than doctrinal.[4]

The Scots claimed to 'show Britain the way' to moral improvement in a number of areas but were not happy when the success of their ideas in the South threatened to jeopardize their control.

---

[2] W. C. Somerville, *From Iona to Dunblane: The Story of the National Bible Society of Scotland to 1948* (Glasgow, n.d.), 18–21.

[3] W. Canton, *The Story of the Bible Society* (1904), 120.

[4] J. Wolffe, 'The Evangelical Alliance in the 1840s: An Attempt to Institutionalize Christian Unity', in W. J. Sheils and D. Wood (eds.), *Voluntary Religion: Studies in Church History* 23 (Oxford, 1986), 336–9.

Given the pattern of Scottish drinking in the early nineteenth century, it is not surprising to discover from Dr Harrison that the earliest anti-spirits societies originated in Glasgow and Ulster.[5] These societies spread into England through the northern textile centres of Preston, Bradford, and Leeds. Scottish temperance zeal in mid-century was greater than English. William Collins, the Glasgow publisher, and other Scottish temperance enthusiasts came south in order to promote a drinking reformation. More Scotsmen travelled to England on this errand than Englishmen travelled to Scotland. Initially, Wales was even less responsive to temperance advocates, though this deficiency was later handsomely remedied.[6] It was in the North of England that the two most active (and significantly named) temperance bodies in Britain had their headquarters. The prohibitionist United Kingdom Alliance operated from Manchester, and the moral-suasionist British Temperance League operated from Bolton (later from Sheffield). The London-based National Temperance League was less effective. Manchester contributed three times as much to the funds of the United Kingdom Alliance as London. Its most prominent contributors had addresses in Lancashire and Scotland.[7] The Scottish Temperance League, and other Scottish temperance bodies, however, continued to insist on their own autonomy. The Scottish temperance and teetotal advocates were apt to argue that there was something peculiar about Scottish drinking which required separate treatment and their English colleagues did not effectively challenge this contention.

The emergence of separate organizations to cater for 'youth' in the mid- and late nineteenth century gave rise to considerable Anglo-Scottish controversy amongst Evangelicals. It was by no means clear, for example, who 'founded' the YMCA. Was it the Scot David Naismith or the Englishman George Williams? Was it 'really' a Scottish or an English Association? One well-informed writer claimed that in 1844, when the YMCA was formed in London, there was no other association with the same title and objectives known to those involved. He had no hesitation in saying that no such society had ever been dreamed of in Glasgow before 1844.

[5] Harrison, *Drink and the Victorians*, 95.
[6] W. R. Lambert, *Drink and Sobriety in Victorian Wales c.1820–c.1895* (Cardiff, 1983).
[7] Harrison, *Drink and the Victorians*, 219–20.

Glasgow young men felt differently and claimed to have evidence to the contrary. In his history of the YMCA Dr Binfield judiciously states that 'the chain of coincidence suggests that somewhere the Scottish societies must have had an impact, however indirect, on the London movement.'[8] The Boys' Brigade, on the other hand, indubitably started in Glasgow in 1883. It spread quickly throughout urban Scotland. The first English company was not formed until 1885 but the movement was then taken up south of the Border by both Anglican and Nonconformist churches. In London, the Brigade idea had strong Presbyterian links because it was taken to the capital by emigrant Scots. By the time of its Silver Jubilee, membership in relation to the male population was strongest in Scotland and the North of Ireland, followed by the South-West of England, Wales, and the North of England. From the beginning, the 'national' headquarters had understandably been in Glasgow. In 1902, however, a London office was established with a full-time Secretary. A lobby then developed in favour of establishing the headquarters in 'the capital of the Empire'. It was further argued that while the headquarters remained in Glasgow Anglican clergy mistakenly supposed that the avowedly interdenominational Brigade was in fact Presbyterian. The solution, in 1914/15, was to move the headquarters to London but to continue to have two official addresses, London and Glasgow, to have a Northern and a Southern Committee with their respective full-time Secretaries. 'This arrangement disregarded the elementary fact that the work did not divide itself naturally between the nations', the Southern Secretary subsequently wrote, 'but in the main was common to the whole movement. As a consequence there was a tendency to re-enact the Battles of Bannockburn and Flodden in alternate rotation.'[9] Such were the hazards in running a 'British' youth movement.

It comes as no surprise, in conclusion, to find that, in general, as regards the external world, the British churches rarely presented a 'British' face. The Presbyterian churches of Scotland had a relationship with the Reformed Churches of the Netherlands, Switzerland, France, and even Hungary which gave them a feeling, if not a strong

[8] C. Binfield, *George Williams and the YMCA: A Study in Victorian Social Attitudes* (1973), 134.
[9] J. Springhall, B. Fraser, and M. Hoare, *Sure & Stedfast: A History of the Boys' Brigade, 1883 to 1983* (London and Glasgow, 1983), 113.

one, that they had an identifiable place in European Christianity.[10] The Church of England, with its increasingly ambivalent stance towards the Reformation, had no such clear identity. In 1875 the World Alliance of Reformed Churches was founded and, although largely English-speaking, it had strong European connections from the outset. It was in Edinburgh in 1876 that its first General Council met. Scotsmen figured among the Alliance's first presidents.[11] By contrast, the Lambeth Conference of the Anglican Communion, which first met in 1867, had no significant European dimension.[12] Anglicans tended to assume that within the British Empire the religion of Britain was Anglican. Presbyterians impatiently pointed out that this was not the case.

Victorian missionary societies were rarely 'British'. The Anglican societies were largely English and the Presbyterian largely Scottish. Their activities were not co-ordinated and the missions they established in different parts of the world frequently had an English or Scottish flavour.[13] Only the London Missionary Society was conspicuously an integrated 'Anglo-Scottish' organization. It is not surprising to find the largely English Congregationalists disagreeing with the largely Scottish Presbyterians about which form of church order might be most suitable in the South Seas.[14] The best-known missionary of the Victorian era, the Scot David Livingstone, originally went to Africa under the auspices of the LMS. Another notable Scottish missionary, James Chalmers, the martyr of the Pacific, was likewise in its service. Reading a moving biography of Chalmers led the English Congregationalist, R. F. Horton, to reflect on the fact that so many supposed 'Englishmen' were in reality 'Scotsmen'. He added that 'when the present Education Bill has wrecked the national education of England, a

[10] See, for example, A. Wemyss, 'La Genève religieuse de 1830 à 1835 vue de l'Écosse et de l'Angleterre', in O. Fatio (ed.), *Genève protestante en 1831* (Geneva, 1983), 197–209; J. H. Mackay, *Religious Thought in Holland during the Nineteenth Century* (1911)—Hastie Lectures delivered in Glasgow. For a continental awareness of Scottish distinctiveness see O. Dibelius, *Das kirchliche Leben Schottlands* (Giessen, 1911).

[11] M. Pradervand, *A Century of Service: A History of the World Alliance of Reformed Churches, 1875–1975* (Grand Rapids, Mich., 1975), pp. xv, 22–3, 26–7; B. Aspinwall, 'The Scottish Religious Identity in the Atlantic World', in Mews (ed.), *Religion and National Identity*, 508–18.

[12] A. M. G. Stephenson, *The First Lambeth Conference* (1967).

[13] E. G. K. Hewat, *Vision and Achievement, 1796–1956: A History of the Foreign Missions of the Churches United in the Church of Scotland* (1960).

[14] R. Lovett, *History of the London Missionary Society, 1975–1985* (1899).

still larger proportion will be.'[15] This gloomy assessment, made at the turn of the century, is an indication that at a time when British Christianity was making its biggest impact overseas its domestic differences were still only too apparent.

[15] C. Binfield, *So Down to Prayers: Studies in English Nonconformity, 1780–1920* (1977), 281.

# 4

## The Business of Politics and the Politics of Business

'A state which is incompetent to satisfy different races condemns itself,' wrote Lord Acton in his 1862 *Essay on Nationality*, 'a state which labours to neutralise, to absorb, or to expel them, destroys its own vitality: a state which does not include them is destitute of the chief basis of self-government.'[1] The previous year, in his *Considerations on Representative Government*, John Stuart Mill had also wrestled with the nature of nationality and its political implications. The civil war in the United States was much in the minds of contemporaries. Could civil war happen in Britain? Mill took the view that one nationality could indeed emerge or be absorbed into another. When it was in an inferior position—he instanced Bretons and Basques in France—such an absorption was beneficial. It was bad for small peoples to sulk on their own rocks, half-savage relics of past times—a judgement he applied to 'the Welshman or the Scottish Highlander as members of the British nation.' He suggested that the greatest obstacles to the 'blending of the nationalities' arose when they were nearly equal in numbers.[2] Henry Sidgwick in *The Elements of Politics* took the view that a nation could be said to exist when people were conscious of being members of one body over and above what they derived 'from the mere fact of being under one government.'[3]

Our argument so far has suggested that such a consciousness both did and did not exist. What it meant to be 'British' admitted of no straightforward answer: everything depended upon context. Diversity in the spheres of broad culture, language, and religion, to mention only those so far considered, could not be denied. Britain might seem to be a multi-national state. Yet, in what was perhaps the crucial area of government, it appeared that political integration was well-advanced. In Britain, a century of 'democratization' did not

[1] Lord Acton, *The History of Freedom and Other Essays* (1907), 298.
[2] H. B. Acton (ed.), *J. S. Mill: On Liberty, and Considerations on Representative Government* (1972), 363-4.
[3] H. Sidgwick, *The Elements of Politics* (1897), 223-4.

lead, as it did elsewhere in Europe, and in Ireland, to the emergence of separate political parties. Party politics was British politics and there were no significant or successful 'Scottish', 'Welsh', or even 'English' parties. If such an absence provides the way to measure 'integration', Britain was an integrated political society. Political groupings solidified around personality, class, and ideology within an apparently homogenous 'national' electorate. British governments were formed by parties who sought support in all parts of Britain. The significance of these obvious facts should not be overlooked, yet they do not tell the full story. After the First World War, separatist political parties did emerge, though they had to wait many further decades before being rewarded with even modest success. The later foundation of such parties does at least suggest that political homogeneity was not complete. It is important to maintain a dialectical balance. We need to see both Scotland and Wales 'in British politics' and British politics 'in Scotland and Wales'.

Walter Bagehot had no hesitation in writing about the *English* constitution, though in the text he occasionally used 'British' as a synonym for 'English'. As a student in London he had lodged with the Scottish holder of the Scottish-sounding 'Chair of the Philosophy of the Human Mind and Logic.'[4] Scotsmen abounded at *The Economist* and he married the daughter of one of them. However, it was apparently not worth mentioning that the British state arose out of a union. Scotsmen felt differently. On the other hand, although the 1707 Act of Union had indeed made certain specific provisions relating to Scotland, it could be argued that they did not fundamentally alter the fact that within the British state English traditions of government and administration held the upper hand. Victorian Scotsmen knew that they had to learn about the historical evolution of the English constitution if they were to understand the conventions of the state in which they lived.[5]

There was one British constitution but, at the beginning of the nineteenth century, there was no such thing as a 'British' electorate. Before 1832, there were some 366,000 voters in England and Wales

---

[4] R. Rose, *Understanding the United Kingdom: The Territorial Dimension in Government* (1982), 11.

[5] M. Ash, *The Strange Death of Scottish History* (Edinburgh, 1980), 150. Scotsmen were guided in their reflections by Prof. D. J. Medley of Glasgow whose *English Constitutional History* had reached a fifth edition by 1913.

(one in eight adult males), but there were 4,500 in Scotland (one in 125 adult males). The Scottish figure highlights the narrowness of the Scottish 'political nation'. Scotland's electorate was expanded by an ill-considered Reform Act which followed the 1832 Reform Act (England and Wales). As a result, one in eight Scottish males possessed the vote, but in England and Wales one in five males now had that right. In aggregate, the Anglo-Welsh electorate was ten times bigger than the Scottish.

The 'Reform' crisis of the early 1830s was British in extent. In earlier decades, West-of-Scotland radicals rarely contemplated a Scottish breakaway. They adopted Magna Carta and the Bill of Rights as documents from their own past.[6] Copies of Tom Paine's *Rights of Man* could be found in Stornoway in the Western Isles.[7] The low franchise in Scotland gave an extra edge to agitation north of the Border, but it is misleading to speak of a distinct 'Scottish' reform campaign. It has been noted, for example, that in the preceding decades Glasgow's political and economic situation 'had more in common with Manchester and north-western England than with the rest of Scotland.'[8] Even so, Tories and Whigs, north of the Border, did not entirely resemble their southern counterparts. In 1880, a correspondent reminded Gladstone that forty-five years earlier he had remarked that 'A Scotch Tory is worse than an English Whig; a Scotch Whig is worse than an English Radical, and a Scotch Radical is worse than the Devil himself.' In reply, Gladstone expressed a certain surprise that he had said such a thing since it seemed to him that Scotch Tories were 'more inclined to extremes than English ones'. He accepted, however, that there had been 'a good deal of violence in Scotch feeling & this simply because the people had not been trained to liberty, of which they had no taste until after the Reform Bill.'[9] For their part, the Scottish Whigs claimed that they had given Scotland 'a political constitution for the first time' and expected the new electorate to be unwaveringly grateful.[10]

In these new circumstances, it behoved British Conservative leaders to interest themselves in Scottish politics. It was not clear,

[6] M. I. Thomis and P. Holt, *Threats of Revolution in Britain, 1789–1848* (1977), 79.

[7] K. J. Logue, *Popular Disturbances in Scotland, 1780–1815* (Edinburgh, 1979), 79.

[8] Thomis and Holt, *Threats of Revolution*.

[9] Matthew, *Gladstone Diaries*, ix. 519–20.

[10] Cockburn's remark is cited and discussed in W. Ferguson, *Scotland, 1689 to the Present* (Edinburgh and London, 1968), 288.

however, how this should best be done. A Scottish Conservative
Association was formed in 1835, largely composed of *ancien régime*
grandees, but it came to nothing. Sir James Graham and F. R.
Bonham in London took a closer interest in Scottish organization
and Peel himself moved on to the Scottish stage. In late 1836, he
was handsomely elected Rector of Glasgow University, the first
British Prime Minister to reach such eminence. Over 3,500 people
celebrated this achievement in a specially built banqueting hall.[11]
Graham was successful two years later. This 'targeting' was very
conspicuous, though the results were not immediately encouraging.
Peel was somewhat at sea in handling the ecclesiastical issues
which were already engaging the Scottish electorate. It is noteworthy, too, that in January 1837 Peel tried to address himself to
'Glasgow' rather than to 'Scotland'. He deliberately refrained, on
this occasion, from going through to Edinburgh.[12] Despite these
efforts, Whigs remained in the ascendancy, particularly in the
burghs, which were now lively centres of political debate. Ironically,
the 'English system' of open nomination and polls, which was
adopted in the Scottish counties, gave scope for extensive magnate
influence. Neither Lord Melbourne nor any other leading English
Whig felt any particular need, during this period, to give special
sustenance to their Scottish brethren. Lord Melbourne may have
felt that his youthful education in Glasgow had given him sufficent
Scottish experience.[13]

Scottish MPs, of both parties, were almost invariably Scotsmen of
no particular distinction. The prevalence of distinctive Scottish
religious controversy may have kept out foreigners—though the
Kilmarnock Burghs constituency was exceptional in electing John
Bowring and Edward Pleydell Bouverie. When the former was
defeated in 1837, there was a local desire to find a 'religious'
replacement 'even if we go to hell to find him'. Bowring, who
combined hymn-writing with editing the work of Jeremy Bentham,
was aggrieved, though he thought Scottish constituencies were
'infinitely less corrupt than in England'.[14] Bouverie's marriage to a

[11] N. Gash, *Peel* (1976), 182. It was not Sir Robert's first visit to Scotland. He had
roamed alone in the wild country of Badenoch after graduating from Oxford. He
was also to spend his last summer, forty years later, in the Highlands.
[12] I. G. C. Hutchison, *A Political History of Scotland, 1832–1924: Parties, Elections and
Issues* (Edinburgh, 1986), 8, 14.
[13] Lord David Cecil, *The Young Melbourne* (1954), 54–6.
[14] Hutchison, *Political History*, 19, 52.

Scottish general's daughter helped him. And it was in odd circumstances that Glasgow accepted Lord William Bentinck in 1834 on his return from India. Despite his reluctance to go north—nine months passed before Bentinck visited his constituency—he came to terms with its radical tone and learnt 'to address large, turbulent crowds in the democratic tone which they wished to hear.'[15]

The Scottish mark in British politics, where visible, was largely made in the first half-century by peers, though their Scottish identity was sometimes ambiguous. Robert Dundas, Viscount Melville, was generally agreed to be a Scot, though he did not greatly enhance the reputation of his nation. Lord Aberdeen, Foreign Secretary under both Wellington and Peel, had been entirely educated in England, though he retained his Scottish home and interests.[16] Peel enrolled other Scottish peers in his second administration—Buccleuch, Haddington and Dalhousie—though they were not very prominent in its affairs. When Lord John Russell succeeded Peel in 1846, he became the second Scottish-educated Prime Minister of the century, but he showed no special regard for Scotland except in so far as he appointed his brother-in-law, the Earl of Minto, Lord Privy Seal.[17] The Duke of Argyll took office in Aberdeen's own 1852 administration. Haphazard though these appointments often were, they testified that Scottish peers expected to play a part in British government. In the offices they held, such men neither expected nor were required to 'speak for Scotland'. They were part of an interlocking British aristocracy which intermarried with scant regard for 'national' considerations. Should one, for example, speak of the Leveson-Gowers as an 'English' family (in England) or as the Sutherlands, a 'Scottish' family (in Scotland)?[18]

In mid-century, therefore, in parliamentary terms, Scotland had an odd presence. Melbourne, Peel, Russell, and Aberdeen all possessed by marriage, education, travel, or birth, unusually strong connections north of the Border. Such links were not vital for a British Prime Minister, but they certainly helped him. However, the

[15] J. Rosselli, *Lord William Bentinck: The Making of a Liberal Imperialist, 1774–1839* (1974), 328–35.

[16] M. Chamberlain, *Lord Aberdeen: A Political Biography* (1983).

[17] J. Prest, *Lord John Russell* (1972), 11.

[18] E. Richards, *The Leviathan of Wealth: The Sutherland Fortune in the Industrial Revolution* (1975), 11.

contrast between the presence of Scottish peers in the higher reaches of government and the absence of Scottish MPs is striking, even granted the continuing aristocratic tone of Cabinets. It has been asserted that the quality of Scottish MPs reflected the fact that the ablest Scots did not go into politics—but did the ablest Englishmen? It may be, however, that the legal and practical difficulties confronting Scottish MPs have been underestimated.[19] The distance from Scotland could cause acute domestic and accommodation difficulties. There was a sense of which West-minster was an alien English world, to which it was not easy to adjust. Some did not try very hard to do so.

The extent of cross-border political activity, however, should not lead to the conclusion that national sensibilities vanished. An Association for the Vindication of Scottish Rights was formed in 1853, though it did not survive the outbreak of the Crimean War three years later.[20] James Grant, the military romantic, who threw himself into this cause, later suffered the ignominy of dying in London. Scottish grievances were various and, to a degree, ambivalent. It was allegedly time for a Scottish minister to head a reformed and separate Scottish administration. Scotland should receive a larger number of seats at Westminster and benefit from a more just proportion of United Kingdom expenditure. The argument, it would appear, was not about the Union itself but about the terms of its operation. This complaint surfaced frequently in subsequent decades, particularly when London governments seemed to think Ireland more important than Scotland. However, the Scottish agitators sometimes found themselves in a difficulty. They generally agreed that the alleged neglect of Scotland stemmed from English ignorance of Scottish peculiarities rather than from malevolence, but they were often not anxious to explain why it was that these mysterious peculiarities should survive.

The 1867 and 1868 Reform Acts (for England and Wales, and

[19] H. J. Hanham, *Elections and Party Management: Politics in the Time of Disraeli and Gladstone* (1959), 57 n: Sir John Hope wrote to Sir John Clerk on 20 Apr. 1851, concerning his standing for parliament, that 'If I found that I could afford to live in or near London, my accepting would be a matter of course . . .'. He was not the only potential candidate or MP to be exercised by such problems. J. I. Brash (ed.), *Papers on Scottish Electoral Politics, 1832–1854* (Edinburgh, 1974), 207.

[20] H. J. Hanham, 'Mid-Century Scottish Nationalism: Romantic and Radical', in R. Robson (ed.), *Ideas and Institutions of Victorian Britain* (1967), 164–9.

Scotland respectively) arose, to some extent, from joint Anglo-Scottish agitation, though it was not until September 1866 that a Scottish National Reform League began its work, two years later than its southern counterpart. John Bright, the chief orator in the campaign, again benefited from his excellent Scottish contacts—McLaren had just been elected to parliament—to take his speech-making north of the Border. He addressed a reputed crowd of 150,000 on Glasgow Green and afterwards stood at a hotel window to acknowledge the cheers.[21] The Acts increased the electorate of England and Wales to nearly two million and that of Scotland to some 230,000. Scotland gained a further seven seats in the Commons at the expense of England. 'The Scotch shall have no favours from me', Disraeli had remarked in 1866, 'until they return more Tory members.'[22] In 1871, however, he was elected Lord Rector of Glasgow University, and received a warm reception in the city two years later, although in the 1868 general election the Tories had won only eight out of the sixty Scottish seats.[23] Scottish Conservatism seemed in a precarious position—the National Union only operated south of the Border and it is not surprising that Scottish constituencies looked for first-class agents 'trained in England'.[24] The Scottish National Conservative Association had been founded in 1867, but it was the despair of Keith-Falconer, the able Scot who masterminded party fortunes in London. Lairds and advocates in Edinburgh could apparently not conceive that Glasgow businessmen might be, or might become, Tories. Highlanders simply ignored letters, whether sent from London or Edinburgh. The Tories gained twenty Scottish seats in 1874 but then dropped back to seven in 1880 and ten in 1885. The Third Reform Act produced a Scottish electorate of 550,000 (three in five adult males) while that of England and Wales grew to 4,380,000 (two in three adult males). There were now seventy Scottish MPs but, after a good showing in 1900, the Tories could only elect seven or eight MPs before the war. However, in the twenty years between 1886 and 1906, a difficult working relationship with Liberal Unionism in Scotland gave the Tories a more respectable position

[21] K. G. Robbins, *John Bright* (1979), 186.

[22] Cited by J. T. Ward, *The First Century: A History of the Scottish Tory Organization, 1882–1982* (Edinburgh, 1982), 8.

[23] J. T. Ward, 'The Origins of Scottish Toryism', *Contemporary Review* (July 1986), 39.

[24] Hutchison, *Political History,*, 112.

than the figures might otherwise suggest, though their minority status could not be disguised.

In these circumstances, the articulation of 'British Conservatism' was never easy. The Liberal Unionist Chief Whip even complained that 'Scotland gives us more trouble than the rest of the United Kingdom put together.'[25] Liberal Unionists and Conservatives would not work together 'as they do in England'. From time to time a certain prickliness developed since Scottish Tories resented English advice, while English officials were exasperated by the conflicts between the Tories of Glasgow and Edinburgh. However, some modest 'British' initiatives were undertaken. Around 1900, for example, Scottish Tories were told that 'In co-operation with the English Central Office the services of a Working-man Speaker are available for Constituencies, and in suitable weather his movements are facilitated by the use of a van.'[26] This speaker would no doubt do his best, but a more likely source of Tory support were Orangemen, some of whom had already thoughtfully established the Beaconsfield Purple Guards Lodge. They were an increasingly potent influence after the 1870s, and served as a reminder that the character of urban Scotland was itself changing. The Irish dimension had entered into the Anglo-Scottish relationship and was subtly transforming it.

The links between a Westminster under Conservative ascendancy and a non-Conservative Scotland were maintained in several ways. From the 1880s onwards, British Tory leaders were persuaded by the National Union to speak in Scotland. Lord Randolph Churchill needed little persuasion, but others needed encouragement. Stafford Northcote spoke in Glasgow in 1882 and he also acquired the Rectorship of Edinburgh University and a Scottish son-in-law. Salisbury spoke in Glasgow in 1884, but could not be cajoled into coming again for another decade. He declined in 1890 on the grounds that the city was a long way away and had an awful climate.[27] His grasp of Scottish affairs was assisted by his brother-in-law, the Earl of Galloway, and his nephew Arthur Balfour. A Scottish Grand Council of the Primrose League was formed in 1885, but the movement, in general, lacked the appeal which it possessed in England.

[25] Hutchison, *Political History*, 207.
[26] Ward, *Scottish Tory Organization*, 15.
[27] Hutchison, *Political History*, 198.

It was Salisbury who established the post of Secretary for Scotland in 1885, a step occasioned by the need to assert ministerial responsibility over the various supervisory boards that had grown up in Scotland over the previous half century. The object, the Prime Minister declared, was 'to redress the wounded dignities of the Scottish people—or a section of them—who think that enough is not made of Scotland.' His choice fell upon the Duke of Richmond and Gordon: 'It really is a matter where the effulgence of two Dukedoms and the best salmon river in Scotland will go a long way.'[28] Richmond thought the office quite unnecessary, but was prepared to take it on. The post was unpopular with the Lord Advocate, the Home Office, and the Treasury but it survived, despite arguments about its legal and educational responsibilities. Correspondence (to London) on Scottish business trebled in five years. The Scottish Secretary became a member of the Cabinet in 1892. This institutional identity, though its administrative presence in Scotland itself was exiguous, was widely welcomed as a necessary recognition of Scotland's distinct place in the British political system.[29]

It was ironic that it had fallen to Salisbury to establish the Scottish Office since the cause had been espoused by the Convention of Scottish Burghs and a group of Whig/Liberal aristocrats, of whom Lord Rosebery was the chief. The parliamentary strength of the Scottish Liberals caused as much difficulty to British Liberalism as the weakness of the Scottish Tories caused for British Conservatism. Scottish Liberals were not disposed to believe that they needed advice from England on their affairs. Edward Ellice, for example, long-time member for the St Andrews Burghs, urged his friends 'to decline the suggested interference of an English agency in their local political affairs' after the electoral set-back of 1874.[30] The strength of Scottish Liberalism rendered it liable to schism since political debate in Scotland, in a sense, took place within the party, rather than, as in England, between Liberals and Tories. Scottish church questions also gave a distinctive twist to Scottish Liberalism. Yet, in the person of William Ewart Gladstone, a remarkable man emerged who made Liberalism truly British.

---

[28] H. J. Hanham, 'The Creation of the Scottish Office, 1881–1887', *Juridical Review* (1965), 229.

[29] J. S. Gibson, *The Thistle and the Crown* (Edinburgh, 1985).

[30] Hutchison, *Political History*, 142.

Entirely Scottish by descent, he was always acutely aware of his ancestry, for all that he was English by upbringing and education. He visited Scotland frequently and with pleasure. The nuances of Scottish church politics were not beyond his understanding. He was committed to Scottish Episcopalianism but was prepared to attend services both in the Established Church and the Free Church. He read Scottish tales with enjoyment. He served as Lord Rector of both Edinburgh (1859–65) and Glasgow (1877–9) universities. Thistles flanked his bust at the head of his campaign engine in Scotland. He actually enjoyed the walks around Balmoral. His election for Midlothian represented a kind of home-coming, even though he declared that he had come among his constituents as a stranger. No other Victorian politician could emulate Gladstone's personal binding of the British body politic.

Certainly, no other British Liberal leader could match Gladstone's grasp of peripheral complexities. There is, for example, a note of desperation in Hartington's plea—'give me a safe sentence or two on Scottish Church matters'—prior to his Scottish tour as party leader in 1877.[31] Rosebery himself was not invariably sure-footed on these issues, but both he and Sir Henry Campbell-Bannerman confirmed the grip which Scotsmen had gained upon the leadership of the British party. Even Asquith, who was impeccably English, sat in the Commons for East Fife and sealed his Scottish connection by marrying Margot Tennant. Asquith was not the only Liberal from the South who found a safe Scottish constituency.[32] H. A. Bruce, Gladstone's first Home Secretary, reached a haven in Renfrewshire in 1869; John Morley became the member for the Montrose Burghs; Winston Churchill found refuge in Dundee; G. O. Trevelyan, who became the first Liberal Scottish Secretary, was an Englishman who sat for the Hawick Burghs; the list could be extended.[33]

[31] Hutchison, *Political History*, 143.

[32] When Asquith recommenced his political life after his defeat in East Fife in 1918 it was another Scottish constituency, Paisley, that gave him, albeit temporarily, a home. His defeat, a few years later, was, however, reputedly in an atmosphere 'full of fervour for Scotland'. According to her biographer, Margot Asquith, 'Scot to the backbone' though she was, 'never felt at home among such people.' D. Bennett, *Margot: A Life of the Countess of Oxford and Asquith* (1984), 341–2. Asquith had shared the representation of Fife, for a time, with Augustine Birrell, who did have a more authentic personal claim to a Scottish connection. See A. Birrell, *Things Past Redress* (1937).

[33] G. M. Trevelyan, *Sir George Trevelyan* (1932). In 1886, Trevelyan stood as a

Yet Scottish Liberalism remained a self-contained phenomenon, not least organizationally. Chamberlain's 1877 National Liberal Federation did not operate north of the Border. There, two distinctly more Whiggish bodies, the East and North of Scotland Liberal Association, and the West and South of Scotland Liberal Association, held the field. These two bodies came together to form the Scottish Liberal Association in 1881. Even so, important figures in Scotland declined to accept it as the authentic voice of Scottish Liberalism. Its espousal of Scottish Home Rule was always contentious. Rosebery argued that it was 'difficult to go far in the direction of Scottish HR without doing an infinity of harm in England, where we shall hear the cry of the "Heptarchy" again.'[34] Nevertheless, it was Scottish influence which persuaded the National Liberal Federation to pronounce in favour both of Scottish disestablishment and Home Rule. Gladstone himself, whose majority in Midlothian fell sharply in 1892, was reluctant to embark on such legislation, though the demand for it never entirely died.

In the decades before 1914, therefore, Scottish politicians faced in two directions with some distinction. Earlier, Bagehot had spoken of his belief that British politics would gain from an infusion of Scotch determination 'which may be described as sternness, but is really the result of a stronger habitual relation between thought and action.' That was precisely what English Liberalism needed to 'give it bone'. He wanted to see Scotch members taking a more prominent part in matters affecting England and increasing their influence generally in British politics. 'They reason', he suggested, 'while the English are often only feeling, and the reason, if expressed, would often make of the feeling a more active and determined force.'[35] The composition of the Liberal governments after 1905 discloses a very strong Scottish presence. Unionism in Scotland did not make the come-back in Scotland which it achieved in England in the general elections of 1910—the interference by the peers with Scottish land legislation over the previous few years may help to explain this contrast in fortune. Scotsmen had been particularly prominent in the Liberal League—though that body

Liberal Unionist and lost, but in the following year he bounced back, being returned for another Scottish constituency, Glasgow Bridgeton, as a Liberal.

[34] Hutchison, *Political History*, 173.

[35] W. Bagehot, 'The Uses of Scotch Liberalism', in *Collected Works*, ed. N. St John Stevas, vol. vii (1974), 180–2.

had flourished in Scotland at a slightly different date from England. And the Scottish presence was not restricted to Liberalism. Andrew Bonar Law succeeded A. J. Balfour in 1911 as Leader of the Opposition. G. K. Chesterton summed up the position when he noted: 'It is one of the paradoxes, so typical of England, that many of the men who have understood and summed up her policy came from Scotland.'[36]

At the beginning of the nineteenth century there appeared to be little that was distinctively Welsh about the parliamentary representation of the principality. The prevailing trend seemed to be still in the direction of removing any lingering 'anomalies' in its administration and government. The Court of Great Sessions was abolished in 1830. It would have been unthinkable to have accorded Wales a separate Reform Act two years later. The 1832 measure increased by five the number of Welsh seats to a total of thirty-two, nearly equally divided between county and borough constituencies. In some of the South Wales borough constituencies, industrialists were able to gain nominations, but in the other seats landed influence was largely maintained by such families as the Wynns, the Mostyns, and the Bulkeleys in the North. Such families may have thought of themselves as Welsh, but they were closely linked by marriage and life-style to English society.

Inevitably the growth of religious Dissent had political consequences. By no means all Nonconformists inherited the political radicalism of some of their eighteenth-century ancestors, but they had specific grievances concerning such matters as the payment of tithes and the burial- and marriage-laws. They could not attend English universities. Such grievances were no different from those of English Dissenters, but the waxing strength of Welsh Nonconformity made it more effective in airing them. In addition, the Merthyr Rising of 1831, the Chartist Rising in Newport in 1839, and the activities of the Rebecca Rioters between 1839 and 1843 demonstrated that there was, in South and West Wales at least, a seething discontent which existed quite outside the framework of parliamentary politics.[37] For three decades after the 1832 Act, 'official' and 'unofficial' politics in Wales seemed scarely to meet.

[36] A. L. Maycock (ed.), *The Man who was Orthodox: A Selection from the Uncollected Writings of G. K. Chesterton* (1963), 104-5.
[37] G. A. Williams, *The Merthyr Rising* (1976).

Immediately prior to the 1867 Reform Act there were roughly 62,000 Welsh voters and as a result of it the electorate nearly doubled. The distinctive parliamentary voice of Wales has frequently been dated from the results of the 1868 General Election. In particular, the victory of Henry Richard in volatile Merthyr Tydfil has been thought symbolic. In his *Letters on the Social and Political Condition of Wales* (1867), Richard, born at Tregaron in Dyfed, had denounced the 'feudal' character of Welsh politics. Yet, for over thirty years, Richard had worked in England as a Nonconformist minister. His prominence in Britain as a whole derived from his work for the Peace Society. He had recently married an English wife and saw his role as being 'in some humble measure an interpreter beween England and Wales.' 'I have kept up my acquaintance with our old language and flourishing literature,' he told the Merthyr electors, 'I know your many social and religious virtues'— the transition from 'our' to 'your' in that extract is noteworthy.[38] Nor should the extent of the 'Welsh revolution' be exaggerated. Dr Kenneth Morgan points out that more than two-thirds of Welsh MPs after 1868 were landowners.[39] Besides Richards, only two other MPs were Nonconformists. In North Wales, in the Denbigh county constituency, George Osborne Morgan defeated one representative of the old order, Colonel Biddulph of Chirk, but Sir Watkin Williams Wynn headed the poll. In addition, it is scarcely possible to speak of an 'all-Wales' campaign for parliamentary reform in 1866/7. Moves towards setting up a 'provincial department' of the Reform League for Wales failed. Little cohesion has been identified between the branches located in individual towns. A League lecturer in Wales found that 'In money matters I am flogging a dead horse with a vengeance . . .'. However, it has been argued that 'The links established between outlying areas and large cities, and the penetrations of radical English newspapers carrying news and correspondence from the localities, helped to break down insularity and localism, serious impediments to the growth of political consciousness.'[40] Reform, in other words, was a thoroughly 'Anglo-Welsh' phenomenon.

---

[38] C. S. Miall, *Henry Richard MP: A Biography* (1889), 17, 152.

[39] K. O. Morgan, *Wales: Rebirth of a Nation, 1880–1980* (Oxford and Cardiff, 1981), 12.

[40] R. Wallace, 'Wales and the Parliamentary Reform Movement, 1866–1868', *Welsh History Review*, 11 (1982–3), 486.

Even so, the stage was set for what Dr Morgan calls the transformation of Wales into 'an impregnable stronghold of the British left' in the period up to (and beyond) the First World War. The politics of Wales, he argues, 'followed a unique rhythm'.[41] At the electoral level, this was certainly the case. In 1880 Liberals won all but four of the Welsh seats. A little earlier, Welsh Liberal MPs had been particularly active in campaigning for the introduction of the secret ballot, producing mostly well-founded stories of landlord victimization in Wales as justification for it. The 1884 Reform Act and the erosion of Welsh Whiggery, accelerated by the Irish Home Rule split, helped to confirm the almost complete triumph of a Liberal/Radical/Nonconformist political tradition. In 1906, not a single Welsh Conservative was elected—there were thirty-three Liberals and Keir Hardie in Merthyr. This particular result can largely be explained by the vehemence of Nonconformist opposition to the 1902 Education Act (England and Wales) which was even greater in Wales than in England. These electoral successes—which were also repeated in the sphere of local government—meant that the pendulum of politics, which produced alternating majorities in England, did not operate in the principality. This strength also meant that pressure could be exerted to extract from Westminster specific Welsh legislation for the first time since the Acts of Union. The first such measure was the 1881 Sunday Closing Act but it was followed, as has been noted earlier, by important legislation relating to Welsh education and, eventually, to Church Disestablishment. The diversity of Wales had received legislative recognition.

On the other hand, close analysis of internal Welsh political organization indicates how difficult it was, even in the late nineteenth century, to think of the principality as a coherent political entity. To an extent, 'Welsh Liberalism' was a façade. It proved impossible to establish one Welsh Liberal Federation. Instead, in 1886, two regional federations were set up in the North and South respectively—which did not prevent complaints that mid-Wales was being ignored. The Welsh National Council, formed in 1887, was supposed to fill the policy-making gap between these two federations in Wales and the 'Welsh Parliamentary Party' at Westminster. It was not an easy task. In the House of Commons,

[41] K. O. Morgan, 'The Welsh in English Politics, 1868–1982', in R. R. Davies *et al* (eds.), *Welsh Society and Nationhood* (Cardiff, 1984), 234–5.

Welsh Liberals attached individual and fluctuating significance to their 'Welshness' and their 'Liberalism'. The tragically short career of T. E. Ellis demonstrates the difficulties of a divided inheritance. After a Welsh-speaking country upbringing, and education, on the one hand in the new college of Aberystwyth, and the old New College of Oxford on the other, Ellis spent some time in London before succeeding the locally resident Scotsman, Henry Robertson, as MP for Merioneth. Ellis threw himself into the work of 'Young Wales'. He claimed that, within the United Kingdom, Wales was making greater progress 'than any of the other three nationalities'. There were, however, two views of his decision to accept the post of Liberal Chief Whip in 1892. Some Welshmen saw it as a betrayal of the Welsh national aspirations Ellis had so firmly espoused: others saw it as a compliment to Wales for its 'faithfulness' to Gladstonian Liberalism[42] Ellis himself, realizing that the Welsh Liberals in 1892 held the key to the government's survival, was able to extract a charter for the University of Wales and a royal commission to enquire into Welsh land problems. Recognition of Welsh diversity would be more likely to be achieved by promoting the politics of integration.

The divisions in Wales on this issue were reflected in the tensions surrounding *Cymru Fydd* in the mid-1890s. It appeared at one stage as though a comprehensive national/cultural movement for Welsh Home Rule might become dominant within Welsh Liberalism. In the end, however, it came to nothing, collapsing, as much as anything, because of the deep differences of perception about the future of Wales between prominent figures in the North and South and the respective hinterlands on which they drew. There were many in the North who echoed the mother in Kate Roberts's Welsh-language novel *Feet in Chains* who seemed to believe that South Wales was on the other side of the world.[43] The blending of

[42] Robertson was one of a number of Scotsmen who were active in quarrying and railway development in North Wales and who then played a part in local public life. See G. G.Lerry, *Henry Robertson: Pioneer of Railways in Wales* (Oswestry, 1949). English businessmen, like William Rathbone and John Platt, also represented North Welsh constituencies which contained a majority of Welsh speakers. It was the custom of some English businessmen to employ 'Scotch' agents—against whom local animosity was no less directed. See Jones, *North Wales Quarrymen*, 60 and W. Jones, *Thomas Edward Ellis* (Cardiff, 1986), 51–9.

[43] Roberts, *Feet in Chains*, 101. Division in Wales was not restricted to that between 'North' and 'South'. In the quarrying districts of Arfon, there was a strong prejudice against Anglesey people, who were referred to on occasion as 'moch Sir

Wales proved a difficult, indeed an impossible, business. It was ironic that for many years the key role in establishing a Welsh Liberal identity was played by the English Anglican arms manufacturer, Stuart Rendel, who became MP for Montgomeryshire ('neither North nor South'). In his draft resignation speech, he complimented his fellow-members of the 'Welsh Parliamentary Party' on their skill in knowing 'how to blend loyalty to the Liberal cause and the Party with paramount duty to the Welsh cause.' As a result, he claimed, Wales had acquired the place and power in the House of Commons 'to which the purity of its Nationalism and the versatility, eloquence and public spirit of its men entitles it.'[44] The other side of the coin was that, unlike the Scottish Liberal Federation, the Welsh Liberal Federations were directly affiliated to the National Liberal Federation. Their organizational compliance may therefore have brought the Welsh greater influence in British Liberal circles than their independence brought the Scots.[45] Nor should it be forgotten that Welshmen had long been successful in getting themselves elected for English constituencies, from Cumbria to Cornwall. If the 'cymricized Scot', Donald Maclean, is counted among them, there were, for example, a dozen Welshmen representing English constituencies in 1906.

At the highest levels, of course, it was again that extraordinary Briton, William Gladstone, who both integrated and diversified. He married into a Welsh family and his home at Hawarden brought him into contact with the life of North-East Wales. He regularly holidayed further along the North Welsh coast at Penmaenmawr. He attended eisteddfodau. On several occasions, most notably at Swansea in 1887, Gladstone addressed Welsh audiences on aspects of their language and culture in most sympathetic terms. Until the emergence of Lloyd George, no Welshman came near to approaching the impact on England that this 'Englishman' made on Wales.

It is appropriate, however, to leave the last word with the Manchester-born Welsh-speaking Welshman. As his career blossomed at Westminster, his early enthusiasm for Welsh Home Rule faded. In England, not invariably to his advantage, he appeared to

Fôn' (Anglesey pigs) because of their rural background and habits. R. M. Jones, *The North Wales Quarrymen, 1874–1922* (Cardiff, 1982), 22.

[44]   G. V. Nelmes, 'Stuart Rendel and Welsh Liberal Political Organization in the Late Nineteenth Century', *Welsh History Review*, 9 (1978–9), 483.

[45]   M. Barker, *Gladstone and Radicalism* (Brighton, 1975), 116–28.

be the epitome of a Welshman but, deep down, he was ambivalent about what he referred to privately as the 'stunted principality'— unless to be ambivalent about Welshness is itself characteristic of Welshmen. He exchanged a Welsh wife for an English mistress. He was deeply attached to Wales but could not be confined to it. In 1914 he was about to embark on a course which, unpredictably, was to make him the first British Prime Minister whose mother tongue was not English.

The place occupied by Wales in British politics had therefore changed considerably, though there was no Welsh Secretary in the British Cabinet on the analogy with Scotland. The status of Scotland, however, was something which Welshmen were coming to aim at. Talk of 'Celtic nations' is not very helpful, but the common characteristic shared by Scotland and Wales was a commitment, in the later nineteenth century, to a political party which could only in 1885, 1886, and 1906 produce a majority in England. Scottish Conservatism struggled on, not without some success but, with the exception of 1874, when Welsh Conservatives gained nearly one third of the Welsh seats, their condition appeared parlous. It is worth remembering, however, that even in the disastrous year of 1906 one Welsh voter in three voted Conservative. Welsh Conservatism is not quite as exiguous as its neglect by historians would imply. However, in parliamentary terms, the fundamental polarity in British politics seemed to be firmly established. British Liberal governments could not normally be formed without the presence of Scottish and Welsh Liberal MPs at Westminster. It was a fact which did not please English Conservatives. British Conservative governments, on the other hand, normally ruled Britain without majorities in Scotland and Wales. It was a fact which did not please Scottish and Welsh Liberals. English Conservatives sometimes wished that they were not saddled with the problems of Scotland and Wales. Scottish and Welsh Liberals sometimes wished that they were not saddled with the problem of England. The balance between integration and diversity was at the heart of British politics. Their reconciliation could never be complete or permanent but, by 1914, the equilibrium seemed to suggest, at least at the parliamentary level, that the small 'British' political élite of the pre-1832 era had been transformed, successfully, into a British political nation.

When we move from the world of parliamentary politics to that of pressure-groups, trade unions, and the emerging labour movement we find a frequent desire to 'think British' coupled with a common inability to agree, functionally or organizationally, how this might best be done.

'The cause of the operatives', declared John Doherty in his appeal to English calico-printers on behalf of their Scottish colleagues, 'is the same throughout the United Kingdom.' His paper *The Voice of the People* did indeed have agents in London, Glasgow, and certain English provincial cities, but his National Association singularly failed to exist nationally.[46] Cross-border co-operation was more difficult at the popular level than at the parliamentary. A few further trade-union examples illustrate the point. The Northern Typographical Union, formed in 1830, was strongest among printers in the North of England, though societies as far south as Gloucester and Monmouth affiliated to it. The suggestion of a union for all United Kingdom printers was mooted in 1840, but nothing came of this northern initiative.[47] In the case of ship-building, the first recorded trade-union meeting of the boiler-makers took place in Manchester in 1834. However, the Scottish boiler-makers organized themselves separately. They bitterly resented it when the English society opened its first branch at Greenock in 1849. In this instance, however, confrontation did lead to a 'British' amalgamation. The United Society of Boiler Makers and Iron Shipbuilders was formed three years later. There was a strong desire, however, despite the adhesion of the London boiler-makers, to keep the union's centre of gravity in the North. Its offices were eventually located in Newcastle upon Tyne.[48]

The first meeting of the trade union 'Congress' in June 1868 was held, significantly, in Manchester, on the initiative of the local Trades Council. This step, however, was also the culmination of a burst of trade union activity in different parts of Britain: the London Trades Council had been formed in 1860; the Glasgow Trades Council had played a prominent part in the lobbying which produced the Master and Servant Act of 1867; a 'United Kingdom

[46] R. G. Kirby and A. E. Musson, *The Voice of the People: John Doherty, 1798–1854* (Manchester, 1975), 207, 275.

[47] A. E. Musson, *The Typographical Association: Origins and History up to 1949* (Oxford, 1954), 37 and 57.

[48] J. E. Mortimer, *History of the Boilermakers' Society, vol. i, 1834–1906* (1973), 50–1, 101.

Alliance of Organized Trades' had been formed in 1866. It began to look as though truly national inter-union bodies might at least be possible after so many abortive efforts in previous decades.[49] Nevertheless, provincial/metropolitan antagonisms were still rife. The Manchester meeting in 1868 was ignored by most London trade union leaders. The next 'Congress' was held in Birmingham, but it was with some difficulty that the third was arranged in London. It was only after the Nottingham meeting in 1872 that even the rudiments of a continuing 'national' bureaucracy were set up, together with a parliamentary committee which was to be the enduring executive organ. Its first chairman was Alexander McDonald, newly elected MP for the Stafford Boroughs, who had disconcerted some of his constitutents both by his Scottish accent and his occasional habit of punctuating his remarks by spitting on the floor.[50] No English miners' leader, however, had been a university student—as McDonald had been at Glasgow. A disposition to spit was apparently no obstacle to academic advance, at least not in that university.

Yet notwithstanding its willingness to hold its meetings in major urban centres up and down Britain in the latter decades of the century, the 'national' authority of the TUC was still only feeble. That was inevitable at a time when individual unions maintained a 'national' coverage only with difficulty and competition was endemic. The mining industry provides one example, though others could be cited. Back in the early 1840s, the Miners' Association of Great Britain and Ireland had briefly been able to embrace all the major coalfields, though the centre of gravity had moved to Lancashire by the time its last national conference was held—in 1847.[51] The Miners' Federation of Great Britain was formed in 1889, largely on the initiative of Yorkshire and Lancashire Miners, but Durham did not affiliate until three years later, and differences of outlook and interest between areas of England, Scotland, and Wales remained. In 1910, the annual conference accepted a Scottish motion that miners should seek 'one Conciliation Board' to operate 'throughout Great Britain' with a 'uniform standard and agreement

[49] R. M. Martin, *The TUC: The Growth of a Pressure Group, 1868–1976* (Oxford, 1980), 19–22.

[50] G. M. Wilson, *Alexander McDonald: Leader of the Miners* (Aberdeen, 1980), 1.

[51] A. J. Taylor, 'The Miners' Association of Great Britain and Ireland, 1842–48', *Economica* 22 (1955).

for all districts'.[52] That objective had still to be attained in 1914. The railway industry also had its union difficulties. In 1872, the first delegate meeting of the Amalgamated Society of Railway Servants took place, but no representative from Scotland was present and, for twenty years until fusion in 1892, there was a separate union in Scotland. The English organization of the ASRS also had its problems. Provincial distrust of London resulted in the establishment of eleven districts, with the result that the central office of the union was short of funds and unable to act 'nationally' to assist those districts with poor resources.[53]

Slowly but surely, a pattern of 'British' unions did seem to be emerging in the late century but, at the 'national' level, Scottish dissatisfaction with the 'British' TUC was mounting. It was not that the Congress refused to come to Scotland. Beatrice Webb spent part of her honeymoon observing its deliberations in Glasgow in 1892. She left the city 'with no regrets. The working-men leaders here are an uninteresting lot; without enthusiasm or much intelligence.' That was not a view held by Scottish trade unionists. When, in 1895, the TUC altered its standing orders so as to exclude Trades Councils there were strong protests north of the Border. These bodies had played a more important role in Scotland than in England and the decision seemed 'insensitive'. It was against this background that the first meeting of the Scottish TUC was summoned in March 1897. The new president was nevertheless at pains to declare that the new organization was not 'got up in opposition to the British Trades Union Congress, but because they believed that if they wanted anything well-done they had to do it themselves.'[54]

The Scots were more vociferous on this issue than the Welsh who did not, during this period, press for a separate Wales TUC. That did not mean, however, that 'Welshness' was absent from trade union affairs. In 1874, for example, 'Red Dragon' unions were established in South Wales by dissident members both of the

[52] R. Moore, *Pit-Men, Preachers and Politics* (Cambridge, 1974), 36–9; H. A. Clegg, *A History of British Trade Unions since 1889*, vol. ii, *1911–1933* (Oxford, 1985), 82.
[53] P. S. Bagwell, *The Railwaymen: The History of the National Union of Railwaymen* (1963), 62–3, 73, 148–9.
[54] B. Drake and M. I. Cole (eds.), *Beatrice Webb, Our Partnership* (1948), 31–3; W. H. Fraser, 'Trades Councils in the Labour Movement in Nineteenth Century Scotland', in I. MacDougall (ed.), *Essays in Scottish Labour History* (Edinburgh, 1978), 1–2, 23.

Amalgamated Association of Miners and of the National Amalgamated Association of Ironworkers. The English leader of the latter body was heckled at a meeting in Rhymney by some of his members who were 'diametrically opposed to the continuation of the connection of Wales with the English Executive.' 'What is the old union?' was the question asked (in Welsh) by one supporter of an all-Welsh union. The answer was 'worship of the English, waste and tyranny'. A vigorous debate followed. Critics of the breakaway saw it as a device to weaken class solidarity. 'Our strength lies in union with England;' argued one local editor, 'in independence lies our weakness and our destruction.'[55] In North Wales, the quarrymen in relatively isolated Gwynedd conducted their union affairs almost entirely through the medium of Welsh.[56] In one form or another the 'independence' debate surfaced in many industries but, on balance, 'union with England' through the British TUC was in the ascendant.

Throughout Britain, however, the industrial unrest of the decade before 1914 demonstrated that in every part of the country trade union 'localism' was still strong. The tone and temper of disputes, whether in the docks or on the railways, varied considerably from one region to another and it is difficult to speak of an 'English', 'Scottish', or 'Welsh' pattern. Differences in pay, hours, and conditions of service could differ considerably from region to region. They made the notion of 'national' solidarity difficult to sustain, whatever the aspirations of those trying to direct the struggle.

The tension between integration and diversity was similar on the other side of industry. Although there had been some spasmodic attempts in mid-century to form 'associations of masters', they rarely extended beyond local areas, be it the West Riding of Yorkshire or South Wales. In the latter instance, the President of the Ironmasters' Association told the Royal Commission in 1867 that he and his colleagues only met every fifteen months or so, and had no paid officer. Thirty years later, however, there was more evidence of organizations which transcended localities.[57] The Clyde shipbuilders formed an association in 1889. Shortly afterwards, Carlisle was the appropriate venue for an attempt to set up a

[55] A. Jones, 'Trade Unions and the Press: Journalism and the Red Dragon Revolt of 1874', *Welsh History Review*, 12 (1984–5) 217–19.
[56] Jones, *North Wales Quarrymen*.
[57] H. Phelps Brown, *The Origins of Trade Union Power* (Oxford, 1983), 104.

Federation of British Shipbuilders.[58] The most conspicuous and successful 'national' body, however, was that created by Colonel Dyer, of Armstrong and Whitworth, arising out of that company's dispute with the Amalgamated Society of Engineers. This struggle has been seen as a landmark in British industrial relations 'because it extended collective bargaining in a major industry from the district to the national level' and the number of firms affiliated to the employers' federation nearly tripled. Yet, in the aftermath, neither union nor employers at 'national' level found it easy to deal with 'local encroachments' on the 'national' agreement.

In general, it would appear that despite technological innovation and growing international competition, British employers were still unwilling, for better or for worse, to combine together effectively on a British basis.[59] The fact remained that, whilst national combinations of employers could strengthen their collective hand in dealing with increasingly national trade unions, a 'national' stance (on pay or conditions) frequently had sharply differing consequences for particular individuals, companies, industries, or regions. A variety of factors still seemed to make local bargains more satisfactory—to both sides of industry. National parity could be viewed, from one perspective, as the achievement of national 'fairness'; from another, it could spell intolerable costs, even bankruptcy, in specific situations.

Earlier in the century, the two best-known examples of 'pressure from without' had encountered not dissimilar problems of balance and co-ordination. Both the Chartists and the Anti-Corn-Law Leaguers, aware of the common interests of the major British urban and industrial centres, endeavoured to organize on a British basis. The Charter demanded the 'just representation of the people of Great Britain' and the movement developed out of artisan and middle-class radicalism in London and Birmingham. Relatively speaking, however, London Chartism was a disappointment.[60] It is not implausible, indeed, to argue that British Chartism was launched in Glasgow in 1838.[61] The Chartist Convention in London in February 1839 met in the appropriately named British Coffee

[58] Mortimer, *Boilermakers' Society*, 118.

[59] Phelps Brown, *Origins*, 105–12.

[60] D. Goodway, *London Chartism, 1838–1848* (1982).

[61] S. Checkland and O. Checkland, *Industry and Ethos: Scotland, 1832–1914* (1984), 71, 87.

House. However, the divisions on tactics and strategy displayed on this occasion were to be repeated throughout Britain. The Newport Rising can be seen, with a little imagination, as the Welsh element in a protest which might also have occurred in England or Scotland.[62] Up to a point, Scottish Chartism can be seen as a movement apart in its origins, ideals, and policy, though the divisions between Glasgow and Edinburgh in turn make it difficult to speak about 'Scotland' as a Chartist entity.[63] Up to a point, too, there was a Welsh Chartism—but studies have also made it abundantly clear that the precise character of 'English Chartism' varied considerably from area to area. The *Northern Star*, itself significantly named, pointed to the concentration of support for the National Charter Association in South Lancashire and the West Riding of Yorkshire. The location of Chartist activity provided by Mrs Thompson in the appendix to her book is very illuminating. It leaves no doubt that the failure of Chartism was the failure of a British movement, kaleidoscopic though it was.[64]

The 'success' of the Anti-Corn-Law League was equally the success of a British movement. Manchester was its pre-eminent organizing centre, but the League's efforts built upon pre-existing opposition to the Corn Laws both north and south of the Border. A flourishing Anti-Corn-Law Association, for example, existed in Glasgow in 1833, though there was much debate in its ranks about the relationship between its specific objective and more general political issues. It has been noted that Glasgow sent delegates to all the main conferences and co-ordinated petitions and propaganda, though it showed a regrettable disposition to promise money more often than it paid it.[65] William Weir, editor of the *Glasgow Argus*, sent his paper to 'popular persons' in Sheffield, Leeds, Birmingham, and elsewhere in England. When his enthusiasm for the cause proved too much for his proprietor, Weir moved to London, but he remained a vital linkman between Scotland and England.[66] Both Bright and Cobden made extensive tours in Scotland. They

[62] D. Thompson, *The Chartists: Popular Politics in the Industrial Revolution* (1984), 84–5.

[63] L. C. Wright, *Scottish Chartism* (Edinburgh and London, 1953), 5, 20; A. Wilson, *The Chartist Movement in Scotland* (Manchester, 1970).

[64] Thompson, *The Chartists*, 341–68.

[65] F. Montgomery, 'Glasgow and Corn Law Repeal', *History*, 64 (1979), 377.

[66] K. J. Cameron, 'William Weir and the Origins of the "Manchester League" in Scotland, 1838–1839', *Scottish Historical Review*, 58 (1979), 70–91.

received an enthusiastic response in the burghs. In January 1843, Cobden was proud to be made a freeman of the City of Glasgow—it should also not be forgotten that he married a Welsh wife and frequently resorted to Anglesey. The only disappointment the Englishmen felt with their Scottish trips was their discovery that an appeal for money at the close of a meeting dispersed the audience as quickly as if the Riot Act had been read.[67] Duncan McLaren, the Edinburgh Radical, threw himself into the work of the Anti-Corn-Law League, and Anglo-Scottish co-operation was later consummated by his marriage to Bright's sister.[68] There was even a flourishing branch of the League in the Shetland Isles. J. B. Smith of the Manchester Chamber of Commerce got himself elected to the House of Commons by the Stirling Burghs in 1847. The response to the League's propaganda was largely determined throughout Britain by the underlying agricultural realities. It happened to be the case that only in two Scottish counties did the grain acreage reach the English average.[69] This fact may explain why, when the Corn Laws were repealed in 1846, and the Tory Party split, there were roughly twice as many Protectionists as Peelites in England, whereas in Scotland there were a few more Peelites than Protectionists. It was a division that further weakened the already weak Scottish Tories.

Later in the century the 'centre of gravity' troubled the nascent British labour movement. 'Depend upon it', declared the president of the Bradford Labour Union, reflecting on the moves in the early 1890s to form a new political party, 'no executive will suit the provincials that they have had no part in forming.' He told the Londoners to 'come say to Bradford, a central town, where you will find plenty of food for reflection.'[70] However, in the event, the organizations represented in that northern town came overwhelmingly from the North (eighty-six), while fourteen came from London, six from the Midlands, and three from the South and South-West of England. There were eleven Scottish representatives. Metropolitan intellectuals might despise the provinciality of the new Independent Labour Party, but for many of its

[67] Robbins, *Bright*, 49.
[68] J. B. Mackie, *The Life and Work of Duncan McLaren* (Edinburgh, 1888), i. 49–53.
[69] Hutchison, *Political History*, 86.
[70] D. Howell, *British Workers and the Independent Labour Party, 1888–1906* (Manchester, 1983), 288–90.

founding members its strength in industrial England was a source of pride.

Three of the 'Big Four' in the party's leadership—Hardie, MacDonald, and Glasier—were Scots, and Snowden came from the North of England.[71] The relationship between the party in Scotland and in England was of great significance—and it was contentious. Keir Hardie had founded his Scottish Labour Party some years before the ILP was established. There was naturally a feeling that Scotland 'led the way'. In addition, the new Scottish TUC was unambiguously in favour of 'independent' labour politics, at a time when that could not be said of the British TUC as a whole. For this reason, a Scottish Workers' Parliamentary Committee came into existence before the Labour Representation Committee was set up in England. The hopes of Scottish Labour were high, though in 1900, the year in which the ILP held its party conference in Glasgow, the MPs returned to Westminster by the city were all Unionists. Organizational inventiveness, therefore, did not indicate massive support in Scotland. The Scottish Workers' Representation Committee (as it was renamed in 1900) appeared from England to be a failure. Labour did not do well in the 1906 general election in Scotland—the 1903 Gladstone/Macdonald pact did not apply north of the Border. Certain Scottish trade unions, seeing the London-based Labour Representation Committee as the more effective body, sought to affiliate to it, though technically they could not do so because it was English. In the end, however, it was MacDonald himself (long since domiciled in England) who pressed for the ending of this embargo. Eventually the SWRC voted in February 1909 to dissolve itself.[72]

This was an important development because it helped to ensure that there would be only one British Labour Party. Once again, the Anglo-Scottish relationship had been the most difficult. The ILP in Wales made less fuss about the issue. Keir Hardie himself, of course, had come as a Scotsman to be one of the MPs for Merthyr Tydfil.

---

[71] Glasier's views on the Irish, however, should guard against notions of a Celtic solidarity. He felt that there was 'a flaw—a fatal lesion—in Irish character that unfits the people for rational and progressive life.' That point of view made him friends and enemies in the West of Scotland. L. Thompson, *The Enthusiasts: A Biography of John and Katharine Bruce Glasier* (1971), 106.

[72] Hutchison, *Political History*, 253; W. H. Fraser, 'The Labour Party in Scotland' and P. Stead, 'The Labour Party in Wales', in K. D. Brown, (ed.), *The First Labour Party, 1906–1914* (1985), 38–88.

He made generous gestures in the direction of Welsh sentiment and oozed Celticism at appropriate moments but it is worth remembering that he did not head the poll. Both Hardie and MacDonald professed a belief in Home Rule for Scotland (and Wales) but Labour would have to organize itself as a British party in order to obtain power in Britain. When, after the First World War, the Glasgow-born North-Easterner Arthur Henderson had little sympathy for alleged 'national' considerations in drawing up appropriate organizational structures for the party in Britain, he was merely reinforcing a tendency which had already established itself. Keir Hardie had to sustain his vision of Britain by cultivating Ayrshire daisies and Welsh leeks in his little garden patch in King's Bench Walk in the heart of London.

The 'business of politics' was, to an extent, self-contained, but we also need to see it in the context of the 'politics of business'. At the beginning of the nineteenth century we might perhaps speak of an English economy and a Scottish economy. By 1914, we might more appropriately speak of a British economy, albeit with strong regional features. How far it is possible to speak of a Welsh economy is problematic. The field of this short concluding discussion is, therefore, primarily Anglo-Scottish.

Professor Smout concludes that, through the nineteenth century, the previous gap between 'rich' England and 'poor' Scotland narrowed, and almost disappeared. Although too much reliance should not be placed upon the figures, in 1798, when the first income tax was introduced, per head of population Scotland paid about 68 per cent of what England paid, but in 1911 Scotland paid about 95 per cent. Such aggregates, of course, reveal little about the prosperity of particular regions and individuals within Scotland or England. However, using Schedule D income-tax assessments to measure middle-class wealth, it seems that in 1880 only London and Manchester made higher returns than Edinburgh. The fourth and fifth highest cities were Liverpool and Glasgow. Aberdeen and Dundee made higher returns than Leeds and Sheffield.[73] The Scottish bourgeoisie was not inferior.

However, in the last decades of the century, comparisons between 'England' and 'Scotland' perhaps become less meaningful.

[73] T. C. Smout, *A Century of the Scottish People, 1830–1950* (1986), 109–10.

The contrast that emerges may be between London and the Home Counties on the one hand, and the rest of Britain on the other. Dr Rubinstein sees the percentage of British business and professional incomes of £100 to £150 located in Lancashire and Yorkshire rising from 10 per cent in 1806 to reach a peak of 23 per cent in 1860 and then slowly falling away to about 18 per cent in 1911. The London and Home Counties reached a low of 33 per cent in 1851, but had climbed up to 47 per cent in 1911.[74] It has been noted that the growing importance of the English South-East and the decline, at least relatively, of the industrial North, occurred at the time when Britain's position in the world economy was becoming more dependent upon 'invisibles'. However, this early contrast between a 'financial' South-East and an 'industrial' North may be overdrawn.[75] There is danger in supposing that London was totally bereft of industry. In any event, there is always great difficulty in identifying wealth and its transmission. Rubinstein has pointed out that only fourteen millionaires died in Glasgow and Clydeside between 1801 and 1914, compared with forty in London merely between 1900 and 1914. On the other hand, Clydeside had more millionaires than any other single region of Britain and some 'London' millionaires had started their careers in the West of Scotland. It is also quite possible that Scottish millionaires were both more successful in transmitting wealth to their descendants, and also less ostentatious in their possession of it, than their southern counterparts.[76] There were certainly great fortunes made in engineering and shipbuilding, in coal, iron, steel, cotton, linen, and jute. The North British Locomotive Co. in Glasgow was Britain's largest in this particular line. Dundee jute, Paisley thread, and Kirkcaldy linoleum established dominant positions in the British market and, of course, beyond. The men who presided over these enterprises were their own masters, frequently content, even if they received titles, to live modestly and remain within their original communities. The manifest dynamism of the West of Scotland reduced, though it did

[74] I owe these figures to Dr W. D. Rubinstein in a paper presented at the University of Glasgow in May 1986.

[75] P. Cain, 'J. A. Hobson, Financial Capitalism and Imperialism: Late Victorian and Edwardian England', in A. N. Porter and R. F. Holland (eds.), *Money, Finance and Empire* (1985), 12–20.

[76] M. S. Moss, 'William Todd Lithgow—Founder of a Fortune', *Scottish Historical Review*, 62 (1983), 47, 71; N. J. Morgan and M. S. Moss, 'Listing the Wealthy in Scotland', *Bulletin of the Institute of Historical Research*, 59 (1986), 189–95.

not remove, the incentive to seek business success elsewhere in Britain, and beyond.[77] There were, however, comparatively few incomers from elsewhere who penetrated into this Scottish commercial élite. Before the First World War, however, there were signs that such important figures as Sir Charles Tennant or William McKinnon had to link themselves to 'the City' to provide the resources and contacts they required. Scotland was not big enough.[78]

At the other end of the scale, in the first half of the century, Scottish wages were generally below English levels. On average, in 1860, they were about one-fifth below those prevailing in England in the same trades—a major factor, so it was alleged, in the ability of Clyde-built ships to compete internationally. A quarter of a century later, however, the disparities between Scottish and English levels were diminishing and, in the decade before 1914, the central belt of Scotland has been classified as one of the four highest wage regions in Britain. These conclusions are not beyond dispute and it may well be that, amongst other factors, higher rent, food, and fuel costs in Scotland meant that the actual standard of living was below comparable English regions. Even if this is the case, however, it was certainly more plausible to think of a 'British' standard of living than it had been a century earlier.[79]

In the world of finance, Scottish holders of securities issued by English companies or foreign concerns, and non-Scottish investments in Scottish enterprise, encouraged, in the view of one recent

[77] Checkland, *Industry and Ethos*, 177.

[78] R. H. Campbell, *The Rise and Fall of Scottish Industry, 1707–1939* (Edinburgh, 1980), chap. 4; E. H. Hunt, *Regional Wage Variations in Britain, 1850–1914* (Oxford, 1973); G. Gordon (ed.), *Perspective on the Scottish City* (Aberdeen, 1985); R. G. Rodger, 'The Invisible Hand: Market Forces, Housing and the Urban Form', in D. Fraser and A. Sutcliffe (eds.), *The Pursuit of Urban History* (1980), 190–211.

[79] Scottish entrepreneurs were active in England. They sometimes brought with them the skills they had learnt at home or, early on in their careers, had come to England for training and had stayed on. One Scottish example from many is the firm of M'Connel and Kennedy, cotton spinners, of Manchester. Their chief rivals in that city were their own compatriots, Adam and George Murray. Significantly, too, Liverpool shipping had a heavy Scottish component—with such names as Macgregor Laird, Alexander Elder, and John Dempster prominent, though it was also possible for a Welshman, like Sir Alfred Jones, and even the occasional Englishman, to have some influence in the city. C. H. Lee, *A Cotton Enterprise, 1795–1840: A History of M'Connel and Kennedy, Fine Cotton Spinners* (Manchester, 1972), 15–16, 27–8, 112; P. N. Davies, *Sir Alfred Jones, Shipping Entrepreneur Par Excellence* (1978), 16–17; R. A. Cage (ed.), *The Scots Abroad: Labour, Capital, Enterprise, 1750–1914* (1984).

scholar, 'the creation of one central market with offshoots throughout Britain, rather than the existence of separate, but inter-
connected, markets'. Around the turn of the century, there was a
continuing need for a separate Scottish stock exchange, but its
appeal was diminishing. The Glasgow Stock Exchange was the
second largest in Britain, but even it could not provide a complete
market for speculation. Brokers had to pass on some of their clients'
business to London. Edinburgh, Glasgow, and London were linked
by telegraph in 1846/7 and, over the next decade, it became an
essential tool for the stockbroker. Other changes meant that, in the
words of one writer in 1910, 'The telegraph, the telephone and the
express train have carried the destruction of time and space far
enough for this island to be practically one market area.' The
London Stock Exchange was by far the largest such institution, but
there was still room for some provincial specialization—in the case
of Glasgow, for example, in mining securities and North-American
railroads. On the other hand, London was the market for British
government securities. On balance, therefore, it was still possible to
suggest that Scottish stockbrokers were an independent professional group rather than merely the country agents of a central
share market.[80]

Despite the increasing interpenetration of business, no British
banking system or accountancy profession emerged. In 1844, there
were nineteen banks in Scotland and 441 in England and Wales. By
1900, the figures had reduced to nine and 106 respectively.[81]
Neither north nor south of the Border, therefore, was it accurate to
speak of particular banks possessing an entirely 'national' coverage,
but the trend towards merger was clearly established and, in the
Scottish case, Edinburgh remained the dominant banking centre,
despite Glasgow's attempts to wrest that supremacy away. The
number of English banks dropped to forty in 1913 and the
dominance of London was firmly established. The Birmingham and
Midland Bank took over the Central Bank of London in 1891 but,
although the former was wealthier, the latter made amalgamation
conditional on London becoming the headquarters of the new
bank. The directors abandoned their half-yearly meeting in
Birmingham in 1912. The District Bank in Manchester and Martin's

---

[80] R. C. Michie, *Money, Mania and Markets: Investment, Company Formation and the
Stock Exchange in Nineteenth Century Scotland* (Edinburgh, 1981), 159–60.
[81] M. Gaskin, *The Scottish Banks: A Modern Survey* (1965), 21.

Bank in Liverpool maintained, for the time being, their provincial independence.[82]

It comes as no surprise, in these circumstances, to discover some Anglo-Scottish banking friction. Did not consolidation within England and Scotland in turn point to a single British banking network? Professor Checkland notes that the responsibility of the Bank of England to the British money system as a whole was accepted north of the Border by the early nineteenth century, but that did not preclude much debate on how that responsibility should be discharged. There were various crises. In 1826, when the government moved to prohibit all notes in England under £5 and extend that provision to Scotland, opposition north of the Border was so fierce that the Scots were left in possession of their small notes. A couple of years later, the banking border was reinforced by preventing such Scottish notes being used in England—they were quite frequently used in Border areas.[83] Another contentious issue was whether Scottish banks should be allowed to open branches in England.[84] After a number of abortive attempts, in which a number of Scottish banks co-operated, the Bank of Scotland opened a London office in 1867 and, after a special Act of Parliament, the Royal Bank did the same in 1874. In the same year, the Clydesdale Bank opened branches in Cumberland and had its eyes on the major English northern cities. English bankers backed a parliamentary bill which threatened, by way of retaliation, to remove from such Scottish banks as opened branches in England their right of note issue in Scotland. The bill was dropped when the Clydesdale Bank was persuaded to desist from its 'aggression'. By 1883, the seven large Scottish banks had all opened London branches, but they did not open up elsewhere, being still worried about threats to their note-issuing in Scotland. The spectacular failure of the City of Glasgow Bank in 1878 perhaps affected Scottish banking nerves at the critical moment. Into the twentieth century, therefore, the two

---

[82] B. Robson, 'Coming Full Circle: London versus the Rest, 1890–1980', in G. Gordon (ed.), *Regional Cities in the UK, 1890–1980* (1986), 220; A. R. Holmes and E. Green, *Midland: One Hundred and Fifty Years of Banking* (1986).

[83] S. G. Checkland, *Scottish Banking: A History, 1695–1973* (Glasgow and London, 1975), 276, 318–19; A. B. Erickson, *The Public Career of Sir James Graham* (Oxford, 1952), 62–3.

[84] M. Gaskin, 'Anglo-Scottish Banking Conflicts, 1874–1881', *Economic History Review*, (1960), 2nd Ser., 12, 445–55.

banking systems eyed each other warily, each suspecting the other of poaching intentions.

In insurance, on the other hand, it was possible for a British market to develop and for Scottish companies to take a prominent part in it. The burgeoning insurance companies of the early nineteenth century, as their names frequently indicated, had regional roots. In 1797, it was reported that 55 per cent by value of property insured by the Sun Fire Office was in the Home Counties and another 14 per cent in adjacent southern counties. Its Scottish business amounted to only 5 per cent. However, it boldly employed a woman as its Glasgow agent and described her as being 'very active and as attentive to the business as a female can possibly be expected to be.' Power to transact business in Scotland was only very recent. The Norwich Union found it difficult to break into the London market and started to look northwards. However, Scottish companies were equally energetically looking south. The Standard Life Assurance Company, founded in Edinburgh in 1825, had become one of the three principal offices in the United Kingdom by 1850, measured in terms of annual new business. That new business was largely being achieved in England. The company's English new business exceeded its new Scottish business for the first time in 1853/4: a decade later English business was worth nearly three times the Scottish business. By this stage, the struggle for a British insurance market was truly joined, with Scottish companies more than holding their own territory. The Scottish Widows' and the Standard Life both survived strongly into the late-century era of large-scale insurance enterprise.[85]

The term 'chartered accountant' was first used in Scotland. In the 1850s and 1860s, three societies were established in Edinburgh, Glasgow, and Aberdeen with essentially local memberships. Comparable societies were formed in the 1870s in London, Liverpool, Manchester, and Sheffield and the Society of Accountants was also established in England. The royal charter of the Institute of Chartered Accountants of England and Wales was granted in 1880. 'Many members of the Scottish Institute are original members of the English Institute', a writer in *The Accountant* noted a little later, and they regretted that it did not embrace 'all the members of the profession in the United Kingdom. We

[85] O. Westall (ed.), *The Historian and the Business of Insurance* (Manchester, 1984), 13, 24, 62, 95–9.

cannot but echo this regret.'[86] However, the Scottish societies neither linked with the English Institute nor, during our period, united among themselves, though in 1898 an Association of Scottish Chartered Accountants in London was formed![87] Part of the explanation for the fact that a British chartered accountancy profession did not emerge lies in some differences in the tasks which Scots Law required accountants to perform, though that is not the whole story.[88]

The area of business which had the maximum public British impact, however, was retailing. In matters of dress, 'tartanitis' antedated the royal presence at Balmoral, though it was boosted by it. Englishmen and women increasingly sported various weaves. These products did not need to be 'made in Scotland' to be advertised as authentic. It was apparently a clerk in James Locke's Scotch Tartan Warehouse in Regent Street who gave the name 'tweed' to Border woven cloth—the Scottish word was 'twill'. A Scotch Tweed Warehouse, also in Regent Street, was the result. And, lest the customer be starved for choice, Her Majesty's Royal Tartan Warehouse was also located there. It had a giant thistle over the doorway which was, in reality, an elaborate gas bracket which lit up as dusk fell. The first Scotch Wool Shop opened in Greenock in 1881 and by 1901 there were two hundred branches across Britain.[89] And, most importantly, it was the Glasgow firm of Charles Mackintosh who patented a process for textile waterproofing in 1823. Production began in Manchester. Not to be entirely outdone, Welshmen brought some of their traditional skills to the English market. The Llanelli-born D. H. Evans bought 320 Oxford Street in 1879 and developed a substantial business beyond his original expertise in lace. Although class differences in clothes were still apparent, the remaining British peculiarities of 'off-duty' regional dress lost more ground. A weekend suit looked much the same whether worn in Cardiff or Newcastle upon Tyne.

Expectations of 'national' pricing accompanied the spread of the

---

[86] Cited by H. Howitt, *The History of the Institute of Chartered Accountants in England and Wales, 1880–1965* (1966), 345.

[87] Anon., *A History of the Chartered Accountants of Scotland from the Earliest Times to 1954* (Edinburgh, 1954), 155.

[88] E. Jones, *Accountancy and the British Economy, 1840–1980: The Evolution of Ernst & Whinney* (1981), 81–2.

[89] These examples have been drawn from A. Adburgham, *Shops and Shopping, 1800–1914* (1964).

retailing revolution. An 1892 *Handybook of Shopkeeping* noted that 'In Edinburgh, as in London, haggling is now gone out of date in all respectable establishments and so it is in Glasgow.'[90] The practice had formerly been to spend at least half an hour bargaining over the price. Sir Thomas Lipton, who started his business in Glasgow, achieved remarkable success throughout England and Wales.[91] Indeed, in retailing generally, developments tended to start in the North and then move south. Michael Marks started his 'Penny Bazaars' in the North of England. The first British branch of F. W. Woolworth opened in Liverpool in 1909—which city also gave birth to Lewis's department store.[92] In another line. W. H. Smith became a familiar name throughout England and Wales: in Scotland its equivalent was J. Menzies.[93] By 1914, it has been suggested that there was practically no important consumer goods trade which lacked multiple shop retailers.[94] And there were few such retailers which did not aspire to 'British' coverage, either by establishing branches or by taking over existing local firms. The first company in Britain to operate more than ten retail butchers' shops—John Bell and Sons of Glasgow—then directed its attention to London. The process of nation-wide coverage was still not complete, and it was slower in some lines (shoes, for example) than in others. Nevertheless, truly national 'brand loyalties' were firmly established. And there was a nice irony in the fact that southerners had to send their dirty clothes to Johnson's of Liverpool or Pullar's of Perth if they wished to maintain their superior external appearances. British businesses gave fresh encouragement to British bodies.

In general, therefore, business and commerce within Britain shared in the broad process of integration throughout the Victorian age. The traveller in the decade before 1914 would have recognized many more 'household names' throughout the country than would his predecessor a century earlier. There were, however, important enterprises existing independently in the English provinces and

[90] Cited by J. B. Jefferys, *Retail Trading in Britain, 1850–1950* (Cambridge, 1954), 37 n.

[91] A. R. Waugh, *The Lipton Story* (1951).

[92] A. Briggs, *Friends of the People: The Centenary History of Lewis's* (1956).

[93] C. H. Wilson, *First with the News: A History of the W. H. Smith Clan since 1792* (1986).

[94] The account of the relationship between the North of England and Glasgow Co-operators provided in J. Kinloch, *History of the Scottish Co-operative Wholesale Society Limited* (Glasgow, 1981), 32–3 indicates that the structures that did emerge were often fortuitous: Jefferys, *Retail Trading*, 26–7.

Scotland. The City, however, was becoming inexorably more significant and with it the tendency for corporate decision-making to drift to the capital. Independent Scottish banking for a time masked the fact that Scottish business was subject to the same influences. The politics of business pointed in the direction of integration. Technical advances in communication could occasionally reinforce local decision-making capacity but they also accelerated the bunching of information and expertise in London. There seemed increasingly little room for diffused centres of business excellence.

# 5

## Education, Science, and the Moulding of the Mind

In Thomas Love Peacock's novel *Crotchet Castle*, Dr Folliott, an English clergyman, admitted to Mr MacQuedy (i.e. QED), a Scotsman, that Scotland was 'pre-eminent in the glory of fish for breakfast'. Such an admission did not satisfy the Scotsman, who proceeded to list other areas of pre-eminence:

Morals and metaphysics, politics and political economy, the way to make the most of all the modifications of smoke, steam, gas and paper currency; you have all these to learn from us; in short, all the arts and sciences. We are the modern Athenians.'

Folliott insisted that he was only prepared to take lessons in the matter of fish for breakfast.[1] This elaborately contrived exchange was designed to explode the notion that a 'British mind' existed; The 'Scotch Intellect', as identified by Buckle, pursued its strange concerns while Englishmen looked on with disdainful contempt. It is, of course, a caricature, yet there were occasions when the growth and dissemination of knowledge took place in Anglo-Scottish contexts where the banter was barbed and the antagonism but lightly concealed. When the march of mind was considered, the 'steam intellects' of the North often saw themselves in the van.

There were, indeed, more than hints in Victorian Scotland that the country had an especially intimate relationship with Education. It was a notion which had a certain currency in the South. When government ministers got themselves into a muddle as to whether the 1833 educational grant for Great Britain should only apply, on its renewal, to England, Lord Althorp at first explained 'that England not having had any provision at all made for the education of the people, the proposed experiment ought rather to be tried

---

[1] D. Garnett (ed.), *The Novels of Thomas Love Peacock* (1948), 657; M. Butler, *Peacock Displayed* (1979), 189–90; Sydney Smith's complaint against 'Scotch philosophers in general' was that they reasoned upon man as they reasoned upon 'X'. Bell, *Smith*, 19–20.

here than in Scotland.'[2] The government later changed its mind, but the assumption still prevailed that Scotland's system of parochial education was superior to anything on offer in England and Wales. 'Sandy Mackaye' in Kingsley's *Alton Locke* was only one of a number of Victorian literary representations of the superior Scot. 'My father was a Hieland farmer', Sandy told the young Radical tailor, 'and yet he was a weel learned man: and . . . he used to say "a man kens just as much as he's taught himself, and na mair."' Sandy added 'And mony's the Greek exercise I've written in the cowbyres.'[3] Kingsley may have suspected that such scholarly activity did not go on in English cowbyres. It has recently been argued by Dr Anderson, however, that the 'democratic' character of Scottish education and the exceptional abilities of its products became, in the nineteenth century, a 'powerful historical myth'. The 'myth' was not false, but it became 'an idealization and distillation of a complex reality.'[4] The subject of education became entangled, at all levels, in the general relationship between England and Scotland.

The maintenance of a separate Scottish educational system appeared to many Victorian Scots to be a vital element in the preservation of Scottish identity. It was a comforting reinforcement of this basic necessity to believe that Scottish education was superior. Prima facie, the case was plausible. Higher levels of basic literacy, and the sense of self-discipline needed to achieve it, would not be surprising in a country poorer in natural resources than its southern neighbour and accustomed to the idea of exporting a segment of its population. 'It is especially in mediocrity that the Scotch are great', wrote one provocative commentator in 1842. Scots were 'first-rate second-rate men' and they swarmed in counting-houses and engineering-shops and the subordinate departments of government offices throughout the British Empire.[5] One of Hugh Miller's landladies took it for granted that the only reason for his visit to England was to look for work. It happened that she was a Scotswoman herself, long settled and married in the West Midlands. She obviously repeated conventional wisdom when

---

[2] Cited by D. G. Paz, *The Politics of Working-Class Education in Britain, 1830–1850* (Manchester, 1980), 14.

[3] C. Kingsley, *Alton Locke* (1881), 34–5.

[4] R. D. Anderson, *Education and Opportunity in Victorian Scotland: Schools and Universities* (Oxford, 1983), 1.

[5] J. M'Turk, 'Scotsmen in London', in C. Knight (ed.), *London*, vol. iii (1842), 323–4.

she took the view that the Scotch people, unlike the Irish who remained drudges, had both the character and scholarship to become 'overseers and book-keepers, sometimes even partners in lucrative works, and were usually well liked and looked up to.'[6] He reflected further that his travels convinced him that the minds of the English common people were 'much more profoundly asleep than those of the common people of Scotland. We have no class North of the Tweed that corresponds with the class of ruddy, round-faced, vacant English, so abundant in the rural districts, and whose very physiognomy, derived during the course of centuries from untaught ancestors, indicates intellect yet unawakened. The reflective habits of the Scottish people have set their stamp on the national countenance.'[7]

The Scottish schoolmaster was available in generous quantities to assist in the awakening of the English intellect. He was not as universally admired as he would have desired. In *Hard Times*, Dickens gave him the unflattering name of Mr McChoakumchild. A London schoolgirl recorded in her memoirs that her teacher was 'the typical sandy-haired, raw-boned dominie, in long frock-coat and skull cap.' Education in Scotland might well have been marvellous, she thought, but 'his only method was to make us learn a great deal of rubbish by heart ... Beautiful maps we certainly drew ... Scotland was the usual subject of these, varied by the Holy Land ...'.[8] Scottish schoolmasters were sometimes asked to demonstrate their ability to 'say something in Scotch'. One dominie in Sheffield replied emphatically 'Fat are ye after noo, ye shochlin vratch?' (What are you after now, you wriggling wretch?) but his lady questioner was quite delighted with the demonstration.[9] North of the Border, the founding directors of Edinburgh Academy explained in their brochure that it was their intention to appoint a master for English 'who shall have a pure English accent', though the circumstance of his being born within the boundary of England was not to be considered indispensable.[10] Boys at Glasgow Academy, taught by Englishmen, immediately picked them out as alien because of an inability to pronounce 'which' in the Scottish

[6] Miller, *First Impressions*, 64.
[7] Ibid. 336–7.
[8] Hughes, *London Family*, 64–5.
[9] MacDonald, *MacDonald*, 163.
[10] *Statement by the Directors of the Edinburgh Academy Explanatory of the Scheme of that Institution, December 1823* (Edinburgh, 1824).

manner.[11] South of the Border, some cricketing members of Rugby School felt that their 'Scotch' master, John Campbell Shairp, 'Must be mad' because he had walked across 'bigside' and right through a cricket match, so engrossed was he in Tennyson's *In Memoriam*. As an undergraduate at Balliol, the same man had endeavoured to convey the essence of Oxford to his Scottish friends. 'There is another place,' he wrote, '"All Souls". It is difficult fully to explain the nature of the Fellowships there.'[12]

It was almost equally difficult to convey to England the unique qualities of the Scottish parochial school. Scots themselves, however, continued to assert that it was the source of national eminence. It appears to be the case that in the North-East, such schools had a 'symbiotic relationship' with Aberdeen's universities.[13] Elsewhere, however, the picture was not as glowing, particularly in the urban Scotland that was emerging. Once again, it proved difficult to disinter educational, financial, and national issues. 'In all but our parochial schools', declared George Lewis, speaking to the Glasgow Education Association in 1834, 'we have lost our nationality. In these alone we survive as a nation—stand apart from and superior to England. ... These are the only institutions around which linger Scottish feelings and attachments ...'.[14] In the 1850s, various attempts were made to provide for 'national' education in Scotland by providing new schools in places where none existed and by countering the trend to separate denominational schools which had occurred after the Disruption. They failed, largely because of the opposition of the Established Church.

It was increasingly believed in Scotland that education was 'a science separate and distinct from all others' and individual Scotsmen, most notably David Stow, devoted themselves to the training of teachers. The fame of these efforts reached England. In 1839, the Wesleyan Conference sent English Methodist students to Glasgow in increasing numbers, until they opened their own college in London in 1851. Stow himself, however, had to admit that 'the largest proportion of our best educated and most accomplished teachers have gone to England, where larger salaries have been

[11] *The Glasgow Academy: The First Hundred Years* (Glasgow, 1946); see also J. Bridie and M. McLaren, *A Small Stir: Letters on the English* (1949), 16.

[12] Knight, *Principal Shairp*, 78.

[13] Anderson, *Education and Opportunity*, 9.

[14] Cited by W. M. Humes and H. M. Paterson (eds.), *Scottish Culture and Scottish Education, 1800–1980* (Edinburgh, 1983), 63–4.

offered.'[15] Scottish teachers, however, firmly resisted the notion that they might belong to a 'British' profession. The Educational Institute for Scotland was founded in 1847 and, over the ensuing decades, regularly pronounced on the peculiar features of Scottish education and why they needed to be preserved.[16]

The recommendations of the Newcastle Commission—whose work did not extend to Scotland—and the subsequent 'Revised Code' for educational grants of 1861/2 caused a furore. Exception was taken to 'payment by results', to the assumption that all teachers were 'elementary', and to the restriction of grants to the offspring of manual workers. All three notions cut across practice in Scotland and aroused opposition. In these circumstances, the government was forced to set up the Argyll Commission in 1864 to enquire generally into Scottish education. Its report, published three years later, contained detailed proposals designed to strengthen what was called 'the ancient theory of Scottish National Education.'[17] Attempts at legislation for Scotland in the wake of the report failed. The 1870 Education Act (England and Wales) occupied the centre of parliamentary attention. There was no suggestion at this time that a British Education Act would be either feasible or desirable.

The Education (Scotland) Act was passed in 1872. Unlike the provision south of the Border, education was to be compulsory until the age of thirteen. And, since nearly all Presbyterian schools transferred to the new school boards—there being public provision for religious instruction according to 'use and wont', a national system came into existence in Scotland without the English division between Voluntary and Board Schools, though Roman Catholic schools remained outside the system.[18] Scotland was therefore not involved in the controversies that raged thirty years later in England and Wales over the 1902 Education Act. When Halley Stewart came north a little later to campaign at Greenock in the Liberal cause he was firmly told that he had no business to attempt to influence the Scottish mind concerning matters in England which were no concern of Scotland. However, since the 1872 Act

[15] M. Cruickshank, *History of the Training of Teachers in Scotland* (1970), 47.
[16] A. J. Belford, *Centenary Handbook of the Educational Institute of Scotland* (Edinburgh, 1947).
[17] Anderson, *Education and Opportunity*, 103–6.
[18] Koss, *Nonconformity* (1975), 19.

did abolish the parish schools as a separate category, some Scottish educationalists described it as 'the application of English ideas to Scotch education.' There was also at this time some emerging demand for public funding for secondary education in Scotland, or at least the release of certain endowment funds for this purpose. 'Primary and secondary education', Lyon Playfair argued, '. . . are so thoroughly ingrained in Scotland that you cannot deal with them separately, nor would Scotchmen give one farthing for a system of national education in which they were separated.'[19]

The failure to tackle Scottish secondary education in the 1872 Act was sometimes attributed in Scotland to a mistaken belief in the South that the findings of the Taunton Commission in England would apply in Scotland. The belief that only Scotsmen could understand the nature and needs of Scottish education led to the view, in the mid-1880s, that the Committee of Council on Education, which had come to be referred to as the Scotch Education Department, should come under the control of the new Scottish Secretary—though both minister and department would continue to operate in London. The issue touched many raw nerves. Sir William Harcourt stated to Gladstone that 'The Scotch people are deeply dissatisfied with the English administration of their Education. They say it is extravagantly conducted without knowledge or regard of the local circumstances of the country. I believe they are quite right in this opinion.'[20] However, Scottish opinion was more divided than Harcourt made out. The Church of Scotland and the Free Church were both internally split on the matter and Roman Catholics were against transfer. Only the United Presbyterian Church was in favour. Even the EIS opposed the removal of Scottish education from the administrative machinery which then controlled education in England. 'No country can less afford than Scotland', declared Playfair, 'to narrow the ambition of its educated classes or to parochialize its institutions. If it separates itself from England in administration and education it need not be surprised if in time England becomes less of an outlet for Scotch enterprise.'[21] But he lost the battle. The new Secretary for Scotland became the first Vice-President of the Scotch Education Department.

The first Permanent Under-Secretary at the Scottish Office, Sir

---

[19] Cited by Anderson, *Education and Opportunity*, 108.
[20] Cited by Hanham, 'Creation of the Scottish Office', 217–18.
[21] Ibid. 219.

Francis Sandford, and the first Secretary of the Scotch Education Department under the new arrangements, Sir Henry Craik, have both frequently been described as 'Anglicizers', but the debates in which they were involved suggest that this description is not very helpful. Likewise, it is an over-simplification to see the great debates on the curriculum, degree structure, and internal constitutional arrangements which took place in Scottish universities in terms of a struggle between 'Anglophile' and 'patriotic' parties. Contrary to the thesis advanced in Davie's celebrated *The Democratic Intellect*, Anderson convincingly suggests that the advocates of increased specialization were not motivated by principles of social exclusivism which made them hostile to a democratic tradition in which philosophy filled a central role. He concedes, however, that Davie is right to see changes made in 1892 as confirmation of the view that the Ordinary degree pointed to a 'Scottish' career and the Honours degree pointed to a 'British' one. In this context, it has also been noted that the debate between 'specialists' and 'generalists' was going on quite independently in the United States at this time.[22] It was unfortunate that the merits of both cases were obscured in Britain by their representation as 'English' and 'Scottish' solutions respectively.

On the other hand, it was easy to see how this identification could be made. Both Sandford and Craik made their way to London Scottish eminence along an established path to greatness—the University of Glasgow and Balliol with the aid of a Snell Exhibition. They both distinguished themselves academically. Sandford was a son of Sir Daniel Sandford, Professor of Greek at Glasgow and Craik was a son of a Glasgow parish minister and later moderator of the General Assembly. Craik married an Englishwoman and sent his three sons to Eton. Sandford married a Scotswoman and died in London. It would be tedious to list all the other Snell Exhibitioners, but a high proportion of them made a significant contribution to British academic and public life.[23] Many of them never returned to

[22] G. E. Davie, *The Democratic Intellect: Scotland and her Universities in the Nineteenth Century* (Edinburgh, 1964); Anderson, *Education and Opportunity*, 358–61; M. E. Finn in Humes and Paterson, *Scottish Scottish Culture*, 188–9.

[23] W. Innes Addison, *The Snell Exhibitions from the University of Glasgow to Balliol College, Oxford* (Glasgow, 1901). One of their number was Andrew Lang. Many Victorians first looked into his prose translations of Homer. See R. Jenkyns, *The Victorians and Ancient Greece* (Oxford, 1983), 195–7; R. M. Ogilvie, *Latin and Greek: A History of the Influence of the Classics on English Life from 1600 to 1918* (1964), 161.

appointments in Scotland, but it is instructive to look at the attitude of Shairp, who did. At St Andrews he tried to graft aspects of the English tutorial and collegiate system on to the life of a Scottish university. He was not an aggressive 'anglicizer' but he did believe— too optimistically as things turned out—that a British university which blended the best in both the English and Scottish traditions was better than either existing system.[24] Men of his generation and experience were hostile to the comparison between Scottish and English schools—and, by extension, education as a whole—made by the experienced Scottish HMI when he wrote:

We have less of the repose of manner and absence of effort on the part of teacher, and less of the politeness and refinement on the part of the pupil. Scotch discipline is not less effective for purposes of work. That it is somewhat wanting in gentleness and finish is probably due to the native ruggedness characteristic of the more northern race.[25]

Snell men, therefore, whether they became bishops or bankers, barristers or poets, or merely professors, contributed a blend of qualities which penetrated deep into British professional life. On the surface there could scarcely be a stronger comparison than between the ambience of late-Victorian Oxford and late-Victorian Glasgow, yet the men who moved between them could never shake off the legacy of both places. A few months after his arrival in Glasgow, Walter Raleigh wrote to George Prothero, who had been in Edinburgh, asking how it was possible to survive in a Scottish university. 'So stimulating,' he wrote, 'they tell me, a hundred and eighty bright keen young spirits must be. And they are; but one can't live on gin. And I get no time to feed the mind . . .'. He was glad to accept the Oxford Chair four years later: less money, but fewer lectures. There was time for tutorial whimsy.[26] Raleigh's own successor in the Merton Chair was eventually to be George Gordon. As an undergraduate at Oriel, however, Gordon had complained of the bored demureness of Oxford undergraduates at a lecture compared with the liveliness of Glasgow.[27] The Scots applauded or displayed dissent. When the Merton Chair was established in 1885 John Nichol of Glasgow dreamed that he might

[24] Knight, *Principal Shairp*, 189.
[25] Cited by Cruickshank, *Training of Teachers*, 106.
[26] Raleigh, *Letters*, 80, 105.
[27] M. C. Gordon, *The Life of George Gordon, 1885–1942* (Oxford, 1945), 8.

occupy it and relive his youth. 'Glasgow needs the best man,' his publisher consoled him, 'Oxford might be satisfied with a second or a third.'[28]

Scottish educationists might protest against what they regarded as subversive English influences sapping the structure and content of their system, but there was at least an undercurrent of resentment at the Scottish influence, particularly in the realm of theory, on education in England. In this respect, the crucial moulder of minds in the late century was Edward Caird who, after a distinguished career at Glasgow and St Andrews, came to Balliol in 1860. He then returned to Glasgow as Professor of Moral Philosophy in 1866, remaining there until he became Master of Balliol in 1893.[29] He gathered about him in Glasgow a formidable group of men—J. S. Mackenzie, John MacCunn, Henry Jones, and J. H. Muirhead in particular—who subsequently distinguished themselves in university posts in England, Scotland, and Wales. They enthusiastically applied idealist philosophy to educational issues and dominated the London Ethical Society in the mid-1880s. It was a formidable academic network, perpetrating upon the unsuspecting English a potent gospel of 'citizenship'.[30] This Glasgow–Balliol link was exceptionally strong, but it was but one particularly influential example of a widespread transfer of intellect, usually in a southerly direction. Between one-quarter and one-third of all Aberdeen graduates in the years from 1871 to 1911 found jobs in England and Wales immediately after graduation.[31]

[28] Knight, *Nichol*, 209.

[29] In a sermon on 'Queen Victoria's Jubilee' in 1897, Caird stated that 'Favoured by their insular position, the British people were among the first in Europe to attain the unity and solidarity of a nation.' E. Caird, *Lay Sermons Delivered in Balliol College* (Glasgow, 1907), 89–90.

[30] P. Gordon and J. White, *Philosophers as Educational Reformers: The Influence of Idealism on British Educational Thought and Practice* (1979), 11, 146. Scots consistently contended that Scottish universities were more relevant to the needs of the age than any other. In the 1860s, James Bryce was appalled that the great English cities lacked an institution like a 'Scotch university', and, in the next generation, it was R. B. Haldane who proclaimed throughout England, Scotland, and Wales that a nation's status depended upon the enlightenment supplied by its universities.

[31] D. I. Mckay, *Geographical Mobility and the Brain Drain: A Case Study of Aberdeen University Graduates, 1860–1960* (1969), 97; study of T. Watt (ed.), *Aberdeen Grammar School: Roll of Pupils, 1795–1919* (Aberdeen, 1923) reveals a comparable pattern of British and international dispersal. A leader in the *Scots Observer*, edited by the Englishman, W. E. Henley, launched in 1889 a controversial attack on 'Aberdonianism', claiming that the scholars of that city had become, from an early age, the 'Competition Wallahs' of Scotland, The *Scots Observer* shortly afterwards moved

Earlier in the century, of course, Scots, along with their Bentham-ite and Unitarian associates, had been prominent in establishing a university in London. The new institution had incorporated supposedly 'Scottish' features: emphasis on lectures, non-residential students, absence of religious tests, and the payment of professors from class-fees. Whether the chief credit for the arrangements should go to Thomas Campbell or Henry Brougham is a matter of opinion, but it seems that Scotsmen were particularly disturbed by the fact that, uniquely in Europe, England's capital lacked a university.[32] Throughout the century, therefore, there was a steady academic interchange which moulded the British mind. Institu-tional differences, however, still remained, though it has been persuasively argued that Anglo-Scottish differences were less profound than combatants, north and south of the Border, supposed. It comes as little surprise to find that when some Scots were attacking the English for basing their education on facts rather than speculation, some Englishmen were attacking the Scots on precisely the same grounds.[33]

Fact and speculation was much in evidence in Welsh educational controversy. British and National Schools, for Dissenters and Anglicans respectively, had made only modest attempts to grapple with Welsh educational needs in the 1820s and 1830s. Much energy was spent in debating a voluntary system's merits as opposed to state intervention. By the middle 1840s the inadequate provision for Welsh education attracted considerable public discussion. William Williams, a Carmarthenshire boy who had become a wealthy London merchant and then entered the Commons as MP for Coventry, pressed for a royal commission on the subject in 1846. Instead, three commissioners appointed by the Privy Council began taking evidence in the principality and produced a nearly two-thousand-page report in the following year. Their indictment of

south, changing its name to the *National Observer*, but not even an illuminating series of articles on 'Golf Greens near London' could secure its viability. J. Connell, *W. E. Henley* (1949), 157–8 and A. Sullivan (ed.), *British Literary Magazines: The Victorian and Edwardian Age, 1837–1913* (Westport, Conn., 1983), 389–93.

[32] R. Stewart,*Henry Brougham, 1778–1868: His Public Career* (1985), 195–7: H. H. Bellot, *University College London, 1826–1926* (1929), 8; T. Kelly, *George Birkbeck: A Pioneer of Adult Education* (Liverpool, 1957); Chitnis, *Scottish Enlightenment*, 169–71.

[33] C. J. Wright, 'Academics and their Aims: English and Scottish Approaches to University Education in the Nineteenth Century', *History of Education* (1979), 91–7.

Welsh educational standards appeared to be the indictment of a nation. Nonconformists, and some Anglicans, thought the report grossly unfair and insensitive and there were bitter protests.[34] Yet, behind the protests, there was an unresolved question. In what sense and to what degree was education in Wales to be Welsh education. Was there a Welsh mind which required separate treatment? Despite the 'Treason of the Blue Books', the answer seemed to be in the negative, even as far as most Welshmen were concerned. The system applied under the 1870 Education Act was 'wholly English'. Sunday Schools—attended by adults—remained, by contrast, 'truly Welsh'. A decade later, the Aberdare Departmental Committee inquired into the intermediate and higher education provision in Wales and, eventually, the Welsh Intermediate Education Act was passed in 1889 setting up a completely new structure and type of school for Wales alone. The administrative evolution of Welsh education followed a tortuous course over the next two decades. There was talk of a 'National Council' for Welsh Education but the Liberal government finally settled in 1907 for a Welsh Department of the Board of Education with its own Permanent Secretary and Chief Inspector. The Department would have responsibility for all grades of education in Wales and Monmouthshire. Part of the impetus behind these changes had stemmed from concern about the educational position of the Welsh language, but that was by no means the only issue. Englishmen took a prominent part in these developments and shared in their ambiguity. In Caernarfonshire, for example, the new system owed a great deal to A. H. D. Acland, the Liberal MP for Rotherham, who had a home in the county. What was being attempted in Wales was Welsh but it also had a potential significance elsewhere. 'When Wales has worked out its own salvation', wrote A. J. Mundella in 1893, 'it will have the effect of leavening the larger and more inert mass of Englishmen. I always desired to see Wales become a model for our national system . . .'.[35]

Wales could not work out its own mental salvation until it had its own universities or university. St David's College, Lampeter apart,

---

[34] P. T. J. Morgan, 'From Long Knives to Blue Books', in Davies (ed.), *Welsh Society*, 209.

[35] L. W. Evans, *Studies in Welsh Education: Welsh Educational Structure and Administration, 1880–1925* (Cardiff, 1974) is a thorough treatment. Mundella's comments are cited on p. 16.

the lack of any such institutions increasingly grieved Welshmen educated elsewhere in Britain. After much dispute and rivalry as to location, three small university colleges were set up at Aberystwyth, Cardiff, and Bangor in 1872, 1883, and 1884 respectively. The University of Wales was given its charter in 1893: a new national institution had been created. But what role was it to occupy in the intellectual map of Britain? The Scottish influence was widespread. John Nichol of Glasgow, asked to advise on the early development of Aberystwyth, wrote emphatically on what he believed to be the advantages of the Scottish system as opposed to the English model. He declined to be considered for Principal.[36] Each constituent institution rather went its own way but did not depart too far from Mundella's view that 'Wales requires local colleges which will afford education as cheaply and be as accessible to the people of the Principality as the Scotch colleges are to Scotchmen.' Scotch colleges, however, did not have to wrestle with the position of the Welsh language. Bangor, which had successfully brushed aside its rival Wrexham's claim to be the town which spoke English 'with a purer accent than almost any in England,' took slow but deliberate steps to secure the teaching of Welsh literature and language under the guidance of its Moravian-descended Anglo-Irish Principal. Perhaps because of his own mixed origins, Sir Harry Reichel liked to dabble in racial analogies. The Welshman was 'the Teuton of the Celts' and might be able to supply the deficiency caused in Britain by the fact that the Englishman had 'so little respect for the intellectual side of life'.[37] Despite this judgement, however, even under the new dispensation, Welshmen did not seem averse to coming to Oxford. Once there, however, they could safeguard their Welsh heritage by joining the Dafydd ap Gwilym Society, whose centenary is celebrated in this academic year.[38] Whether in England or Wales, the Welsh mind was being more adequately prepared than ever before to break the apparent Anglo-Scottish monopoly of the intellectual life of Britain.

Peacock's Mr MacQuedy made a handsome list of fields in which he believed Scotland to be supreme, though other Scots might even

[36] Knight, *Nichol*, 203–4.

[37] J. G. Williams, *The University College of North Wales: Foundations, 1884–1927* (Cardiff, 1985), 30, 43, 224–5.

[38] Jones, *Ellis*, 25–7.

have found it a restricted one. Before considering intellectual life in more detail, it is worth pausing before the phenomenon of the Victorian 'sage'. It was Francis Bacon who had said of the Scots that if they were at a disadvantage in respect of 'the external goods of fortune', nevertheless, 'for the goods of the mind and body, they are *alteri nos*, other ourselves.'[39] Scottish ratiocination, however, could often seem to the English to be excessively disembodied, and some Scotsmen agreed. Principal Shairp of St Andrews thought the teaching of history in Scotland would 'give something of the concrete to the Scotch mind, which is so tremendously apt to run off into abstractions, metaphysics, and logic.' Giving evidence to the 1876 Royal Commission on the Scottish universities, he added 'the utter blank of history, and the absence of all that is meant by the historical spirit and the historical method, is the greatest want in Scotch education.'[40] It may be that the work of the history departments that were set up in Scottish universities over subsequent decades has modified what Emerson called 'the insanity of dialectics' which he found in Scotland.[41]

On a cognate theme, Walter Raleigh deplored the admiration for 'aggressive eccentricity' which he found among the Scots.[42] Yet it seemed that English life needed the advent of a prophet from the North at regular intervals, even if his message could not be assimilated or even comprehended. The most celebrated Victorian Scottish sage lived in Chelsea. 'London is the heart of the world' Carlyle told Emerson, though it was a conclusion he had reached after six years of Craigenputtoch gloom and acerbity. 'On the whole,' he had earlier written to his brother John, 'this London is the most *twilight* intellectual city you could meet with: a meaner more utterly despicable view of man and his interests than stands pictured even in the better heads you could nowhere fall in with.'[43] Residence in London helped him, at a distance, to appreciate the merits of Scotland. 'Scornfully as I used to speak and think of Scotland in my hours of bitterness and irritation,' he wrote, 'I never fail to stand up manfully in defence of it thro' thick and thin, whenever a renegade Scot takes upon him to abuse it.'[44] Carlyle

[39] Cited in K. Miller, *Doubles: Studies in Literary History* (Oxford, 1985), 430–1.

[40] Cited by A. L. Brown, 'History in the Making', *Glasgow College Courant*, 29, no. 58 (1977), 6–11.

[41] Emerson, *English Traits*, 55.    [42] Raleigh, *Letters*, 84–5.

[43] Cited by I. Campbell, *Thomas Carlyle* (New York, 1974), 78.

[44] Cited by F. Kaplan, *Thomas Carlyle: A Biography* (Cambridge, 1983), 100.

found it necessary to make regular pilgrimages to Annandale. The last essay he wrote was on 'The Portraits of John Knox'. It turned out to be the case that the authentic portrait of Knox was one which closely resembled a portrait of Thomas Carlyle.[45] The offer of burial in Westminster Abbey was declined and Carlyle's body returned to Ecclefechan.

Carlyle was not alone in his prophetic role. Sparks had likewise flown when his 'friend' Edward Irving had taken London by storm. Looking back, thirty years later, Thomas concluded that Irving 'had tried to do what no man may do and live—to gaze full into the brightness of the Deity, and so blindness fell upon him.'[46] Such men disrupted English modes of discourse with an uncomfortable northern existential urgency. They oscillated, Kierkegaard-like, between the 'Everlasting Yea' and the 'Everlasting No'. And, although he had not actually been born in Scotland, it was a similar disconcerting light, perhaps trembling on the verge of madness, that the London Scotsman, John Ruskin, directed upon English cultural life. He had been baptized in the Caledonian Chapel, Hatton Garden—though before Irving became its minster. His Latin grammar, which he had memorized at home, was thrown back at him by his London schoolmaster with the dismissive words: 'That's a Scotch thing'. When James Hogg, the 'Ettrick Shepherd', paid his last visit to London, he drove out to Herne Hill to meet the young Ruskin. However, John declined an invitation to go north, though he confessed 'the very name of Scotland is sweet to me.'[47] It remained so, from afar, through all the troubles of his life. It was certainly a more potent reality for him than it was for John Stuart Mill, though, as has been observed, James Mill was following in a Scottish tradition by giving his eldest son such careful instruction. It was another Scottish tradition—extreme reticence—that Mill's biographer, Alexander Bain, honoured when he could not bring himself to tell his dying father that he had been offered the chance to teach the Moral Philosophy Class in the University of Aber-

[45] Kaplan, *Thomas Carlyle: A Biography*, 513.
[46] Cited by H. C. Whitley, *Blinded Eagle: An Introduction to the Life and Teaching of Edward Irving* (1955).
[47] T. Hilton, *John Ruskin: The Early Years, 1819-1859* (New Haven and London, 1985), 28-30; H. G. Viljoen, *Ruskin's Scottish Heritage* (Urbana, 1956) gives a full account. Leslie Stephen's discussion of the relationship between Ruskin's work and Carlyle's is printed in J. L. Bradley (ed.), *Ruskin: The Critical Heritage* (1984), 422-3.

deen.[48] It comes as no surprise to learn that one of the first things the young Bain did when he came to London was to visit Carlyle. Scotland could not fully hold the energies and ambitions of such men, but England could not fully absorb them either. The peculiar tensions of these divided minds contributed powerfully to Victorian culture. Dr Jekyll and Mr Hyde, it might be thought, had long been installed in Cheyne Walk. It is, finally, no accident that it is to Carlyle, according to the *Oxford English Dictionary*, that we owe the meaning of the word 'environment' in the sense of 'the region surrounding something'. Carlyle and his fellow Scots had an acute sense of the English environment in which they lived precisely because it was not the environment in which they had been born.[49]

During his visit south of the Border, Hugh Miller was struck by what he called 'the immense extent of range across the intellectual scale' which he found in England. There was

an order of English mind to which Scotland has not attained: our first men stand in the second rank, not a foot-breadth behind the foremost of England's second-rank men; but there is a front rank of British intellect in which there stands no Scotsman.[50]

It was not an admission which the learned men of Edinburgh would have readily made in the late eighteenth and early nineteenth century. The heady brew of 'Scotch knowledge' concocted there was thought, at least by its exponents, to be in advance of anything available in England.[51] Political economy was a major part of that concoction. It is significant that Peacock chose to focus his fire particularly on Scottish economists. Besides Mr MacQuedy, he also invented Mr MacFungus, Mr MacBorrowdale, and Mr MacPuzzle-head. There were some economists in England who might have been attacked, but it was the combination 'Scottish Political

---

[48] W. E. S. Thomas, *The Philosophic Radicals: Nine Studies in Theory and Practice, 1817–1841* (Oxford, 1979), 152; A. Bain, *John Stuart Mill: A Criticism with Personal Recollections* (1882); W. L. Davidson (ed.), *A Bain*; *Autobiography* (1904), 110.

[49] J. D. Rosenberg, *Carlyle and the Burden of History* (Cambridge, Mass., 1985), 35–6. While a sense of duality can also be located within Scotland itself, and within the contrary imperatives of two 'languages', Karl Miller properly observes that 'there are double tongues and different languages in the South too,' Miller, *Doubles*, 436. See also his criticism in his *Cockburn's Millennium*, 216–17 of Edwin Muir's thesis that Scotsmen felt in one language and thought in another.

[50] Miller, *First Impressions*, 334.

[51] A. C. Chitnis, *The Scottish Enlightenment and Early Victorian Society* (1986), 74–82.

Economy' which he found especially repellent.[52] It was a sentiment shared to the full by William Cobbett. It stemmed, perhaps, from a dislike of the market and of the belief that every man and every object had a price. In *Headlong Hall*, Peacock has Mr MacLaurel explaining that 'poetry is a sort of ware or commodity, that is brought into the public market wi' a' other descriptions of merchandise.' A man was 'pairfectly justified' in getting the best price he could for his article.[53]

The actual Scot being pilloried by Peacock was probably J. R. McCulloch. He published his *Essay on the National Debt* in 1816, five years after graduating from Edinburgh. It gained him a considerable reputation, but after the attempt to establish a Chair of Political Economy for him at Edinburgh had failed, he moved to England. He made a living by writing and teaching until Lord Melbourne made him Comptroller of the Stationery Office in 1838, a post he occupied until his death in 1864.[54] His insatiable didacticism, coupled with his propensity to quarrel with other 'Scots'—Mill and Brougham—made it easy to type-cast him and discredit his work. 'Since the time that Scotsmen began to repair in considerable numbers to our capital', wrote one commentator in 1842 'they have come lecturing and to lecture, and that John Bull cannot abide.'[55] McCulloch was not a man easily to be deterred. In his *Discourse on the Rise, Progress, Peculiar Objects and Importance of Political Economy* (1824) he asserted that:

The price of all sorts of commodities—the profits of the manufacturer and merchant—the rent of the landlord—the wages of the day labourer—and the incidence and effect of taxes and regulations, all depend on the principles which Political Economy can alone ascertain and elucidate.[56]

Although they did not accept such 'Scotch' doctrines in their entirety, even Englishmen had to come to terms with the fundamental requirements of a commercial society. The impetus provided by the successors of Adam Smith was an important element in the development of British economic thought.

[52] W. D. Grampp, 'Scots, Jews and Subversives among the Dismal Scientists', *Journal of Economic History* (1976), 545-7.

[53] Garnett (ed.), *Novels of Peacock*, 31. It may be noted that *Headlong Hall* was set in Snowdonia and that Peacock was married to a Welshwoman.

[54] D. P. O'Brien, *J. R. McCulloch: A Study in Classical Economics* (1970).

[55] M'Turk, 'Scotsmen in London', 323-4.

[56] Cited by B. Fontana, *Rethinking the Politics of Commercial Society: The Edinburgh Review, 1802-1832* (Cambridge, 1985), 109-10.

Both in general and in particular disciplines the world of nineteenth-century science also offers a series of Anglo-Scottish encounters, not all of them harmonious. In the first place, the organization of the 'age of science' had to be attended to. In the late 1820s, a number of English and Scottish scientists saw the need for 'a new Association to stir up the slumbering spirit of British science.'[57] The Royal Society of London was judged to be 'gone', and the condition of its Edinburgh counterpart was little better. David Brewster wrote from Melrose in February 1831 urging that 'the cause of science in England would derive great benefit from a meeting of British men of science.'[58] The obvious place for a meeting, as he wrote to the Secretary of the Yorkshire Philosophical Society, was York—'as the most centrical city for the three kingdoms.'[59] If there was to be a truly British Association for the Advancement of Science, its inauguration should not take place in either Edinburgh or London. The meeting duly took place in September 1831 and the new body was launched. 'I think a larger admixture of southern stars with such a galaxy of northern lights would have added to the splendour of the occasion,' William Buckland wrote from Oxford, but he presumed that at the next meeting to be held in Oxford the proportions would be reversed.[60] Before the Association met again in York, in 1844, it had gathered in Oxford, Cambridge, Edinburgh, Bristol, Liverpool, Newcastle, Birmingham, Glasgow, Plymouth, and Manchester, together with two meetings in Ireland. Such a rotation was not a diplomatic exercise. It reflected the fact that 'Science' was creating a new British balance.

Early in the nineteenth century, it was still commonly supposed that in 'Science', Scotland held the British lead. The work of Joseph Black in the previous century had given Edinburgh and Glasgow universities a high reputation in the field of chemistry. Classes of 500 students were not uncommon in this subject. In Edinburgh, however, chemistry was taught solely through lectures. Practical classes failed.[61] That was not a happy augury for the

---

[57] J. Morrell and A. Thackray (eds.), *Gentlemen of Science: Early Correspondence of the British Association for the Advancement of Science*, Camden Fourth Series, 30 (1984), 129.

[58] Ibid. 33.

[59] Ibid. 34.

[60] Ibid. 79.

[61] D. S. L. Cardwell, *The Organization of Science in England* (1972), 32–3.

development of research. Even so, the belief in northern supremacy attracted Englishmen to Scotland. Among them was Charles Darwin, but he was disappointed with what he found. With the sole exception of T. C. Hope's chemistry lectures in 1825, instruction by this means was 'intolerably dull'. It was much better to read than to go to lectures, though he told his father that 'all the Scotchmen are so civil and attentive, that it is enough to make an Englishman ashamed of himself.'[62] Charles and Erasmus Darwin borrowed more books from Edinburgh University Library than any other students! Glasgow students amazed Erasmus. They actually played at football within the precincts of the college: 'you never did see such a set since you was born & please God never again.'[63]

The reaction of the Darwins throws some light on the Anglo-Scottish tensions which were never far below the surface in Victorian science. Englishmen recognized in the Scots, a little disparagingly, a great capacity for collecting, compiling and listing, whether rocks, plants, or animals. It is perhaps no accident that it was Carlyle who defined genius as 'a transcendent capacity of taking trouble'. On this definition, there were many scientific men of genius in Scotland. In this light, it comes as no surprise to find that the author of a *History of Classifications of the Sciences* (1904) was the painstaking Robert Flint of Edinburgh. Scotsmen, on the other hand, considered English scientists less well-grounded in their general intellectual formation, though they could grudgingly admit that what was called English flare and imagination could penetrate more swiftly to the heart of a problem.

It is, of course, difficult to measure scientific distinction with any accuracy, though one writer sees the period from 1830 to 1870 as the 'Golden Age' of Scottish scientific discovery. Scottish Fellows of the Royal Society of London 'peaked' during roughly this period.[64] Even to make that assertion, however, runs at once into the familiar difficulty of defining a 'Scottish scientist'. William Thomson, later Lord Kelvin, was an Ulsterman, but he was elected to the Chair of

[62] G. de Beer (ed.), *Charles Darwin: Thomas Huxley: Autobiographies* (1974), 25–8. The scientific establishment of England did not take seriously Robert Chambers's *Vestiges of the Natural History of Creation*.

[63] F. Burkhardt and S. Smith (eds.), *The Correspondence of Charles Darwin*, 1 (Cambridge, 1985), 18, 33.

[64] A. G. Clement and R. H. S. Robertson, *Scotland's Scientific Heritage* (Edinburgh and London, 1961), 124–7.

Natural Philosophy at Glasgow in 1846 at the age of 22 and remained in that university for the rest of his career, publishing in the fields of electromagnetism and thermodynamics. It would not be wrong to call him in his time 'the doyen of British physicists'. James Clerk Maxwell, on the other hand, arguably an even greater physicist, divided his time between Cambridge and his Scottish estate, with intervals in Aberdeen and London. Although always a very independent mind, his career and contacts rendered the Border insignificant.[65]

Among lesser figures, the scientific drift southwards was a constant feature. An examination of science in Victorian Manchester, for example, discloses the existence of a remarkably high number of Scottish names in the city's scientific and technical institutions.[66] Young men who had studied in Glasgow (either at the university or at the Andersonian) saw and took opportunities for themselves in the cotton industry in Lancashire. By the 1830s, it looks as though a strong nexus of personal connections had been established to facilitate this process. The supply of Scots diminished in the mid-century period, but it had proved a vital element in that region's industrial progress. It comes as no surprise to find William Jack as Professor at the new Owens College in Manchester, until he returned to Glasgow to edit the *Glasgow Herald*. That such a switch of career was possible was taken to confirm Scottish versatility.

The functioning of this informal scientific network depended on the ability of certain individuals to operate acceptably north and south of the Border. Lyon Playfair was perhaps the most conspicuous of such figures. After St Andrews University, he studied medicine at Glasgow and Edinburgh before pursuing research in chemistry in Germany. Elected to the London Royal Society at an early age, he had a spectacular career in London in the scientific circle around the Prince Consort. He returned to Edinburgh as Professor of Chemistry in 1858 and became one of the Scottish University MPs a decade later. There were few educational or scientific issues which did not come to Playfair's attention. He formed an admirable go-between, keeping himself abreast of both English and Scottish developments to an unusual extent. He helped

[65] D. M. Knight, *The Age of Science* (Oxford, 1986), 173-5.
[66] R. H. Kargon, *Science in Victorian Manchester: Enterprise and Expertise* (Manchester, 1977), 100.

to keep 'British Science' together, although well aware of the difficulties that existed in such fields as geology or medicine.[67]

In an essay in 1871, Sir Archibald Geikie discussed 'The Scottish School of Geology' and argued that James Hutton and his friends in Edinburgh laid the foundations of modern British geology.[68] Dr Porter has identified three respects in which he believes geology in Scotland differed from geology in England: it was a socially homeogenous profession, in practice confined to Edinburgh; it possessed an overriding concern with utility; it saw 'the natural history of the mineral kingdom' as set within a 'philosophy of natural history'. Scottish earth scientists were teaching professors, whereas geology in England emerged from traditions of local amateur observation. Ironically, Porter argues that Hutton himself was not typical of the Scottish approach.[69] It has also been noted that the 'English School' was dominated by clerical academics— Buckland, Conybeare, Sedgwick, and Whewell. It is not surprising that they were more concerned about the relationship between geological discovery and the authority of the Bible than were the Scots. The bitter dispute in Edinburgh between Huttonians and Wernerians had, however, no English parallel. Indeed, Conybeare wrote scornfully of the 'excessive addiction to the theoretical speculations' among the Scots. Their enthusiasm in this respect had, he believed, led to their falling 'far behind the schools of London and Oxford', though such self-evaluations need to be treated carefully.[70]

There is no need, however, to stick too rigidly to the notion of an 'English School' and a 'Scottish School'. Charles Lyell, whose *Principles of Geology* (1830-3) constituted an important stage in the development of geology, was a Scot by descent, though English to outward appearance. One English critic complained that his work contained 'much Scotch amplification. A Scotchman can never write briefly and directly to the point.' The Scottish geologists, however, scarcely recognized Lyell as one of their own.[71]

[67] W. Reid, *Memoirs and Correspondence of Lyon Playfair, First Lord Playfair of St Andrews* (1899).

[68] A. Geikie, *A Long Life's Work: An Autobiography* (1924).

[69] R. Porter, *The Making of Geology* (Cambridge, 1977), 149-56.

[70] Cited by N. A. Rupke, *The Great Chain of History: William Buckland and the English School of Geology* (Oxford, 1983), 16.

[71] L. G. Wilson, *Charles Lyell: The Years to 1841: The Revolution in Geology* (New Haven and London, 1972); Cited by Rupke *Great Chain of History*, 190.

The Geological Survey of Great Britain was for many years in the hands of the Glasgow-born Sir Andrew Ramsay. Based in England, Ramsay visited his staff north of the Border each year and, amongst other things, reminisced about his native country. In 1867, however, the decision was taken that, for geological purposes, Great Britain was to be divided into two. Sir Archibald Geikie took charge of Scotland. Ramsay himself retained England—and Wales, for by this time he had married a Welsh wife, learned a little Welsh, and was captivated by the view of Snowdonia from his home in Beaumaris.[72] Snowdonia, inevitably, came to fascinate Adam Sedgwick and numerous other contemporary geologists.[73] Whatever theoretical interpretations the scientists might want to place upon their discoveries, the geological foundations of Britain as a whole were becoming more comprehensively known than ever before.

In the first half of the century, it has been calculated that almost 95 per cent of British doctors with medical degrees had been educated in Scotland. In no other field of knowledge did Scotland exercise such domination. This position was, in large measure, a calculated exploitation of a gap in the British market. It was not until 1821 that the first of the new London medical schools started teaching. The number of registered medical students in 1815 at Edinburgh and Glasgow universities reached peaks of 820 and 232 respectively. There was then some numerical decline in mid-century, followed by a strong recovery to 2,000 and 800 respectively in 1890. There were also substantial numbers of extramural medical students in both cities, and smaller medical schools at Aberdeen and St Andrews.[74] In the 1830s and 1840s, approximately half of Edinburgh's medical graduates came from Scotland, one-third from England and the rest from 'the colonies'.[75] The medical services of the British forces were dominated by Scotsmen for most of the century. Amongst the successors of Thomas Alexander as Directors-General of the Army Medical Department were Sir Thomas Galbraith Logan, Sir William Muir, Sir Thomas Crawford, Sir William McKinnon, and Sir James Cantlie. The Indian and Colonial Medical Services were also well-stocked with Scots. Sir

[72] A. Geikie, *Memoir of Sir Andrew Crombie Ramsay* (1895).
[73] Charles Darwin spent many happy hours examining the rocks in Cwm Idwal and published his observations on them.
[74] D. Hamilton, *The Healers: A History of Medicine in Scotland* (Edinburgh, 1981), 140.
[75] A. J. Youngson, *The Scientific Revolution in Victorian Medicine* (1979), 57.

Patrick Manson, 'the father of tropical medicine', was an Aberdonian born and educated.[76] Sir Andrew Balfour, Sir David Bruce, and Sir William Leishman were scarcely less-distinguished figures in this field. Drs W. G. Grace, Barnardo, and Arthur Conan Doyle had all received an Edinburgh medical training, though their fame derived from other activities.

Yet, despite this prominence and the widespread belief in Scottish medical prowess, the reality was more complicated, particularly after the half century. Part of the problem stemmed from success. In the 1840s, for example, the Edinburgh surgeon Syme, and the pioneering anaesthetist and obstetrician Simpson, were so outstanding that they attracted patients from England.[77] The major tendency, however, was for surgeons to move south rather than for patients to come north. Financial rewards were greater elsewhere, though Edinburgh doctors were never notably poor. 'An eminent surgeon', wrote Sir Charles Bell, the great neurologist, from London to his former Edinburgh colleagues, 'is received by the first people in a manner most flattering and which I fear, obtains nowhere else. . . . Yestreen I sat between the Chancellor of the Exchequer, the Vice-Chancellor, Sir H. Halford, etc. Can you place me so in Auld Reekie?'[78] In addition to social forces, the standard of English medical education was steadily improving under such men as Richard Bright at Guy's—Bright had originally been trained at Edinburgh.[79] The proportion of Fellows of the Royal College of Physicians with Scottish medical degrees, which was in the 40 per cent band in the decades from 1840 to 1870, dropped to just over 20 per cent in the decade which ended in 1889. The percentage with London degrees rose from under 3 per cent in the 1840s to 32 per cent in the 1880s. A broadly comparable change was also occurring in the education of Fellows of the Royal College of Surgeons.[80]

Nevertheless, the Scottish medical presence, at all levels, continued to be extraordinarily high in England, particularly in the

[76] R. Manson-Bahr, *Patrick Manson: The Father of Tropical Medicine* (Edinburgh, 1962).

[77] J. A. Shepherd, *Simpson and Syme of Edinburgh* (Edinburgh, 1969), 70–1.

[78] G. Gordon-Taylor and E. W. Walls, *Sir Charles Bell: His Life and Times* (Edinburgh, 1958), 150–1.

[79] P. Bright, *Dr Richard Bright* (1983).

[80] M. J. Patterson, *The Medical Profession in Mid-Victorian London* (1978), 50–1, 67.

expanding provincial hospitals.[81] It was sometimes suggested that English medicine profoundly benefited from that Scottish presence in England: different styles and approaches could fruitfully blend to achieve important advances. The problem was that the cross-fertilization of ideas rarely worked in the opposite direction. In a city like Glasgow, for example, the local medical corps was locally trained by men who had themselves been locally trained. It was rare indeed to find a medical 'incomer' from south of the Border.[82] Of course, there were a few outstanding exceptions, most notably Lister, though his appointment had initially been controversial. There was some irony, therefore, in the fact that Lister worked in Scotland for so long, from 1852 to 1877, that he came to be identified in England with 'Scottish medicine'. It may be that Lister moved from Edinburgh to London in 1877 because he felt that only by doing so could he persuade London surgeons to adopt the antiseptic treatment.[83] An additional problem, as medicine became steadily more 'scientific' and equipment more complex and expensive, was that the structural deficiencies in the organization of Scottish medical education became more apparent. The Scottish cause was also not helped by a massive disposition to exhausting litigation—particularly in Glasgow between the university and the Faculty of Physicians and Surgeons. It appeared increasingly that the necessary additional financial resources could only come from the state, but the state was British and might make conditions.

Anglo-Scottish medical tensions were not difficult to detect. The 1815 Apothecaries Act, for example, had caused strong resentment in Scotland. Scottish universities and faculties had not been consulted in its drafting. The difficulty was that, whereas Scots had been used to sending well-qualified surgeon-apothecaries or MD graduates to England, where their qualifications had been accepted, the new act required them to serve another formal apprenticeship in London. The *Edinburgh Medical and Surgical Journal* bitterly

[81] W. J. Ellwood and A. F. Tuxford (eds.), *Some Manchester Doctors: A Biographical Collection* (Manchester, 1984); Chitnis, *Scottish Enlightenment*, 148–63, gives details of the role of medical Scots in northern English cities. See also J. B. Morrell, 'Science in Manchester and the University of Edinburgh', in D. S. L. Cardwell (ed.), *Artisan to Graduate: Essays to Commemorate the Foundation in 1824 of the Manchester Mechanics' Institution . . .* (Manchester, 1974).

[82] M. Lamb, 'The Medical Profession', in O. Checkland and M. Lamb (eds.), *Health Care as Social History: The Glasgow Case* (Aberdeen, 1982), 36.

[83] Youngson, *Scientific Revolution*, 189–90.

criticized the Royal College of Physicians in London, claiming to detect 'a deep, fixed, and determined hatred of the Scottish Universities, and every one who avails himself of their means of instruction.'[84] There were also problems in the broad area of public health and welfare. Disputes concerning procedure frequently meant that Scottish legislation lagged behind that south of the Border. The 1848 Public Health (Scotland) Bill, for example, would have treated Scotland simply as a part of the United Kingdom, with responsibility resting with the Central Board of Health in London. That was too much for the Royal College of Physicians in Edinburgh. It professed 'a high respect' for individual members of the London Board. Sadly, however, these members were wrong in their opinions concerning the diffusion of epidemic diseases, and Edinburgh had no confidence in any measures they might propose for Scotland.[85] The bill was abandoned and, for a time, the 'big six' Scottish cities used private bills of their own to deal with public health matters.

The 1858 Medical Act set up a General Council for Medical Education and Registration, responsible to the Privy Council. It provided for a branch council in Scotland. Medical unity on a British basis was also helped by the fact that, by this juncture, the British Medical Association had become firmly established as the mouthpiece of the profession. Charles Hastings had started the Provincial Medical Association in 1832 in Worcester and by the end of the decade it had united with the Glasgow Medical Association and bodies in the North of England to form the British Medical Association.[86] Initially, however, Scottish branches were not to the fore, and some feeling remained that English doctors did not grasp the complexity of the Scottish context or, if they did grasp it, felt that it ought to be simplified.

One simplification which occurred to some minds was to end the Scottish legal system. It was contended that its continued existence caused so many complications and such duplication of effort, particularly in public health and educational matters, that the sooner it withered away the better. There had always been a body of opinion, chiefly in England, which had considered it anomalous

[84] Cited by Hamilton, *Healers*, 164.
[85] Ibid. 201.
[86] P. Vaughan, *Doctors' Commons: A Short History of the British Medical Association* (1959).

that a unitary state should embrace two legal systems. It would be simpler if English Common Law prevailed throughout Britain. On the other hand, the Scottish legal system was protected under the Act of Union and a direct assault on its status was not politically plausible. In any case, there were some, even in England, who saw benefits in the status quo. 'I have no doubt', wrote F. W. Maitland to Henry Sidgwick in 1888, 'that Scotch experience has improved English law and English experience Scotch law ... On the whole I have been surprised to find how little harm is done by differences between Scotch and English law.'[87] Whatever the truth of this contention, the long-term future of Scots Law was in doubt, for three main reasons. First, by mid-century, there were increasing complaints against the actual administration of justice in Scotland. That was accompanied by the claim in some quarters that 'The fitness of Scotch laws to the Scotch people has scarcely ever been less than at present.' Businessmen, particularly in the West of Scotland, complained about shortcomings in mercantile law, particularly regarding bankruptcy, and urged the advantages of assimilation to English practice.[88] It had also not escaped their notice that Scots Law and Edinburgh lawyers went together. On the other hand, there was a view that in certain other respects Scots Law benefited business. Second, however, it was undoubtedly proving difficult to refresh and develop the sources on which the legal system drew. Legal development was not a task to which the best minds devoted themselves and the defence of what had been inherited against the encroachments of English law was coming to seem a sterile and probably ultimately futile occupation.[89] Third, the attractions of a legal career in England steadily mounted for ambitious men. They bypassed Scots Law altogether and were not averse to creating the impression that those who stayed within the native system were conservative and second-rate, perpetuating an increasingly obsolescent but comfortably enclosed career. Going to London to study law was relatively rare in the eighteenth century. In the nineteenth, for every three Scots who joined the Scottish Faculty of Advocates, two entered one of the London Inns of

[87] C. H. S. Fifoot (ed.), *The Letters of Frederic William Maitland* (Cambridge, 1965), 51.

[88] Hutchison, *Political History of Scotland*, 93–5.

[89] D. M. Walker, *The Scottish Legal System* (Edinburgh, 1981) is the standard authority.

Court.[90] 'Giving evidence of the profoundest abilities in Scotland', declared one of the more egregious Scots to become Lord Chancellor of Great Britain, 'is like a flower wasting its fragance in the desert, or a gem sparkling at the bottom of the ocean, whose lustre is marked only by the stupid inhabitants of the deep.'[91] It may merely be remarked that Lord Campbell did not reach his high office until he attained his eighty-fifth year. The sentiments he expressed, however, help to explain why the Scottish legal system, though it survived, was in a somewhat dubious mental condition.

The moulders of the British mind in the nineteenth century would have had little impact without the ability to correspond with each other and their readers through the post on the one hand, and to publish their articles and books on the other. We read that per capita deliveries of letters in England and Wales grew steadily: four in 1839, eight in 1840, thirty-two in 1871, and sixty in 1900.[92] Mid-Victorians supposed that the true civilization of a people could be gauged by the amount of its correspondence. It has been neatly suggested that Rowland Hill's 'unrestricted circulation of letters' was designed 'to replace the patchwork of private communities by a network of communicating individuals.'[93] It was still the case in the mid-century—in northern mill-towns, for example—that most information was exchanged through conversation, but major towns began to generate substantial internal mail. At the time of the introduction of Penny Post both Radicals and Conservatives, from their different standpoints, had reason to be alarmed about the privacy of the individual and the security of the state. Families and friends could henceforth maintain contact relatively cheaply over large distances. The 1900 Union Postale Universelle statistics showed that, per head, only Americans sent more letters than the British. In 1850, United Kingdom letter deliveries were shared out in the following percentages: London (inland, foreign, and district) 24.7; remainder of England and Wales 55.6; Scotland 10.1, and

---

[90] P. S. Lachs, 'Scottish Legal Education in the Nineteenth Century', in E. W. Ives and A. H. Manchester (eds.), *Law, Litigants and the Legal Profession* (1983), 156.
[91] Cited by R. F. V. Heuston, *Lives of the Lord Chancellors, 1885–1940* (Oxford, 1964).
[92] D. Vincent, 'Communication, Community and the State', in Emsley and Walvin (eds.), *Artisans, Peasants and Proletarians* (1985), 167.
[93] Ibid. 169.

Ireland 9.6. In 1910, the comparable percentages were 24.1, 60.9, 9.4, and 5.5.[94]

It is not easy to assess the consequences of this flow of correspondence. It is difficult to resist the conclusion that it was a means of promoting a sense of British identity and keeping minds in touch with one another. It has been noted that the Post Office was one of the few agencies which possessed a complete British coverage, from John-o'Groat's to Land's End. Only the Army and Navy equalled the reach of the Royal Mail. It also meant that, if they so wished, individuals who migrated within Britain could still maintain contact with their families and home communities.

There was nothing anonymous, however, about the communication across the country provided by newspapers, the periodical press, and books. When it came to purveying knowledge in nineteenth-century Britain Scotsmen stood supreme. When the writer T. W. H. Crosland considered that the time had come for 'the Scotsman to be taught his place', he started with the suggestion that 'to rid the Press of his influence would be an excellent thing for the Press.' It was wrong that 'every newspaper one picks up should contain certificates of character for the Scotch.'[95] Crosland was not a man to show restraint—and he was to suffer the unspeakable fate of having his own biography written by one of the unspeakable Scots—but he could have talked about the Scottish role in the general area of publishing as well.[96]

In the world of journalism, the Edwardian venom of Crosland was particularly directed against Robertson Nicoll, editor, amongst other roles, of the *British Weekly*. Nicoll's various styles—Revd, Dr, Sir—could be tributes to his expertise in devotional literature, detective stories, and in selling the *British Weekly* respectively. Nicoll, however, was only the latest in a long line. Bagehot thought that Scottish education was deliberately designed to train men to write authoritative articles or leaders. He exaggerated, but even in his day there was nothing new about the Scottish 'scribbler'. John Gross points out that the first editors of the *Spectator*, the *Economist*, and the *Saturday Review* were all Scotsmen.[97] The *Edinburgh*

---

[94] M. J. Daunton, *Royal Mail: The Post Office since 1840* (1985), 46, 80, 271.

[95] T. W. H. Crosland, *The Unspeakable Scot* (1912), 191–2.

[96] W. S. Brown, *The Life and Genius of T. W. H. Crosland* (1928).

[97] J. Gross, *The Rise and Fall of the Man of Letters: English Literary Life since 1800* (1969).

*Review*, founded in 1802 with Francis Jeffrey as editor, spread its influence in subsequent decades far beyond the Scottish capital. *Blackwood's Edinburgh Review* (1817) was the riposte of another Edinburgh publisher, and there later followed Chambers's *Edinburgh Journal* (1832). William Cobbett early developed 'a sneaking kindness' for the Edinburgh men as they lashed the 'boobies and bastards' in the South, but it occurred to him that they wished to 'fasten *themselves* upon us' and reluctantly concluded that the existing boobies and bastards were 'likely to suck our blood less unmercifully than those northern leeches would.'[98] The *London Magazine* was explicitly founded as the capital's counterblast against journals emanating from what it called 'secondary towns of the Kingdom'. It was a trifle awkward that its first editor, John Scott, hailed from Aberdeen.[99] Nicoll also came from Aberdeenshire and it was thought in some quarters that Grampian soil was the essential starting-point for a career in London journalism.[1]

Scotsmen were to be found in Fleet Street and in newspaper offices all over the provinces. Charles Dickens found himself virtually the sole Englishman when he began work on the *Morning Chronicle*. Its editor, John Black, surrounded himself with his fellow-countrymen for safety. John Jaffray started the *Birmingham Daily Post*; D. S. Macliver started the *Western Daily Press* in Bristol; Thomas Graham began the *Wolverhampton Evening Star*; these are but a few of the energetic newspaper Scotsmen.[2] Samuel Smiles, urged by his friends to leave Scotland and accept a good opening as a general practitioner in Doncaster, was diverted *en route* into accepting the editorship of the *Leeds Times*. He had learned that the proprietor wished to replace the retiring editor, Robert Nicoll, 'with another Scotsman'.[3] Although no systematic study of this northern penetration exists, Lee's study of the popular press refers to Scotland providing 'an altogether disproportionate part of the personnel of English journalism.' By inference, he explains this fact

[98] Cited by J. Clive, *Scotch Reviewers: The 'Edinburgh Review', 1802–1815* (1957), 86.

[99] J. Bauer, *The London Magazine, 1820–1829* (Copenhagen, 1953).

[1] T. H. Darlow, *William Robertson Nicoll: Life and Letters* (1925); W. Donaldson, *Popular Literature in Victorian Scotland: Language, Fiction and the Press* (Aberdeen, 1986).

[2] A. J. Lee, *The Origins of the Popular Press, 1855–1914* (1976), 141–4.

[3] T. Mackay (ed.), *The Autobiography of Samuel Smiles* (1905), 85; P. R. Drummond, *The Life of Robert Nicoll* (Perth, 1884).

by suggesting that Scotland was 'for long better educated and more democratic than England'—an explanation perhaps vitiated by the fact that there was a 'disproportionate' Irish presence too.[4] The movement was largely, but not entirely, in one direction. The Hull-born Charles Cooper became the first London correspondent appointed by *The Scotsman* and he later became the paper's editor.[5] For many years, the editor of the Aberystwyth-based *Cambrian News* was an Englishman. Such men, however, were exceptional.

The personnel of the industry, however, is only one aspect of the question. How and to what degree the press moulded a 'British mind' is more difficult to determine. The young David Lloyd George tramped fourteen miles to Porthmadog and back to get a London newspaper which contained Gladstone's Midlothian speeches in full. There could be no more apt illustration of a 'British' experience. Central Scotland and North Wales were linked via London.[6] The steady penetration of a 'national', that is to say a London-based, press was one of the features of the nineteenth century. Lucy Brown notes, for example, that the London papers, the *Daily Telegraph* and the *Standard* had greater sales in the Bradford of 1868 than any other paper except the *Leeds Mercury*. Manchester papers also had some sales, but they were the only 'provincial' competition.[7] Some provincial papers could dominate whole regions and make energetic efforts to expand circulation— the *Liverpool Daily Post* prepared a weekly edition for North Wales. For a time, the *Newcastle Daily Chronicle* was able to flourish in Middlesbrough, Stockton, and Darlington because it arrived in these towns by an earlier train than that from London.

Although sampling is notoriously difficult, the London press did not in general seek to include substantial 'provincial' material. Dr Brown suggests that this is true of *The Times* in the 1890s. In the last quarter of 1894, for instance, *The Times* made five references to Birmingham and Manchester, and three to Belfast, but there was no mention of any event in Bristol, Nottingham, Plymouth, Sheffield, or Glasgow.[8] On the other hand, as compared with its previous

[4] Lee, *Popular Press*, 20. A well-known Merseyside Irishman expressed the view that 'We Garvins are in our nature Northerners and flourish better in the cold weather than the hot,' D. G. Ayerst, *Garvin of the 'Observer'* (1985), 3.

[5] C. Cooper, *An Editor's Retrospect* (1896).

[6] S. Koss, *The Rise and Fall of the Provincial Press in Britain*, vol. i (1981), 214n.

[7] L. Brown, *Victorian News and Newspapers* (1985), 41.

[8] Ibid. 258–61.

indifference, the *Standard* had developed a regular news column entitled 'The Provinces'. Provincial news in its estimation, was part of a 'national' newspaper's equipment. But that was not the view, for example, of the *Daily Telegraph*. London newspapers did not establish offices in Manchester or Glasgow until the 1900s, though individuals acted as correspondents for them—Professor Dunbar of Edinburgh for *The Times* and George Combe for the *Courier*.[9]

From the opposite perspective, when the *Scotsman* opened its London office in 1863 it was the first 'provincial' paper to do so. In Edinburgh at about the same date, its news was being received by special telegraph wire. By the 1880s the paper could contain as many as twenty-five columns which had been telegraphed from London during the previous night.[10] Scottish papers had successfully battled alongside their provincial English colleagues to obtain more adequate representation in the parliamentary Press Gallery. Major Scottish newspapers like the *Scotsman* or the *Glasgow Herald* had little doubt that they could withstand the English challenge. They could even, on occasion, overcome political and inter-city rivalries to state a 'Scottish' case when that seemed important. In turn, by the end of the century, their comments on 'British' issues, thanks largely to the telegraph, were far less dependent upon second-hand information gleaned from the London press itself—and sometimes printed with scant acknowledgement of the source!

The 'newspaper revolution', however, was not entirely an Anglo-Scottish affair. Repeal of the 'taxes on knowledge', followed by Gladstone's repeal of paper duties produced what Gwyn A. Williams calls 'an explosion into print'—newspapers, magazines, and quarterlies in both languages flooded across Wales, extended into England and even to Welshmen across the Atlantic.[11] In the Welsh language in the 1890s there were published two quarterlies, two bi-monthlies, twenty-eight monthlies, and twenty-five newspapers.[12] They stimulated an indigenous discussion and debate which was 'national' in character. Yet, at the same time, because newspapers flourished in such small towns as Caernarfon, Denbigh, Carmarthen, and Brecon, debate was also highly 'provincial'. In a

[9] R. M. W. Cowan, *The Newspaper in Scotland* (Glasgow, 1946), 134–5.

[10] *The Glorious Privilege: The History of 'The Scotsman'* (Edinburgh, 1967) 42–6.

[11] G. A. Williams *When was Wales?* (1985), 215.

[12] D. Lleufer Thomas, 'Bibliographical, Statistical, and other Miscellaneous Memoranda', *Report of the Royal Commission on Land in Wales and Monmouthshire* (1896), App. C, pp. 195–7.

country that lacked a capital, regional cacophony was perhaps inescapable. It was, however, a press which in tone was more authentically 'Welsh' than it had been in the 1820s when, surprisingly, the Seventh Earl of Shaftesbury helped to found the *Cambrian Quarterly*. On the strength of some weeks spent in Aberystwyth he expressed in its columns an editorial determination 'to save our poets from night, our manuscripts from the flames and our venerable tongue from contempt.' This short-lived journal was published in London. So, in 1911, was the new journal *Wales* which was distributed to readers in the principality from England. The history of these two enterprises encapsulates the wider point: in the very act of supporting individuality they drew attention to integration.[13]

A comparable paradox existed in the world of books. From the early nineteenth century, Scottish publishers had been in the forefront of their trade, dealing in encyclopaedias, biographies, novels, and textbooks for the British and English-language foreign markets. The standard of Edinburgh printing was also extremely high, with substantial London contracts.[14] Among the most notable names of this period are A. & C. Black, Blackwoods, and Constables. William Collins expanded his business from Glasgow as did the Blackies. The latter enterprisingly started publishing Welsh-language books in the 1860s[15] In addition, some Scotsmen, among them the founders of John Murray and Macmillans, started their businesses in the South. By the mid-century, however, a London office had come to be deemed essential by the Scottish publishers—Blackwood in 1840 and Blackie in 1837, for example. But was that sufficient for commercial needs? Adam W. Black took the view in 1889 that the company's future would be better assured from the centre of the publishing trade, that is to say from London. If it remained in the North it would be in danger of running down.[16] And, in the decades that were to come, most of that generation of Scottish publishers did either move down or see their business run down. It seemed that, in the last analysis, even the moulding of the mind could not be exempt from the manipulation of the market.

[13] Sullivan, *British Literary Magazines*, 88–93, 447–50.
[14] The *Encyclopaedia Britannica* was first published in Edinburgh in 1768–71. See the section on printing and publishing in J. Mackinnon, *The Social and Industrial History of Scotland from the Union to the Present Time* (1921), 205–12; C. Clair, *A History of Printing in Britain* (1965), 248–9.
[15] Keir, *Collins* (1952); A. Blackie, *Blackie and Son, 1809–1959* (Glasgow, n.d.), 25.
[16] *Adam and Charles Black, 1807–1957* (1957), 50.

# 6

## Sport, Patriotism, and the Will to Win

The emergence of 'sport' in its modern form in the 1860s had unexpected consequences for the maintenance and reinforcement of national and regional loyalties within Britain. It did not prove an easy matter, in particular games, to establish 'leagues' or to decide whether they should seek to embrace the entire country in a single competitive framework. The tensions which have become familiar in other contexts reappeared in the world of sport. It proved difficult to strike a balance both between north and south within the 'home' countries and between England, Scotland, and Wales. Sport and patriotism were indeed linked, but not in a straightforward fashion. Many contemporary schoolmasters saw a clear link between the sports-field and the field of battle. 'Team spirit' was a sign that in a crisis the nation would pull together. 'Games in which success depends on the united efforts of many, and which also foster courage and endurance are the very life-blood of the public school system,' wrote Hely Hutchinson Almond, Headmaster of Loretto in the 1890s. Praising Rugby football, he feared that self-indulgent games would 'cause public schools to fail in their main object, which was taken to be the production of a grand breed of men for the service of the "British nation".'[1] Paradoxically, however, our discussion of the sporting life makes it clear that it divided as much as it united the 'British nation'.

The progress of 'Association football' in the latter decades of the century was almost invariably attended by controversy. There was disagreement both about the rules of the game and about its appropriate organization. It would be wrong to interpret these disagreements as simply a further manifestation of rivalry, within England, between North and South, nevertheless that rivalry was certainly present. In London and the South of England there was,

---

[1] Cited by J. A. Mangan, *Athleticism in the Victorian and Edwardian Public Schools* (Cambridge, 1981), 56; B. Haley, *The Healthy Body and Victorian Culture* (Cambridge, Mass., 1978).

initially, fierce resistance to professional players and clubs.[2] Attempts were made to 'outlaw' them. As a result, it was in the Midlands and the North of England that the Football League flourished. For example, in the season 1892-3, of the twenty-eight clubs in the First and Second Divisions, ten were situated in Lancashire, six in Staffordshire, two each in Warwickshire, Yorkshire, Lincolnshire, Cheshire, and Nottinghamshire, and one each in Durham and Derbyshire. At this juncture, it was scarcely a 'national' game in which the fortunes of particular teams were followed across England. By the end of the century, however, professionalism had made great strides in the South of England, though clubs there, with a few exceptions like Arsenal and Bristol City, played in a separate Southern League. 'The tendency is in the direction of a national League', wrote one commentator in 1905, 'but this is more likely to come by evolution than revolution.'[3] So, eventually, it proved, though the process of integration was tortuous.

Clubs from the Football League and the Southern League did, however, compete in the Football Association Cup but that, too, proved difficult to organize. The headquarters of the Football Association was in London. The Association was determined that the Cup Final should be played in London, despite the fact that clubs from the North of England tended to dominate the competition. Surrey County Cricket Club, for a time, made their pitch at Kennington Oval available for the final, but were somewhat distressed by the consequences of their hospitality. In 1893 and 1894 the Cup Final took place in Manchester and Liverpool respectively, but the FA was not happy with this arrangement. From 1895 until the First World War the final was staged in the South at the Crystal Palace.

Although there were 'difficulties', Association football did manage to avoid the division between North and South becoming so serious that two separate games emerged. That fate befell Rugby football. It was in 1895 that twenty-one northern Rugby clubs, unable to persuade the game's southern-based English ruling body that players should be compensated for money lost by taking time off from work to play the game, decided to go their independent

[2] T. Mason, *Association Football and English Society, 1863-1915* (Brighton, 1979).
[3] Cited by J. Arlott (ed.), *The Oxford Companion to Sports and Games* (Oxford, 1975), 343.

way. The Northern Union—the title Rugby Football League was not adopted until 1922—flourished in the North of England as its title explicitly indicates. There were some attempts to establish the new professional game in the Midlands and in South Wales, but they were not very successful. The actual rules of the game came to diverge significantly from those of Rugby Union. The Northern Union game seemed very exotic to those southerners who ever encountered it. Of course, the Northern Union did not capture the North of England entirely, and Rugby Union clubs re-established themselves in the region, but the game's appeal in the small towns of Lancashire and Yorkshire was an expression of distinctiveness.

In the two most widespread winter games in England, therefore, no coherent, universally accepted 'English national' framework existed, though signs pointed in that direction. It was clear, on the other hand, both in Association football and Rugby Union that leagues and competitions would not be organized on a 'British national' basis. There was, however, nothing inevitable about this outcome. Events could have taken a different turn. For example, the first Scottish football club, Queen's Park in Glasgow, formed in 1867, contributed one-sixth of its annual income—one guinea—towards the Football Association's expenses in purchasing the Cup Trophy. When it was first competed for, in 1870, Queen's Park FC travelled down to take part. They drew their semi-final tie in London, but could not afford to travel for the replay and had to scratch. A 'British' competition was not inherently implausible, but, at this juncture, distance and expense rendered it unlikely. In addition, resistance to professionalism in the game continued longer in Scotland than it did in England. Partly for this reason, the Scottish Football League was not formed until 1890. Thereafter, the game flourished in Scotland, though the distribution of the country's population made it difficult to prevent success being restricted to a small number of clubs. Rugby Union also came to Scotland and developed a particularly strong following in the small towns of the Borders. Their success gave Scottish Rugby a somewhat different social tone from that which prevailed in England.

The winter games likewise penetrated into Wales, though again in a somewhat lop-sided fashion. For reasons that are not immediately apparent, it was Rugby football, a more 'gentlemanly' game, at least in southern England, that caught the imagination and enthusiasm of players in South Wales, many of whom were not gentlemen. Skill at Rugby rapidly came to be thought a 'Welsh' characteristic, but in fact the game did not catch on to a similar degree in North Wales—it may have been mining rather than Celtic blood which linked Rugby men from South Wales with those of Cornwall. In North-East Wales it was Association football that became the popular game. Inevitably, therefore, the regional nature of their support posed problems for the organizers and players of both games. Ambitious clubs, like Cardiff City FC, did not wish to be confined to the principality, and successfully entered the English Southern League. Likewise, it proved difficult to arrange a Welsh Cup competition. In 1877, for example, of the nineteen entrants, there was only one club, Swansea, which came from South Wales and, somewhat ignominiously, that side scratched to Aberystwyth in the first round. Wrexham came to think of itself as the football capital of Wales, but this position was resented in South Wales. South Wales clubs bitterly resented the holding of the semi-finals and finals of the Welsh Cup in Wrexham, despite the fact that there were sometimes no northern clubs surviving in the competition. It was indeed the President of the English Football league who was bold enough to remark in Cardiff in 1906 that the Football Association of Wales had not 'paid as much attention to the southern part of the country as they might have done.'[4] It was the reverse of the complaint made by northern clubs in England about the English League. Despite this gentle hint, however, North-East Wales remained determined to resist any shift in footballing power to Cardiff.

The fact, therefore, that, despite anomalies, both Rugby and Association football had come to be organized with distinct governing bodies in England, Scotland, and Wales, paved the way for 'international' competition within Britain rather than for the formation of 'British national' teams. The first England–Scotland soccer match took place in 1872, and thereafter continued annually, alternating between the two countries. England first played Wales in 1879. Scotland first encountered Wales in 1882. In Rugby Union, the same phenomenon occurred at almost the same dates. The first England–Scotland match took place in 1871 and that between

---

[4] B. Lile and D. Farmer, 'The Early Development of Association Football in South Wales, 1890–1906', *Transactions of the Honourable Society of Cymmrodorion* (1984), 197, 212; D. Smith and G. Williams, *Fields of Praise* (Cardiff, 1980).

England and Wales a decade later, while the first game between Scotland and Wales occurred in 1883. From time to time, under both codes, disputes arose about the rules and caused international matches to be cancelled. It was most often the case that the Scots declined to accept English practices, where they differed from their own, as definitive, though the Scots usually gave way in the end. In another respect, underlying economic realities had important consequences for the developing sporting balance of power within Britain. Scottish and Welsh clubs, for the most part, were not in a financial condition to prevent the drift of some of their best (and worst) players to England. In the decade before 1914, for example, it was rare for northern English clubs to be without players of Scottish origin. Movement north of the Border was virtually unknown. It is significant that, between 1895 and 1914, Scotland never fielded an international side entirely composed of men who played in the Scottish League. Scottish and Welsh international footballers were frequently 'British' in their experience in a way that was not true of English international footballers, whose experience was normally confined to England. The issue of payment did not, of course, arise in Rugby Union, nevertheless Scottish and Welsh players appeared in England, as the formation of both the London Scottish and London Welsh Rugby Football Clubs testified. Both teams on occasion contributed players to the Scottish and Welsh teams respectively. In Rugby Union, too, it did prove possible to combine a domestic international tournament with 'British' overseas representation. The 'British Lions', as they came to be called, went on tour for the first time in 1888 when they visited New Zealand.

Cricket, like the winter games, spread into Scotland and Wales from England and in some quarters in both countries it was taken up with enthusiasm. Cricket scores appeared in the *Perthshire Advertiser* from the early 1830s onwards, but they did not feature in the Edinburgh and Glasgow press until mid-century. There was no doubt, however, that England remained the heartland of cricket, partly, it was alleged, for climatic reasons. It was the English county championship which was the centre of British cricketing enthusiasm. A Welsh county, Glamorgan, was admitted to that championship just after the First World War. The disparity in playing strength meant that a tripartite 'home countries' cricket championship was never feasible—the height of a Scottish cricketer's ambition lay in representing his country in the annual encounter with Ireland. Test matches against 'the colonies' steadily developed after 1880, but the problem of the national label was avoided by the convenient device of the Marylebone Cricket Club.

The sporting initiative did not, however, rest entirely with English—originated games. We learn from the *Glasgow Chronicle* of 3 January 1822 that a team of London Scots demonstrated a game of shinty at Blackheath. It has to be confessed that this brave demonstration did not lead to mass enthusiasm for shinty among the English. In the case of golf, however, matters were different. The game had been played for centuries in Scotland, but it was not until the last decades of the nineteenth century that it spread into England. It was often the case, in the first instance, that exiled commercial or medical Scots took the initiative in forming golf-clubs, but then the game boomed among the English (and Welsh) middle classes. The best Scottish golfing professionals were lured south and they had a generation of domination before English golfing professionals challenged their hold on the market. The London Scottish Golf Club was founded at Wimbledon in 1865. The Oxford and Cambridge Golf Clubs came into existence a decade later. Scots oscillated between desiring the game's popularity and anxiety lest they should lose control of its direction. From the start, at Prestwick in 1860, the premier golf championship was the *British* Open, but it was not until 1894 that the first championship was held in England.[5] Four years earlier, the fortunately named John Ball became the first Englishman to break the stranglehold of the Scots and carry off the title. The 1897 British Open was staged at Hoylake—relatively convenient for both Scots and English players. It is interesting to note that in this year approximately half of the professional entrants were Scots—drawn almost equally from English and Scottish clubs. In the years that followed, however, the proportion of Scots to other nationalities steadily decreased.[6] Nevertheless, despite the game's popularity in England, Scots succeeded in retaining the direction of its fortunes. The Golf Committee of the Royal and Ancient Club at St Andrews yielded to no English claims. It was also the case in these years that golf proved an admirable game for British women, though not all of

---

[5] D. Steel (ed.), *Guinness Book of Golf: Facts and Figures* (1982).

[6] G. Cousins, *Golf in Britain: A Social History from the Beginnings to the Present Day* (1975), 64.

them emulated that notable Scotswoman, Mrs Asquith, who played in a black 'afternoon' dress and satin toque.[7] Other British women knew how to cause her husband's colleague, Mr Lloyd George, severe distress. In 1913 they launched an attack on his golfing cottage in order to draw attention to the merits of female suffrage.

It is difficult to estimate the 'national' significance of this major expansion of 'British' sport. The games that have been discussed linked the British people in common enthusiasms. In Ireland during much the same period the Gaelic Athletic Association attempted to make Irish games a further talisman of national distinctiveness, but that rift did not exist within Britain. Nevertheless, as we have noted, while the games were common, with only minor exceptions, the era of mass sport reinforced national identity at the popular level in a quite novel fashion. It was conspicuous in Association football particularly that there was little sense of 'British' solidarity. Diversity was emphasized in this way at just the moment when other tendencies pointed in the direction of uniformity. The uncomfortable legacy of this development survives to the present. The United Kingdom is the only sovereign state which contrives to have no less than four 'national' sides competing internationally.

By 1914, in the eyes of many commentators, 'sport' had come to occupy an ambiguous place in British life. For some, the large crowds of 'fans' who attended football matches in the major urban centres reflected the decadent life of the city. For others, the competitive stimulus provided by games kept the nation alert and ready to face the even more serious challenge of war. When that war came, both reactions were apparent. Sir George Young, in 1915, for example, was scandalized by the continuation of professional football 'with huge "gates" of loafing lads as spectators.'[8] The loafing lads ought to have something more serious to do, he added, 'how slow we English are!' Lord Derby, however, endeavoured to transfer the team-discipline of footballers from the pitch to the battlefield.[9] He urged them to 'play for England now'. And many zealous sportsmen did make the transition. The Clifton College Cricket XI of 1914 'certainly played the game': all of them fought in the war; five were killed, one died of disease, and four were wounded:

[7] Bennett, *Margot*, 354.
[8] Cited by T. Wilson, *The Myriad Faces of War* (Cambridge, 1986), 261–2.
[9] P. Fussell, *The Great War and Modern Memory* (Oxford, 1975), chap. 1.

From the great Marshal to the last recruit
  These, Clifton, were thyself, thy spirit in deed
Thy flower of chivalry, thy fallen fruit,
  And thine immortal seed.[10]

These lines by Sir Henry Newbolt reflected deeper emotions than even those engaged when the spectators anxiously watched to see whether the last man in could gain the necessary runs to achieve victory. However, before we move on to consider that 'real battle', it is appropriate to probe certain other aspects of patriotic expression.

In 'God save the King', the British people had the oldest 'national anthem' in the world. In a strict sense, however, it was a prayer for the monarch rather than a celebration of the virtues of either land or people. It was appropriate in 1914 to seek to confound the 'knavish tricks' of the enemy but, by the end of the nineteenth century, 'God save the King' had its limitations as a 'British' anthem, not least in sporting contests which seemed to require some musical means of encapsulating English, Scottish, or Welsh sentiments. Percy Scholes, the author of a history of the national anthem, records that in September 1914 he himself was due to lecture in Dublin, Cork, and Wexford on the history of British music. In the new circumstances, he sent sheets of the 'National Anthems of the Allies' in advance and suggested that a certain amount of singing would be appropriate. On arrival in Ireland, he was told that the 'national anthem' had not been sung at any public gathering in Ireland for years. Scholes pressed ahead regardless and was apparently rewarded by a good deal of national anthem singing.[11]

It was not only in Ireland, however, that the 'national anthem' was a source of division rather than unity. At the National Eisteddfod held in 1891 at Swansea, for example, Prince Henry of Battenberg, Queen Victoria's son-in-law, was well received, but there was some hissing when 'God save the Queen' was played. It was about this date that the anthem 'Hen Wlad Fy Nhadau' (The Land of My Fathers), composed in South Wales in 1856, was coming to be thought of in Wales and beyond as 'the Welsh

[10] Cited by D. Winterbottom, *Henry Newbolt and the Spirit of Clifton* (Bristol, 1986), 70–1.
[11] P. A. Scholes, *God save the Queen! The History and Romance of the World's First National Anthem* (1954), 221–3.

national anthem'.[12] By the First World War, it had firmly rooted itself in Wales and functioned in uneasy harmony alongside 'God save the King' on public occasions. Even English-speaking Welshmen seemed to accept with equanimity the view that the land of their fathers had been exclusively peopled, in the words of the anthem, by warriors, singers, and bards. Notwithstanding the Welsh example, the Scots during this period singularly failed to find a song which, by general consent, could qualify as 'national', though there were a number of runners in the field. 'God save the King', lacking as it did any identification of the 'us' over whom the monarch reigned, was 'British'. Unlike the Welsh, therefore, the English and Scots lacked agreed national anthems of their own, though works of William Blake and Robert Burns respectively could sometimes serve when there was an occasional need to laud England or Scotland. The Great War, too, confirmed that a considerable number of Englishmen showed some familiarity with 'Auld Lang Syne' and were able to sing at least the opening lines with a certain vigour on poignant occasions.

Wales possessed an anthem, but on the other hand it received no recognition in the national emblem, the Union Jack, which contained the crosses of St George and St Andrew and, after 1801, of St Patrick. It must be admitted that the heraldic reconciliation of a red dragon with an array of superimposed crosses would have defeated any designer! Even so, the absence of any formal acknowledgement of the existence of Wales in the flag of the Union was sometimes seen as a slight. By 1914, something emblematic had to be done. In October, orders were placed on behalf of the Welsh Army Corps for metal badges for new recruits which bore a design of the Welsh dragon on a green and white background.[13] At this point, however, the College of Arms became bellicose. It complained that this particular badge was only one of several which were personal to Henry Tudor. It suggested that the true arms of Wales were the red and gold lions of Llewellyn the Great. The lions, it is true, had been used in 1911 at the investiture in Caernarfon Castle of the Prince of Wales—though dragons challenged the lions even on this occasion. Pomp and pageantry had then accompanied

[12] D. Smith, *Wales! Wales!* (1984), 39.
[13] C. Hughes, 'The Welsh Army Corps, 1914–1915: Shortages of Khaki and Basic Equipment Promote a "National" Uniform, *Imperial War Museum Review*, 1 (1986), 96–7.

the revival, after three hundred years, of the 'investing' of the Prince of Wales, the eldest son of the monarch, tutored for the occasion by the eminent local MP, David Lloyd George.[14] In general, it can be said that the dragon defeated the lions and he became increasingly familiar in the rest of Britain.

The English, by comparison, were somewhat bashful about banners. Flying the Cross of St George alongside or as a substitute for the Union Jack was advocated, paradoxically, in certain Anglican and Socialist circles, but it seemed rather an artificial exercise to the general public. The flag of St George could be seen fluttering, a little feebly, from parish churches, but the Union flag was more evident in public places in England.[15] Certain patriots were not happy about the relaxed attitude towards flag-flying which they detected in early twentieth-century England. In *The Town Child* (1907), Reginald Bray detected the Union Jack 'idly flapping' in many English schools and thought 'the flag should be produced only on rare occasions, and then accompanied only with solemn ceremony worthy of an emblem for which men have died.' He added, not untypically, that 'It would probably be wise to substitute for the Union Jack the less vulgarized banner of St George.'[16] Sir Walter Besant, writing of East London in 1901, also complained that their country's flag was never seen by inhabitants of this quarter of the city, except occasionally on the River Thames. He feared that children were not being taught to reverence the flag of their country as a symbol of their liberties and their responsibilities. For a time, indeed, the London County Council did forbid the use of the Union Jack in schools.[17]

These anthems and emblems of Britain reflected, in a typically incoherent and inexact fashion, the mixture of integration and diversity which we have by now become accustomed to discovering. The supreme symbol of integration, however, was the monarchy and, in the nineteenth century, that royal function became an identifiable reality as well as a symbol in a way it had never become before. The long life of George III had enabled him to share in many thanksgivings for his survival. On the occasion of his jubilee in 1809, no fewer than 666 celebrations were reported to be taking

[14] J. Grigg, *Lloyd George: The People's Champion, 1902-1911* (1978), 303-4.
[15] J. H. Grainger, *Patriotisms: Britain, 1900-1939* (1986), 58.
[16] R. Bray, *The Town Child* (1907), 329.
[17] Grainger, *Patriotisms*, 38-9.

place in England alone, with a smaller number in Scotland and Wales. However, despite this rejoicing throughout Britain, the monarch himself was content to receive the loyalty of his people without feeling under any compunction to see for himself what those of them who lived in the North of England, Scotland, or Wales might conceivably be like. The death of the Prince Regent's only legitimate child, Princess Charlotte, in 1817, was marked with mourning throughout Britain, though, perhaps predictably, it was only in Scotland that the holding of a special service caused controversy. The minister of St George's, Edinburgh, refused to hold a commemoratory service, and, for his temerity, received a letter, which was duly published, significantly entitled '... *on the Respect due to National Feeling*'.[18] Eventually, it was George IV who came to Scotland in 1822 to see his Scottish subjects in their proper milieu.[19] He obligingly wore garments thought suitable for the occasion. So little, however, had the royal palace of Holyroodhouse in Edinburgh been in the habit of receiving British monarchs that its state of repair made it inappropriate to install the King in his palace.

It was Queen Victoria, however, who first gave to the British monarchy a truly British dimension. She first visited Scotland in 1842 and found that her reception was enthusiastic. She was particularly struck by the young Scotch fisherwomen she encountered, finding them 'very clean and very Dutch-looking'. She also recorded the useful information that 'they never marry out of their class'. Two years later, on a visit to Blair Atholl, she recorded that she found it 'very different from England: all the houses are built of stone; the people so different,—sandy hair, high cheek-bones; children with long shaggy hair and bare legs and feet; little boys in kilts.' On her return south, the English coast appeared by contrast 'so terribly flat'. She detected a 'great peculiarity about the Highlands and the Highlanders; and they are such a chivalrous, fine, active people.'[20]

The subsequent acquisition of Balmoral enabled her, over many years, to make the greater acquaintance of the Scottish people. The

<hr />

[18] This information is contained in L. Colley, 'The Apotheosis of George III: Loyalty, Royalty and the British Nation, 1760–1820', *Past and Present*, 102 (1984), 113–16. See also her 'Whose Nation? Class and National Consciousness in Britain, 1750–1830', *Past and Present*, 113 (1986), 97–117.

[19] *A Historical Account of His Majesty's Visit to Scotland* (Edinburgh, 1822).

[20] D. Duff (ed.), *Queen Victoria's Highland Journals* (Exeter, 1980), 24, 38, 47.

requirement that her ministers should visit her there brought more politicians to Aberdeenshire than would otherwise be the case. Provided he was allowed to slip away to an Episcopalian chapel, Gladstone was in his element, timing himself on his great cross-country tramps. Disraeli was less energetic, but he accepted a 'Scotch shawl' which the Queen kindly thought Mrs Disraeli might welcome as a souvenir of Scotland.[21] Queen Victoria did not restrict herself to Royal Deeside. She took particular pleasure in recording in her diary after a visit that it was 'the first time the British standard with a Queen of Great Britain, and her husband and children, had ever entered Fingal's Cave.'[22] Her pride in *Britain* is unmistakable. It was entirely appropriate, therefore, that the Prince Consort should be commemorated not only by innumerable statues but also by 'national' monuments in Edinburgh, Tenby (a somewhat exotic Welsh location), and London.[23] While no royal residence was ever established in Wales, the Queen travelled both in North and South Wales. She could truly claim to be the first effective monarch of Great Britain and, although neither her son nor her grandson quite shared her passion for Scotland, the ritual visits north were too firmly established for addicts of Sandringham to abandon them.[24] '*I* feel a sort of reverence in going over these scenes in this most beautiful country,' Queen Victoria wrote of Scotland in 1873. The people had shown such loyalty 'to the family of my ancestors— for Stewart blood is in my veins, and I am *now* their representative, and the people are as devoted and loyal to me as they were to that unhappy race.'[25]

King Edward VII first visited the Highlands of Scotland in 1847, cruising from Cowes by way of the Welsh coast and the Caledonian Canal. He exchanged his sailor's suit for a kilt on his arrival in Scotland. Later, in 1859, he received much serious technical information from Lyon Playfair, having taken up residence at Holyroodhouse for three months to undergo serious intellectual preparation for Oxford. Later still, Scots were to be particularly prominent amongst his financial advisers.[26] At the age of sixty,

[21] I. Brown, *Balmoral* (1955), 215–19.    [22] Duff, *Highland Journals*, 55–6.
[23] E. Darby and N. Smith, *The Cult of the Prince Consort* (1983).
[24] D. Cannadine, 'The Context, Performance and Meaning of Ritual: The British Monarchy and the "Invention of Tradition", *c*.1820–1977', in Hobsbawm and Ranger, *Invention of Tradition*.
[25] Duff, *Highland Journals*, 174.
[26] S. Lee, *King Edward VII: A Biography* vol. i (1925), 23, 72–3, 175.

Edward broke fresh royal ground by visiting Stornoway, the capital of Lewis, and was presented on the occasion with venison. He was much disconcerted, however, to learn that the stag had been shot by a woman.[27] He liked Balmoral, but he liked Sandringham better. He took care to instruct his son not to offend the Scots by using the word 'English' when 'British' would be more correct. Kenneth Rose has noted that Edward took pains with his dress on approaching Scotland. An initial transitional tartan waistcoat perhaps heralded 'the full exuberance of kilt, sporran and skean dhu.'

King George V learned his lesson from his father well and liked Scotland. 'Glad to be in this dear place again', he noted in 1919 on reaching Balmoral again for the first time for six years, '. . . and to see all our nice people again.'[28] In the interval, that great conflict had occurred which tested the integrity of the British state to the full. It was not a good war for emperors and kings but, whether by luck or good judgement, the 'House of Windsor' succeeded, where others failed, in maintaining a role for itself in integrating the British state, at least at the symbolic level.

The peculiarly insular patriotism of Britain was put to the supreme test in the Great War which began in 1914. It was this conflict which, because of the events of Easter 1916, was to destroy the United Kingdom of Great Britain and Ireland. Yet 'Great Britain' itself survived the ordeal intact. The myriad links and connections, outlined in previous chapters, proved stronger than any fissiparous tendencies. Diversity and rivalry coexisted with a sense that, at a point of crisis, the 'British nation' did exist and would survive. There was a collective 'will to win'. It drew sufficiently deeply upon a common stock of symbols, experiences, and institutions to transcend the potential appeal of other focuses of loyalty and allegiance. Propaganda nourished, but could not create, that sentiment.

It is not suggested, however, that 'the British nation' was mobilized without strain. Millions of men, uprooted from their homes and sent to a foreign land in a common British cause were thrown together on a scale for which there was no precedent. Men from Inverness or Plymouth played, ate, drank, sang, and fought alongside each other, but frequently sensed that they were, at one

[27] Lee, *King Edward VII: A Biography* vol. ii (1927), 112–13.
[28] K. Rose, *King George V* (1983), 91 and 287.

and the same time, comrades and strangers. The 'British nation' for which they were about to die was both myth and reality. It was H. G. Wells, who certainly looked upon the world as an English-man, who observed that, unless assisted by a kilt, 'the ordinary Frenchman is unable to distinguish between one sort of British soldier and another. He cannot tell—let the ardent nationalist mark the fact—a Cockney from an Irishman or the Cardiff from the Essex note.' Patrick MacGill, the Irish/Glaswegian, noted the same phenomenon.[29] However galling it might be, foreign soldiers found the distinctions too subtle to be bothered by them.

Amongst 'the British' themselves, however, national and regional loyalties and identities were by no means submerged. One example must suffice. 'We did not move back', wrote a solider in the 7th Cameron Highlanders describing the Battle of Loos, 'until an English Brigade came up and just at that time the Germans made another attack and Holy God what did those damned English do but turn back. . . . There were about 200 Kilties and about 1,000 English and yet they turned.'[30] No doubt he went on fuming about 'those cursed English regiments' for the rest of his life! It was perhaps fortunate, if fortuitous, that the man who was to become Commander-in-Chief, Sir Douglas Haig, was a properly blended Briton, the quintessential Anglo-Scot. It is not possible to under-stand both his strengths and limitations without coming to terms with Clifton College, the English public school which he attended, and the Scottish Calvinist conscience which he inherited.[31]

The military blending of Britain was not, of course, a novelty in 1914. The martial qualities of the Scottish soldier had long been serenaded and the Scottish presence in the British Army had long been notable. In the revolutionary and Napoleonic Wars, for example, among the distinguished British commanders born and bred in Scotland could be mentioned Sir Ralph Abercromby, Sir David Baird, Sir David Dundas, Sir John Hope, Sir Charles Stuart, and Sir John Moore.[32] Scottish soldiers were prominent both in the conquest of India and in the suppression of the Mutiny. Economic circumstances at home had long made the military career an option

---

[29] H. G. Wells, *The War and the Future: Italy, France and Britain at War* (1917), 229; P. MacGill, *The Red Horizon* (1916), 82–3.

[30] Wilson, *Myriad Faces*, 261–2.

[31] R. Blake (ed.), *The Private Papers of Douglas Haig, 1914–1919* (1952), 28–9, 149–50.

[32] A. Brett-James, *General Graham, Lord Lynedoch* (1959), 1.

for Scotsmen. It has been noted that in 1830, 13.5 per cent of British soldiers were Scots at a time when Scots formed 10 per cent of the British population.[33] Scotsmen were widely thought to make admirable NCOs because, generally, they were more literate than English recruits and, in the case of Highland units, were more responsive, in matters of behaviour, to kinship pressures. In the Royal Artillery, for example, in 1840, 16 per cent of the Scots were NCOs but only 11.8 per cent of the English and 9.75 per cent of the Irish. In Scotland, compared to the rest of Great Britain, it has been noted that from mid-century a markedly higher percentage of the available population enrolled in the Volunteers. This cannot be explained by contrasting rural Scotland with urban England for 'even in urban areas the Scots were much keener to join the Volunteers than the English or Welsh.'[34] In the 1860s, it was in the Highlands of Scotland—not in immediate danger, perhaps, from France—that the British people most enthusiastically enrolled in the Volunteers. However, while there was perhaps a more pervasive acceptance of military values in Scotland than in England, the attraction of the British Army as a career began to diminish in Scotland, possibly because emigration or industrial employment offered more attractive prospects. The reality of this development was disguised by the fact that certain ostensibly Highland regiments did not even contain a majority of Scots. As early as 1836, for example, of 677 men in the 1st Battalion of the Royal Scots, 289 were Irish. By 1870, indeed, Scots made up only 8 per cent of the British Army. On the other hand, Scotsmen figured prominently in regiments which could be selective in their recruiting. Of the Rifle Brigade's recruits, for example, overall 27 per cent were illiterate but, whereas 50 per cent of its recruits from southern England were illiterate, only 5 per cent of its Scots were.[35]

By contrast with Scotland, a generation of Welsh politicians had established the notion that Welshmen were peculiarly inclined to peace. Henry Richard was held up for admiration as 'the Apostle of Peace', and indeed, comparatively speaking, it was probably the case that in broad terms the Peace Society found more favour in

[33] H. Strachan, *Wellington's Legacy: The Reform of the British Army, 1830–1854* (Manchester, 1984), 51–2.

[34] H. Cunningham, *The Volunteer Force: A Social and Political History, 1859–1908* (Hamden, 1975), 46.

[35] Strachan *Wellington's Legacy*, 51–2.

Wales than in Scotland. It should not be assumed from the mere fact that a Peace Convention was held in Edinburgh in 1853 that pacific sentiment was particularly evident either in the capital or in Scotland as a whole. It was often assumed, though inaccurately, that Welsh Nonconformity was solidly against war in any circumstances.[36] It was the case, however, in the mid-Victorian period, that there was a conspicuous reluctance among Welshmen to enlist in the army, and that pattern did not change drastically in subsequent decades. In 1843/4, for example, out of 17,450 recruits to the British Army, only 167 were Welsh. The so-called 'Welsh' regiments came to depend heavily on Irish recruits to make up their numbers.[37] An occasional Welsh general surfaced, but the tradition was not strong.

It is against this background that the 'national' response in 1914 must be considered, though there remains ample scope for further investigation. On the whole, 'Britain' did rally 'with one voice'. Lord Curzon liked to believe that he played a part in this process. 'In time of crisis such as this', he declared in Glasgow on 10 September, 'it is the duty of the Government to lead, and it is the duty of the rest of us to follow.' He added that he had been urged to make speeches in the North of England and Scotland, particularly in Scotland, because, allegedly, 'that people, though very shrewd and pertinacious and patriotic, is somewhat slow of mental movement.' However, on coming north, he had to admit that he saw 'no sign of slowness or of any reluctance to rise to the full measure of civic duty.'[38] The City of Glasgow provided 25,000 recruits in a month and there appeared little ground for the southern suspicion that Clydeside was seditious. Indeed, when the Glasgow Trades Council met on 5 August, it was only by a small majority that it even agreed to be represented at a demonstration in the city called to express regret at the outbreak of war.[39] Scotland, it seemed, was determined to be 'the brave'. It was certainly not the case that geographical remoteness brought with it detachment from the military developments in Europe. On the island of Skye, for example, the Territorial Fourth Battalion of the Cameron Highlanders had been preparing

[36] G. J. Jones, *Wales and the Quest for Peace* (Cardiff, 1969); K. O. Morgan, 'Peace Movements in Wales, 1899–1945', *Welsh History Review*, 10 (1981), 398–430.

[37] Strachan, *Wellington's Legacy*, 51–2.

[38] D. M. Chapman-Huston (ed.), *Subjects of the Day: Being a Selection of Speeches and Writings of Earl Curzon of Kedleston* (1915), 389–90.

[39] D. J. Newton, *British Labour, European Socialism and the Struggle for Peace, 1889–1914* (Oxford, 1985), 327n.

for war for years. When it came, as their ancestors had done in earlier conflicts, men marched down to the pier with a swing of the kilt and a skirl of the pipes. The sorrowful crowd sang 'God save the King' as the men disappeared from sight, most of them never to return.[40] The cause, and the rhetoric and preaching that supported it, was thoroughly Scottish/British. No less than 90 per cent of all 'sons of the Manse' volunteered for active service. It was even possible in the Church of Scotland for ministers to enlist as fighting soldiers. An early ministerial casualty from Edinburgh had the perhaps unfortunate surname of Pagan.[41] John Buchan threw himself energetically into the work of British propaganda.[42] There was, in short, no notion in 1914 that 'England's difficulty' was Scotland's opportunity. No submarine landed a treacherous knight off the West Coast of Scotland in an attempt to reverse the verdict of 1745. Agreement on the precise extent of Scottish loss of life is still lacking, but the figure of deaths has been put at 100,000—'equivalent to about 10 per cent of the Scottish male population aged between sixteen and fifty, and probably about 15 per cent of total British war dead.' In putting this figure forward, Smout suggests that the Scottish sacrifice was 'higher in proportionate terms than for any other country in the Empire.'[43]

In Wales, in 1914, the response did not prove significantly different from the pattern that was emerging elsewhere in Britain. In North Wales, the initial reaction does not seem to have been enthusiastic, but it soon picked up and certain influential ministers were willing to appeal for volunteers from their pulpits. Lloyd George himself wavered in his attitude until the last moment, or at least appeared to do so. No doubt his decision to stay in the Cabinet and his eventual strong support of British intervention helped to settle the convictions of many of his fellow-countrymen. Much was then made of Welsh sympathy for small nations, such as Serbia or Belgium, in their struggle against the great states. There were, therefore, several reasons for trying to ensure a specific place for Wales within the overall British war effort. Kitchener, however, was

[40] I. Macdonald, *A Family in Skye, 1908-1916* (Stornoway, 1980), 110.

[41] P. C. Matheson, 'Scottish War Sermons, 1914-1919', *Records of the Scottish Church History Society*, 17 (1969-71), 205.

[42] M. L. Sanders and P. M. Taylor, *British Propaganda during the First World War, 1914-1918* (1982), 62-7.

[43] Smout, *Scottish People*, 267.

hostile to the excessive introduction of ethnic considerations into the structure of the British Army and it was only with great reluctance that he agreed to Lloyd George's suggestion that a new Welsh Division should be formed. It was commanded by the Welsh Liberal MP, Sir Ivor Phillips. Every attempt was made to clothe all recruits in Welsh homespun uniforms, Welsh flannel shirts, and Welsh underclothing. Three Welsh battalions were also raised in Liverpool, London, and Manchester. The commander of the North Wales Brigade, as it was originally known, was Welsh-speaking, and some 195 out of 302 officers of the brigade were of 'Welsh nationality' in August 1915, the remainder being connected with Wales by birth, parentage, or residence.[44] Eventually, the proportion of Welshmen enrolled in the armed services (13.82 per cent) was greater than either the English or the Scottish. In 1914, recruiting posters in the Welsh language thought it quite safe to draw upon patriotic utterances which purported to come from the age of the independent Welsh princes. However, there lingered in Welsh poetry the experience, over many centuries, of Welsh military defeat and it was not altogether easy to link that tradition to the circumstances of the Great War. There was, in addition, an inescapable element of bitter irony when, in Welsh-speaking Wales, mothers received letters from the War Office in London telling them of the death of their sons in a language which some of them could not understand.[45]

Looked at over the country as a whole, by February 1915, '15.6 per cent of the workforce on the land had joined up, compared to 15.2 per cent among all industrial workers.' It seems that the early rush to enlist came from 'most well-paid manual occupations', followed by even higher levels of recruitment amongst non-manual workers. And, by mid-1915, over 230,000 miners—roughly one-quarter of the workforce—had enlisted. The highest rates were 'British', that is to say from Glamorgan, Durham, and Northumberland, and some Scottish coalfields—areas of pre-war militancy.[46] There was some correlation between the levels of enlistment and unemployment in particular cities, but it was by no means

[44] C. Hughes, 'The New Armies', in I. F. W. Beckett and K. Simpson (eds.), *A Nation in Arms* (Manchester, 1985), 117.

[45] Roberts, *Feet in Chains*, 146-7.

[46] J. M. Winter, *The Great War and the British People* (1985), 30-5; Beckett, in Beckett and Simpson (eds.), *Nation in Arms*, 10.

complete. It may be, of course, that even fighting was thought preferable to coal-mining.

Taken in the round, there is little reason to discount the view that in 1914/15 British national unity was complete in its response to the war, or at least it was as complete as is ever likely in such circumstances.

It is more difficult, in national terms, to decide what Englishmen, Scotsmen, and Welshmen thought they were fighting for. Was it 'England', 'Scotland', or 'Wales', or was it 'Britain', or, even, just conceivably, 'the United Kingdom'? 'If one does take a toss,' wrote one officer from Watford, 'there's always the satisfaction of knowing that we could not do it in a better cause. I always feel that I am fighting for England—English fields, lanes, trees, good days in England, and all that is synonymous with liberty.'[47] The further one went north from Watford, of course, the less potent became the image of the leafy lane or the thatched cottage. The urban Englishman was expected by some of his poetically inclined superiors to respond to the sound of church bells ringing out across myriad English meadows, and perhaps he did. It was no doubt possible to dream of strawberries and Cornish cream in Flanders fields, but it was easier to do so if one came from Exeter rather than Hexham. Church bells, being virtually unkown in Scotland, stirred few Scottish hearts.

When Ernest Rhys came to edit the patriotic anthology for the YMCA in his Everyman Library for the use of British troops, he called it *The Old Country: A Book of Love and Praise of England* (1917). He was himself of mixed English and Welsh descent, with an Irish wife.[48] Such a title from such a man for such a purpose points to the ambiguous character of 'Englishness'. It has been persuasively argued that 'As a tribal *patria* England had less definition simply because so much had happened to her, so many had found hope and harbourage within her, so accommodating was her civil society.' Grainger continues in this vein by suggesting that it was because England had been:

for so long the reception centre for true-born Englishmen of all shapes and sizes—quite apart from diffusion or self-effacement in Empire—that England's own sense of identity as the national home and birthright of a

---

[47] Cited by D. Winter, *Death's Men* (1978), 32.
[48] See his significantly entitled autobiography, *Wales England Wed* (1940).

particular people, as a distinctive kith and kin ... was already somewhat blurred.[49]

It was, indeed, in England that the blending of Britain reached its height. It was the country 'where the best in politics and in literature was conceded to stem from a mixture of Anglo-Saxon and Celt conceived as aptitudes, moods and spirit rather than races.'[50] The English, uniquely in Britain, did not possess their own national museum, but it was entirely proper that the British Museum should be situated in England. It is notable that it was the poet Edward Thomas, who had conceived a pure passion for Wales, who could write:

what with Great Britain, the British Empire, Britons, Britishers, and the English-speaking world, the choice offered to whomsoever would be patriotic is embarrassing, and he is fortunate who can find an ideal England of the past, the present, and the future to worship. ...[51]

For H. G. Wells in *Mr Britling Sees it Through*:

Britain was not a State. It was an unincorporated people. The British Army, the British War Office and the British administration had assimilated nothing; they were little old partial things: the British nation lay outside them, beyond their understanding and tradition: a formless new thing, but a great thing; and now this British nation, this real nation, the 'outsiders', had to take up arms.[52]

It was his vision that the war would produce a 'British nation' at a level of popular experience and awareness on a scale never previously known.

It was by no means clear that this would happen. In the very act of democratic incorporation, it might be disclosed that 'the British nation' was a figment of the imagination or merely a temporary political expedient. The nation of the 'outsiders', if they not only took up arms but also took power, might turn out not to think 'British' at all. It might be only the 'little old partial things' that encased the entity of Britain. It was not easy to tell, perhaps it remains not easy to tell, what the ultimate pattern of insular alignments would be. And insularity needs emphasis. The 'island

[49] Grainger, *Patriotisms*, 54.
[50] Ibid. 54–5.
[51] E. Thomas, *The South Country* (1909), 71.
[52] H. G. Wells, *Mr Britling Sees it Through* (1916), 238.

race', in the circumstances of the Great War, lived athwart the continent. If it was in southern England that guns could be heard across the Channel, it was in northern Scotland that the bulk of the British Fleet was concentrated. Danger from the direction of the North Sea linked together Scapa Flow and Felixstowe. Yet the 'Eastern British' did not recognize themselves. Charles Rennie Mackintosh, the Scottish architect and painter, was living with his wife in Suffolk in the summer of 1914. They stayed on after the outbreak of war. Their accents were judged by locals to be 'foreign' and, one evening, they returned home to find a soldier guarding their lodgings. Mackintosh was summoned before a local tribunal and only with difficulty established his good faith.[53] No less extraordinary, at a different level and after the carnage of war, was the letter written in 1918 by an Archbishop of Canterbury, who was a Scot, to a Prime Minister, who was a Welshman, rejoicing in the victory of 'England'. The ambiguities of 'Britishness' at this time of crisis could not be more graphically illustrated.

[53] T. Howarth, *Charles Rennie Mackintosh and the Modern Movement* (1977), 196.

# 7

# Conclusion: A Balanced Blending?

The achievement of victory during the years from 1914 to 1918 drew deeply upon national reserves of energy and emotion. The 'will to win' was sustained at critical moments by shared values and experiences with deep roots. The British nation appeared to be more firmly welded together than ever before by the war, whatever social cleavages were still evident. It was apparent, however, that 'Britain' was a unity in diversity. 'Everything English', Emerson had written in the nineteenth century, 'is a fusion of distant and antagonistic elements.' The language was mixed and the men were of different nations. England was shot through with characteristics which might, in other contexts, make cohesion impossible. He detected 'contemplation and practical skill; active intellect and dead conservatism; world-wide enterprise and devoted use and wont; aggressive freedom and hospitable law with bitter class-legislation; a people scattered by their wars and affairs over the whole earth and homesick to a man . . .'.[1] His analysis has even more point if we substitute 'Britain' for 'England'.

Even in the nineteenth century, historians argued that the making of the 'British nation' had been a long process. Maitland, when asked by Acton to contribute to the Cambridge History, reflected that he was descended from the Maitlands of Kirkcud-brightshire and began, unusually and boldly, by focusing attention upon Scotland. Reflecting upon Mary, Queen of Scots, and the famous casket letters, he felt that religion was not the only matter at stake in this period: 'a new nation, a British nation, was in the making.'[2] Macaulay, too, saw in the growth of British nationhood what John Burrow has called 'the triumph of enduring reconciliation'.[3]

[1] Emerson, *English Traits*, 53.
[2] C. H. S. Fifoot, *Frederic William Maitland: A Life* (Cambridge, Mass., 1971), 221–2.
[3] J. W. Burrow, *A Liberal Descent: Victorian Historians and the English Past* (Cambridge, 1981), 86–7.

Our analysis of religion and politics, of literature and education, of music and the life of the mind, of sport and science, incomplete though it has necessarily been, suggests that through the nineteenth century the 'British nation' was indeed 'made', but it was neither a painless process nor a complete one, Exploration of various indicators of identity suggests, however, that there was no uniform tendency operating in all fields simultaneously. 'England', 'Scotland', and 'Wales' were in certain respects, most notably by improved communications, more closely bound together than they had ever been in the past; yet we have also suggested that heightened contact might as easily increase an awareness of difference as confirm integration. Our investigation has also suggested that it is dangerous to think simply in terms of the extent to which the three 'nations' came closer together, drifted further apart, or maintained the status quo. The 'centralizing' tendencies of the Victorian age upset inherited boundaries and jurisdictions. Meditating on contemporary France, and comparing it with its medieval past, Stubbs saw 'a record of centralization, codification, universal suffrage', and government by policemen. The work of 'simplification', he believed, would never be carried so far in England, but there were signs that the same process was at work. He considered it to be 'a sign of the decline of independent thought and character.'[4] On the other hand, an article in the *Edinburgh Review* in 1847 on 'Centralization' deplored the fact that in both France and England the old administrative units might appear to be perfectly fused whereas in fact 'exclusive local patriotism' still lingered on in both countries. The author deplored signs of 'this miserable spirit' which obstructed all progress in government and administration.[5] In such circumstances, it was not easy to strike the right balance.

The experience of the First World War did suggest, however, that the reconciliation was indeed 'enduring'. At its close, other multi-ethnic, multi-lingual, empires collapsed, to be replaced by states supposedly based upon the principle of 'national self-determination'. Our argument suggests that 'Britain' was both a three-nation unit and a single unit, in different contexts and for different purposes, in a more fundamental sense than either the Austro-Hungarian or Russian empires. Defeat could conceivably have led to disintegration: victory was unlikely to do so.

[4] A. Hassall (ed.), *Stubbs, Lectures on Early English History* (1906), 2.
[5] 'Centralization', *Edinburgh Review* (Jan. 1847), 251.

It is possible to argue that the consolidation of British unity achieved during the nineteenth century was accomplished at too high a price. In the wake of the First World War, J. S. Mackenzie, the Scots philosophy professor at Cardiff, reflected at length on the 'British experience'. Welshmen and Scotsmen did 'tend to regard England in somewhat the same way as the southern Germans have tended to regard Prussia.' They resented its 'self-satisfied assumption of superiority and its somewhat scornful indifference to their modes of thought and life.' There was a case for suggesting that the smaller nations suffered from being too closely tied to a larger one. Yet there was the opposite danger of a 'somewhat morbid concentration upon their own peculiarities'. The existence of 'Britain' helped all its diverse constituent elements keep a sense of proportion and prevent the outbreak of petty rivalries.[6] Since the Irish question was apparently being solved in the 1920s, there was an understandable tendency to suppose that the character of Britain had been moulded into its final form. Few at the time would have suspected that issues of multi-ethnicity and multi-lingualism would reappear in the late twentieth century.[7] In this perspective, the integration achieved by 1914, which appeared to be permanent, may come to seem temporary and transient—the expression of a mistaken European belief that there was something sacred about the notion of a homogeneous nation-state.[8] The balance between integration and diversity has to be struck afresh in each generation. It may be suggested, therefore, that the British identity with which we have been concerned, forged as it was by a government and people firmly conscious of an imperial destiny, reached its apogee around the First World War. Certainly, the 'matter of Britain', both domestically and internationally, has become far more problematic as the twenty-first century approaches than could have been anticipated in 1914. Despite these far-reaching changes, however, it is still the patterns established in the nineteenth century which, for better or for worse, underlie the current relationships between all the people of Britain.

---

[6] J. S. Mackenzie, *Arrows of Desire* (1920), 197–9.

[7] P. B. Rich, *Race and Empire in British Politics* (Cambridge, 1986).

[8] E. Gellner, *Nations and Nationalism* (Oxford, 1983); J. Breuilly, *Nationalism and the State* (Manchester, 1982); R. D. Stack, *Human Territoriality: Its Theory and History* (Cambridge, 1986); W. H. McNeill, *Poly-ethnicity and National Unity in World History* (Toronto, 1986).

# Index